Shamanism
&
Personal
Mastery

Shamanism & Personal Mastery

•

USING SYMBOLS, RITUALS, AND TALISMANS TO ACTIVATE THE POWERS WITHIN YOU

•

Gini Graham Scott, Ph.D.

PARAGON HOUSE
ST. PAUL, MINNESOTA

PUBLISHED IN THE UNITED STATES BY

PARAGON HOUSE
2700 UNIVERSITY AVENUE WEST
ST. PAUL, MN 55114-1016

LIBRARY OF CONGRESS CATALOGING-IN-PUBLICATION DATA
SCOTT, GINI GRAHAM.
SHAMANISM AND PERSONAL MASTERY: USING SYMBOLS, RITUALS, AND TALISMANS TO
ACTIVATE THE POWERS WITHIN YOU /GINI GRAHAM SCOTT.—1ST ED.
P.   CM.
ISBN 1-55778-381-0 (PAPER):
1. SHAMANISM.   2. NEW AGE MOVEMENT.   3. SELF-ACTUALIZATION
(PSYCHOLOGY)   I. TITLE.
BF1611.S39   1991
291.4—DC20   90-29017
CIP

MANUFACTURED IN THE UNITED STATES OF AMERICA

CONTENTS

•

INTRODUCTION

•

Shamanic practices have a long history, stretching back to the dawn of time. People have used them to get control over the unknown and the forces of nature, and in the process, practitioners have built up extensive systems of symbols and procedures which they have found effective in achieving desired results. Shamanism stresses practical results and practitioners have used whatever tools and techniques that seem to work.[1]

These symbols and procedures have proven effective because they help to focus the attention and power of the shaman or magician on the results he or she wants, while providing an established repertoire of methods to guide him or her. A formal system can

---

[1] Shamanism is also closely allied with magical thinking and practice and the terms *shaman* or *magician* are often used interchangeably, although sometimes the associations with these terms are different (i.e., shamans have been associated more with the ancient traditions of helping and healing, magicians with the more recent historical developments of Western magical practice, designed to manipulate reality for the gain of oneself or others). However, since both are in essence based on intuitive thinking and seeing into and working with alternate realities for practical gains, I will be using the terms interchangeably here.

also help to give the practitioner a feeling of confidence, and it helps others accept and believe that the practitioner knows what to do in any given situation.

However, the real driving force that empowers these symbols and procedures lies within the individual practitioner himself, in the form of his belief and his commitment of energy to achieving the desired results. Consequently, people may find a particular shamanic or magical system effective because they have become accustomed to using those symbols and procedures and believe in them; but they could likewise use another system if they like and believe in it also. Or they could draw elements from different systems or create their own, as long as they have the necessary belief and commitment of energy to generate the power needed to gain their objectives.

In fact, often people may be using shamanic or magical methods to achieve desired results without even realizing that this is what they are doing, because they do not call their activities shamanism or magic. They think of shamanism or magic as a practice involving specific procedures that have built up an established tradition, like the system of Western magic espoused by well-known magicians such as Aleister Crowley or John Dee, the shamanic healing practices of Native Americans, or the elaborate rituals of the curanderos of Ecuador and Peru.

Yet underlying all of these traditions is this root power that exists to some degree in each person and can be developed with training. People can, of course, use these traditional systems, but they can develop their own, based on symbols and associations which have particular meaning to them. What is most critical for success is that they draw on and focus this power toward their goals. Moreover, it is important to seek beneficial goals (or face assorted potential dangers) and to use these techniques in pursuit of these goals in a balanced, productive way.

Shamanism and Personal Mastery is designed to present various techniques for tapping this power, including using power objects, power words, and ritual. This book also briefly describes some of the abilities you can develop that will help work with these techniques, such as "seeing" into other realities, being aware of and controlling your dreams, projecting your consciousness into other places and into the future, being in touch with your inner knowing, and knowing how to stay in balance.

Many of the techniques discussed in this book come from my

experiences in working with a master shaman, Michael Fairwell, who has been developing and teaching shamanic and magical principles most of his life. I studied with him for over a year and wrote about him and his teachings in my first book on shamanism, *Shaman Warrior,* and more recently in *The Secrets of the Shaman.*

These teachings represent a modern-day blend of traditional shamanic and magical practices, and draw to a varying extent on the wisdom of the Eastern shamans, the teachings of the Native Americans, and the shamanic traditions described in the writings of Carlos Castaneda. Michael has experimented with these various methods in the field and has synthesized them into an approach to shamanism and magic which the average person can use to gain access to and work with the often mysterious world of unseen energies and forces.[2]

However, while I have drawn on these teachings, the emphasis in *Shamanism and Personal Mastery* is on how you can use the basic principles of shamanism and magic to create the results you want in your life and to experience greater personal power. You can use the particular techniques described here, which have worked for many people, or create your own, using the symbols and associations which have personal meaning for you. As I have noted, the underlying power behind shamanism and magic is created by the personal belief and energy you bring to the process. Therefore, if you find that traditional symbols are especially powerful for you, you can use those; if you like the particular tech-

---

[2] A little about Michael: Michael has generally tried to stay in the background with his work, because at the same time that he has developed his system, he has been working among people who might not be receptive to the subject of shamanism generally. Rather, he has focused on working individually with a few select students and with a small group of especially committed people, which existed for about ten years (until 1989) as the Order of the Divine Flame, or ODF. Now he just works with a few individuals privately. His work with students has involved both teaching long-established practices and exploring and experimenting with new methods to find new working techniques. This approach is very much like the practical approach of the traditional shaman, who, in different cultural settings, has remained receptive to adding new practices over time. Thus shamanism readily becomes a blend of old and new, a process which I observed on a trip to visit shamans and healers among the Colorado, Cayapa, and Otovalan Indians of Ecuador. While the shamans we visited used many traditional devices in their rituals (like tobacco smoke and leaves twisted together, which were shaken to cleanse the individual by drawing out and eliminating any negativity), they used new inventions too (such as bottles of "fire water," a potent local brew, bought in a nearby grocery or trading center).

I originally worked with Michael when he came to the San Francisco Bay Area to teach for a year. Now he is back in Los Angeles, and he has done much of his work in the nearby deserts and mountains, as well as in the city.

niques and procedures described here, you can use these; or if you wish, you can create your own. In short, use the practice that you find most effective. This book is designed to be the map that helps you find the way.

I should also explain that this book represents a blend of these more traditional approaches I used out in the field and methods I have developed to make these traditional techniques more accessible to people on an everyday basis. For many people, many traditional shamanic techniques are not accessible, since they can be be quite strenuous, exhausting, or simply impractical for the typical urban or suburban environment. For example, the average person may not be able to or want to go off into the wilderness to work with power objects and rituals or spend an hour or two sitting alone in the darkness, as I did when I was training with Michael. However, a person can experience a similar, if less dramatic phenomenon by using visualization and imagery to place him or herself at this wilderness site in the darkness and then use a power object, take part in a ritual, or meditate there. With this experience in the imagination, the person then can gain the same sort of knowledge and insights that he or she might in the field and apply these to everyday life. Thus I have combined my work with Michael and my more recent study of other shamanic approaches with work that I have been doing myself for over twenty years: using imagery, creativity, problem solving, mental control, mind power, and other mental and visual techniques.

When I talk about shamanic mastery, I mean having this ability to exercise the mental control to be who and what you want to be in life, and using shamanic techniques to attain these goals. It is also important to remember that while these shamanic techniques involving altered states of consciousness may draw on traditional symbols or use traditional objects and methods, these symbols, objects, and methods are only tools, developed in early times from the few resources available. However, as shamanic practitioners today emphasize, shamanism has always stressed practicality—in simple terms: do what works. You should use these traditional approaches when they work for you, but should not feel limited by them. Today, shamans may use all sorts of aids to move into altered consciousness dimensions—even high-tech devices and manufactured objects. It is the message, not the medium, that is important. In a similar fashion, I have combined many of the basic teachings I learned from Michael with other consciousness-altering techniques that have worked for me.

In turn, *shamanic* mastery can help you achieve *personal* mastery. In other words, by mastering the techniques and methods of shamanism—the means to your desired goals, you can gain that end result which is sought—in this case, a mastery and control of the self—leading to personal excellence. Such excellence, of course, does not mean being perfect; no one can be. But it does mean moving as close as possible to your ideal of what you want to be or achieve. In so doing, one feels a sense of enjoyment and fulfillment that comes from several sources: from the process of achieving as you use these techniques; from experiencing the sense of achievement as you move ever closer to your goals; from the sense of purpose and direction you gain by pursuing a goal or series of goals; and from the final attainment of particular goals, even as you may set new ones for further progress and mastery.

These goals will naturally differ for each person. Some may want to enhance their personal relationships, others their careers; some may seek a spiritual or personal quest; still others may hope to use these methods to help them enrich society. The point is that these methods themselves can be adapted to any number of goals or combinations of goals—as well as helping you clarify what your goals are so you can pursue them with greater commitment.

In particular, some of the goals and benefits for which you can use shamanic mastery techniques include the following:

- to gain a greater understanding of who you are and what you want to do;
- to set goals and enable you to move more firmly toward their fulfillment;
- to feel a greater sense of connectedness to other things and to your present, future, and past;
- to gain an increased sense of empowerment, leading to enhanced feelings of self-confidence, self-trust, and self-esteem;
- to become more in touch with your inner or higher self, and with your sources of guidance or spiritual truth, so you can see yourself, others, and the world more clearly—which will help you make better decisions and know better how to respond in different situations;
- to experience a keener perception of a greater closeness with

others, because of your awareness, knowledge, and understanding;
· to better direct and balance your own energy so, as desired, you can feel more energized or more relaxed and less stressed, even when encountering difficult situations and problems;
· to achieve an increased sense of peace, calm, and serenity in your life.

Chapter 1 provides an overview of some basic abilities that will help you attain and work with the altered state of consciousness fundamental to producing magical results. These abilities include "seeing," dream awareness and control, conscious projection into other places and times, working with your inner knowing, and staying in balance.

The rest of the chapters in Part 1 focus on the key principles you must keep in mind to use the shamanic tools of power, insight, and ritual appropriately. These include the principles of engaging in right action, using self-control, having the courage and commitment to persevere through difficulties, giving true service to others, having compassion, acting with honor, being aware, having a purpose, and having persistence and patience.

In Parts 2 and 3, I reveal specific techniques to be used while applying these principles. Chapters 9 through 12 show you how to use power objects and power words to intensify and direct your own power. They discuss the use of some traditional objects, like the staff, ritual knife, and crystal, and describe how to find or create your own power objects. They also consider both using traditional words of power and developing your own.

The final chapters deal with the variety of specific methods you can use to get information through other modes of knowing. Chapters 13 and 14 describe psychometry, or the intuitive reading of information contained in an object about its past or its owner. And Chapters 15 through 17 examine the use of ritual to contact and direct the forces of nature to help you achieve your goals.

In all of its chapters, this book also emphasizes the dual nature of gaining shamanic knowledge and power—which is based on successfully balancing the passive or receptive side of the self that provides insight and knowledge with the active or willing side that acts to attain results. A key to this end goal of personal mastery is acting in light of this knowledge, which comes from the inner wisdom in each of us.

I should also mention here that I have included very little on healing in this book, choosing instead to emphasize the use of imagery and approaches of shamanism to resolve everyday problems and enrich your everyday life. In the West today much of the tradition of shamanism has been applied to healing, and medical practitioners have found many of these methods that stress the use of natural, holistic techniques (like using herbs and meditation) helpful as alternative forms of treatment. However, traditionally shamanism has also been used to help individuals and the community solve everyday concerns. So shamans have resolved community disputes, helped individuals regain or cope with lost loves, and have otherwise restored harmony and balance. This book focuses on this latter approach, which draws on the techniques of the shaman for knowing, gaining insight, and advising rather than for healing.

To an extent, some of the uses of shamanism described in this book may overlap with the healing area, like using shamanic techniques to relax, overcome stress, and gain more energy. However, beyond these applications, I think that it is more appropriate for someone to use shamanism for healing when he or she has a medical, nursing, or healing background, since in these instances, shamanism becomes a form of practicing medicine. I am not trained as a doctor or medical practitioner, and the person I studied with emphasized the use of shamanism for knowing and problem solving. So that is the approach I have emphasized here.

•

PART ONE

The Major Principles of Achieving Personal Power and Mastery

1
•

The Basic Tools
of Shamanic
Mastery

Although shamanism and magic have long been considered the exclusive practices of medicine men and sorcerers, the basic principles involved are simple, and can be employed by most people. Essentially, both involve the ability to look into the normally invisible world of energies and forces of nature. Also, practitioners may talk of actually entering or stepping into this other world to gain power and use these forces to achieve desired practical ends.

The two terms of shamanism and magic are often used interchangeably, and the main differences seem to be in the types of symbols, the purposes, and historical factors. The term *magic* has commonly been used to refer to the practices of those in the classical or Western traditions of magic, such as in the ancient empire of Egypt or in the Middle Ages, as well as to the practices of witch doctors, healers, and medicine men in small, tribal nonliterate cultures. By contrast, the reference to the *shaman* has usually been confined to the practitioners from these traditional nonliterate, or non-Western cultures, who use these methods to help and heal group members of the tribe or clan. Some of the most well-known examples of shamans today are from American Indian, Mexican, and South American traditions.

However, modern practitioners have created a more eclectic mix, combining practices from many sources, and the meanings of these two terms have blended. Rather than waste time with semantics, I will be using these two terms more or less interchangeably to refer to the process, noted above, of making a connection with another reality through an altered state of consciousness in order to get information or power from this other world. The second step in the process involves taking that information or power in order to produce practical results in the everyday world.

This chapter describes some of the basic tools you can use to get in touch with this other world and tap into this information or power. (If you have already been working with shamanism, you should find this chapter a useful review of the fundamentals.) As you work with these methods, be aware that this information or power itself is neutral: you can use these techniques for good or ill. However, this book is designed to help you achieve only positive and beneficial results. Thus you can gain what you want in a way that is most satisfying to yourself and others; otherwise, you may open yourself up to all sorts of dangers that can result from having a negative intention and working to achieve negative ends (such as having the negativity you direct outward come back to hurt you).

THE BASIC TOOLS

To work with this other world, you need a few basic tools: These basic tools include developing and using your ability to "see" into the other world, getting in touch with your dreams for information and guidance, projecting your consciousness so you can travel into other times and spaces, and tuning into your inner vision or knowing. Further, you must be able to apply these tools in a balanced way to use the powers described in this book. You will find these are techniques which anyone can use, but you must approach learning them with a certain amount of commitment and patience. For in learning shamanism and magic, as with any other skill, regular practice is important to make these techniques an everyday part of your life.

ADAPTING THE BASIC TOOLS OF THE SHAMAN

Many of the common tools of the shaman can facilitate the process of seeing into other dimensions. These tools can also add mystery and magic to the ritual, to intensify the experience.

For example, shamans sometimes use small wooden figures as focusing devices to speak with the spirits. Or they may use repetitive dancing, as in Bali, and singing, chanting, or drumming, as do many American Indian groups, to step into and gain insights from this other world. Other widely used techniques include fasting, sensory deprivation, piercing or pinching the body in elaborate rites (such as in the sun dance of some Plains Indians), sweating in a kiva (an underground chamber heated by rocks like a sauna, as practiced by Indian groups in the Southwest), and similar acts of self-denial or intensification of experience. And many shamans select personal power objects, like staffs and daggers, to help them feel a greater sense of power as they focus and extend their own internal energy or power through that tool.

Yet remember that all of these activities, rites, and objects are just tools to facilitate and enhance the purpose of this shamanic activity—*seeing* and/or *stepping into* this other world of consciousness or alternate spiritual realm, where the shaman is able to gain the information or help he or she needs to apply to this everyday world. Traditional shamans chose their particular objects because they found them accessible and effective in achieving this larger goal. So through continued use, these tools have come down to us as part of this shamanic tradition. However, since we are now living in a very different society, we can use other objects, activities, and rituals, as well as the traditional ones, to see into or step into this shamanic world, as long as they have meaning for us. Certainly, these can be natural objects like the small stones, flowers, or pieces of bark, such as I have collected for ceremonies during shamanic weekends. But they can also be other, more modern objects that have meaning (such as records, coins, photographs, or just about anything)—and modern dance beats and rock music can play much the same role as traditional drumming, dancing, and chanting. What matters is the purpose to which they are directed: they can be used for mere entertainment or to convey us to other realities.

Then too, it is possible to use no physical tools at all—just our active imagination to help us enter this alternate reality. The key to shamanism lies in the *process* of seeing or moving into this other world to seek to gain information, insights, and spiritual help, not in the particular tools or methods used to get there.

And it is here perhaps that shamanism comes very close to blending with the current popular psychology, which features a range of techniques like creative visualization and mental control that may also be applied in shamanism. Certainly shamanism and transpersonal psychology are related: they both draw on the same inner resources that contribute to self-transformation and increased personal power.

Still, I think shamanism brings another dimension to this modern mix—an awe of and sense of connection with the natural world, which sometimes gets lost in the modern process of self-development and transformation. For shamanism draws very heavily on these natural forces and powers to which the individual is connected, and part of the magic and mystery of shamanism, even in its modern, high-tech guise, is that sense of natural awareness that empowers the individual to see into this other world and step beyond the usual boundaries of experience and knowing.

THE ABILITY TO SEE

The ability to see is fundamental to working with magic or shamanism; it is the essential building block on which all else rests. You have to be able to look at and be aware of the other reality before you can begin to work with it to gain information or power.

Basically, seeing involves looking at the spaces around things. Rather than seeing things directly, you are seeing the auras or energies around objects and people. It is a type of unfocused seeing, during which you are looking off in space, rather than at concrete forms.

To get the feeling of this, pick out some object or point on the wall and stare at it for about five minutes. You will find that soon your vision will start turning fuzzy and unfocused, and you may notice changes in the object or point you are staring at. You may see an aura emerge around it, or you may even see it disappear. Or possibly it may change shape or vibrate.

For an even more intense experience of this process of seeing, try looking at another person for five or ten minutes. Pick a point in the center of the person's forehead, but don't look into his or her eyes, because that is too intense. Again you may notice some interesting changes, as you shift from direct looking to seeing into this other space. Sometimes, you may see the person's face turn into a mask. Or the person's face may seem to disappear. From these changes you may pick up insights or information about the other person.

In fact, gaining information about others is one of the major advantages of learning how to see. You may be able to see the others' thoughts or their feelings. In turn, your seeing enables you to gain these insights into others, because it operates like a beam of light or energy (much like a mental laser beam), focusing your intuition to help you tune into the mental workings of the other person. Of course, it may take some time to develop this in-depth perception of the other person—perhaps some weeks or months, depending on your practice and your ability.

Your seeing can also help you get in closer touch with your own inner knowing, teaching when to trust the information your inner knowing is giving you. Again, your seeing can provide these results because it acts like an energy or light beam to cut through the layers of misunderstanding and uncertainty that sometimes surround your interactions with others or your plans to act. You can also think of your seeing as a key to open the door to your inner world.

You get this information through the images you see when you look at something or from the auras you see around physical objects and people. However, these images and auras you see are, in turn, shaped by both the object you are actually observing and the symbols and associations triggered by this object.

For example, when you look at someone you may suddenly see or think of an image or association with that person, such as the image of a lion, that tells you something about this person, depending on how you interpret that image (e.g., the lion might suggest a strong, steadfast, powerful person to you). Or as you look at someone, you may initially just see a plain aura in the form of a white afterimage around the person's body. But as you continue looking, you may start to see colors emerge that suggest qualities about the person too.

These images or colors may be projected to some extent by the energy of the person or object you are observing. Yet, the images and colors you see can also be influenced by your own interpretation of the energy you experience from the person or object. This interpretation can be shaped by your past experiences and the symbols and associations which have meaning to you.

These interpretations can vary greatly among people, because we all have different ways of interpreting energy. As a result, when several people watch someone doing an exercise to generate energy, some may see the energy take one form or shape, while others may see something else. Thus if your own experiences of the energy evoked by a ritual or other magical or shamanic act do not match the experiences of another observer, do not be concerned. We all have our individual ways of responding because of what we bring to the event, so you should expect these differences.

At one time, when we lived in more tradition-based societies, people were all basically part of the same culture and likewise shared the same system of imagery and symbols when they worked with magical and shamanic techniques. Today, however, we all have had so many different experiences and have learned about so many alternative methods for working with altered realities that we can expect to have different images and interpretations. For the same reason, different people may feel more comfortable pursuing different shamanic or magical paths.

Yet as long as you use the basic principles, you can work effectively with a variety of different techniques. You are free to use your own imagery and symbols, creating your own magical universe. I will be describing certain techniques and rituals which have worked for me and others. You should see these simply as tools which will help you in contacting this other world to tap its sources of information and power. With practice, you will be able to choose the tools that work best for you.

To determine which tools will work best, trust your inner knowing—you will feel which ones are most comfortable. It is similar to what happens when some people decide to buy a new house. Suddenly a visceral feeling tells them that this is the one! This feeling really can't be explained logically—there is just this sense of unity and connection that makes the decision feel right. Likewise, when a tool or technique gives you that feeling, you will know it is a good one for you.

PAYING ATTENTION TO YOUR DREAMS

Your dreams are also a key to working with alternate realities. Pay attention to your dreams because they can help you gain insights about yourself and other people.

One way to help you become more aware of your dreams is to keep a dream log. When I started using one, I found that just keeping it made me more conscious of my dreams and I remembered most of them. Before I started the log, I normally forgot my dreams. But once I told myself, You're going to write in the log every morning, I found that when I did spend a few minutes with my log, images from the dream would appear, which otherwise might have quickly faded. So use your log both to inspire yourself to dream and to jog your memory.

You will also find the dream log useful for noticing patterns—certain themes that reappear in your dreams. Recording your dreams may help you recognize these themes. Reading over your past dream notes will provide insights about yourself from these recurring themes. For example, you may discover some fears you want to overcome or wishes you want to fulfill.

Once you get in touch with your dreams, you can use them actively in a number of ways. One possibility is mutual dreaming, in which two people share dreams. Sometimes people who are close may spontaneously have such a dream. However, the two of you can also plan the subject of a dream; and then you may have a dream on that topic. Although you can do mutual dreaming with anyone, it helps to pick someone close to you, someone with whom you have already shared many things, as this closeness helps to produce successful results.

You can also use mutual dreaming to pick up information about someone else. In this case, you focus on the person and tune in to his or her dreams. Then, if you are really aware, you may get a sense of what he or she is dreaming about; and sometimes you can start dreaming that dream as well.

For example, one of the couples in my workshop described how they sometimes had experienced themselves as being in each other's dreams, sensing the other's feelings and desires. The man, whom I'll call Roger, described one dream of being out in the desert, seeing a snake, and suddenly feeling his wife, Joyce, there with him. He knew she shared this fear, and he killed the snake for her. When they woke up and compared notes, he discovered that

Joyce had had a similar, though fuzzier dream of being in a hot environment and feeling frightened. But then she felt her husband beside her and was comforted. According to Roger and Joyce, this dream helped them feel closer; and I noted that their marriage seemed to be an especially intimate, sharing one.

Dreams that tell you about the future are another powerful source of information. You'll commonly feel a certain intensity to such prophetic dreams, which serves as a signal to pay attention— that this is a particularly important dream. Getting this signal is helpful, because often dreams are merely processing random bits of everyday information. But your inner knowing or intuition, once you develop it, can help you pick up this signal.

Dreams can also help you work out problems. This may occur without any planning on your part, when you're trying to deal with a certain difficulty. A dream may come along that provides an answer to this issue. But you can take more active control over your dreams to plan or program what you dream about, so you can consciously seek an answer to your problem in your dreams.

Programming your dreams can be an excellent way to get information and insights, because you are intentionally directing yourself to dream about a certain subject. So besides seeking answers to specific problems, you can seek information about others or about yourself.

You can program your dreams in a number of ways. If you have prepared a tape of suggestions, you can listen to it as you drift off to sleep. Or you might spend a few minutes before you go to sleep at night telling yourself, I want to dream about this; or, I want an answer to this. Either approach works well, because just before you go to sleep, you are in the hypnagogic alpha state in which you are more suggestible. As you fade into sleep with a particular suggestion in mind, you are more likely to have a dream about it. In turn, the more you practice giving yourself such suggestions, the more suggestible you will become, and you will be more likely to have such programmed dreams.

Another way you can control your dreams is through conscious lucid dreaming. This is a little harder to do, because you are not just programming yourself to have a dream or remember your dreams; you are also seeking to stay alert while you are having a dream so that you can direct it. In order to encourage a lucid dream, do the following: As you are on the edge of falling asleep, give yourself the suggestion to have a certain type of dream or to observe your dream, and be ready to step in and guide the dream if it is not progressing as you would like. Then when you fall asleep, you must keep this aware part of yourself awake, so that you can be the dream's "stage manager." This can be an especially difficult exercise, yet there are some people who have developed a real skill for this technique.

One well-known example of this process comes from the Senoi of Malaysia, a tribal people whose culture includes frequent lucid dreaming. The Senoi pay close attention to their dreams and direct them, and train their children to do this as well. Should something in a dream bother them, they take control and change the dream. Suppose a person dreams about a tiger and is afraid of it. He or she might program him or herself to dream about the tiger again, but this time will make it walk away from him or her, or direct it to somehow show it is friendly, or perhaps he or she will talk to it, and so will lose the fear.

In the United States, we generally do not pay much attention to dreams, because we tend to value a rational, conscious orientation and downplay the value of intuition and unconscious. But you can develop this ability in yourself, by paying attention to your dreams and practicing with the self-programming and lucid-dream-control techniques.

However, without the conscious and continued effort to direct yourself to have such dreams, you may find any success with such dreams transitory. I have found this myself. The few times I have specifically directed myself to have a dream about a certain subject or to direct my dream while it was happening, I have been able to do so. Most of these lucid dreams have come when I have been taking a workshop on dreaming, and thus really concentrating on my dreams. But at other times, when I have been paying more attention to other matters I have not had such dreams.

Lucid dreaming can be quite dramatic. I remember awakening once and feeling that I really liked the dream I was having and would like it to continue. Thus I was aware that a certain part of me was watching the dream happening and that this part of me wanted to see more of the dream. So I went back to sleep and continued the dream. I did this by concentrating on the ending of my previous dream and letting it play over and over in my mind as I drifted off to sleep, while at the same time giving myself the suggestion that once I was asleep, I would find myself back in the dream. Though a successful return is not guaranteed, this technique sometimes works. Later, when I woke and reflected on what had happened, I realized that when I was going through this tran·sition from one dream to the other, I was both awake and not awake at the same time. The part of my consciousness (or perhaps more accurately my unconsciousness) that had been dreaming was still asleep, though just waking up, while this other part of me that was watching was awake, though not fully conscious. In other words, for a few moments, I was in a limbo between wakefulness and sleep, and the wakeful part of me had the power to move me in either direction. Since I wanted to see more of the dream, sleep was the direction I chose to go, though this inner director remained awake to direct the dream.

You may find the process similar to meditating, when a part of you remains alert to guide the meditation. The part of you that is receptive to whatever you experience while meditating is like the part of you that is dreaming. On the other hand, the part that is guiding that meditation by keeping you focused is like your wakeful guide in your dream. The two operate simultaneously, so you are both awake yet asleep, receptive yet active and directing too. You have that control over your inner processes, if only you will take it—both when you are awake and in your dreams.

WORKING WITH CONSCIOUS PROJECTION

Another basic technique for developing your shamanic abilities is conscious projection, in which you project your seeing or consciousness to other places or into the future to pick up information. Some other terms used to describe the process include *geoteleportation* and *remote* or *future viewing*. In essence, you are traveling in space, in time (or both), in your mind and then picking up images, sounds, or sensations.

In the last decade, there have been numerous experiments with this technique conducted by parapsychologists, like the remote viewing experiments at Stanford, and they have reported a measure of success: results have been somewhat higher than those which would occur by chance. In these experiments, several people have been sent to a target destination, while the subject being tested for remote vision tries to pick up their whereabouts. Then he or she records any images or impressions, which are compared with the target destination. If there are sufficient similarities—say the subject picks up water when the participants have gone to the ocean, the response is considered a hit.

You can try your own conscious-projection experiments. One possibility from one of our classes, is to go into one room and perform an action (e.g., look at a picture or select an object), while people in another room try to pick up what you are doing. To check results, record your movements, while they write down their impressions. Afterward compare records to see how accurate these impressions were. With practice, your results should improve. Even if they don't, this experimenting will help make you more adept at imagining what it is like to be in another location (i.e.—another city, another house, another room, etc.)—a useful technique for playing out what you might do in different situations which you have not yet experienced (e.g., meeting someone for the first time, or figuring out what you need for a trip by imagining you are already there).

Another way to use projection is to imagine that you have stepped into someone else's mind and try to see the world through his or her eyes. When you do, you can often pick up information about what he or she is experiencing or seeing, or why he or she is acting in a certain manner.

You can also use projection when you meet people, to get a sense of what they are like. Also, you can do this to prepare before an actual meeting, like a job interview. For instance, if you have not met the person yet, but have spoken to him or her on the phone, you can consciously project yourself where he or she is to get a sense of his or her personality. Then you can guide the interview accordingly. For instance, if he or she is a detail-oriented person, you can come to the interview ready to provide the details. Or if he or she prefers a quick overview, you can provide that.

So, too, you can travel to other places mentally just to visit and observe, much like a tourist, except you are traveling in your mind. Go to another city or visit friends and pay attention to your surroundings. Ask yourself questions so you will notice more details.

You can also use projection in a ritual to increase the intensity of your focus. For example, imagine your energy projected outward like a beam of light.

Another use of the process is influencing others. Suppose you are hoping to get a favorable reaction from a prospective employer or someone with whom you are negotiating a business venture; focus on projecting yourself to him or her in a positive light so he or she will have more positive thoughts about you. Or perhaps preview yourself meeting or talking with him or her. Then too, if there is something you want, you can work on picturing it and focusing all your energy and intention on getting it.

PROJECTING YOURSELF INTO THE FUTURE

When you use projection to look into the future, realize that you are looking at a probable future, not one that is fixed in time. So you are picking up information about what is likely to happen, but is not definite. Since these events are only probable, you may be able to have some influence on a particular probability that you see.

You might think of your ability to change the future this way. Every event has a certain likelihood of happening if things continue as they are, and every event can be affected by people who are involved in, or have the power to influence, that event to some degree. For instance, under normal circumstances, there may be a 99 percent chance that the newspaper you subscribe to will be delivered. But then this likelihood can be affected by various people, such as the delivery person, the printers, the banks that finance the paper, the labor unions, and social and natural events, like local protests, earthquakes, and floods. Each of these individuals or factors have a greater or lesser degree of influence on the delivery of your paper.

You may also have some degree of control over something, apart from the likelihood of its occurrence and the influence of others. (For instance, you can call to cancel your paper, or can order another paper if the first one does not come.) In some cases, your control can be direct and fairly certain, regardless of what others do (e.g., when you decide to go to work or not). But in other cases, the event may involve more people (like a big celebration)—so that many people may need to share similar ideas in order to effect a change (like changing the time, purpose, and place of that celebration). Also, some people have more power to change the future than others do (for instance, you alone might not have too much impact on changing a local law, but someone with political connections might be able to call the right people or organize a demonstration to get the law changed more quickly and effectively).

Yet regardless of the nature of the event or the amount of influence you think you have now, projection and the other techniques we will discuss can help you develop more personal power and increase your ability to take charge and thereby influence the course of future events.

Many people misconstrue the process of future projection, because they think a psychic is supposed to be totally accurate or he or she is completely wrong. In turn, when many psychics make predictions, they lead people to make an all-or-nothing interpretation. Predictions that a certain candidate is going to win the presidential race or that one celebrity is going to marry another star often turn out to be wrong, giving the skeptics fuel to bash all psychic prophecies as shams. In truth, these inaccuracies result because the psychics are only predicting a probable future, even though the psychic may not be aware of this and may have a strong feeling of certainty at the time. In other words, each time a psychic makes a prediction, it has a certain probability of happening, so that some predictions are much more likely to come true than others. So perhaps it might be helpful if psychics couched their predictions in these terms (e.g., the presidential win by this candidate is about 40 percent likely). Then the overall outcome of their predictions would be more accurate.

All futures are only probable because everyone has some degree of influence on the future, since we are all interconnected with each other and with the environment. Imagine the whole world and everyone on it as being part of a rubber ball. If you push one place on this ball, you affect everything else. Yet just as a stronger push on the ball will have a greater impact than a weaker one, some people have more ability than others to influence events.

Since future events have varying probabilities and people have varying abilities to influence them, consider these factors when you plan the future. A good first step is to look into the future and determine which events are most probable, and to use intuition to get a sense of how likely they are to happen. Second, sense how able you are to influence the outcome. Then, after weighing these two factors, if you feel that something is almost sure to happen, you can adjust and prepare for it. On the other hand, if you pick up a future outcome and see this is something you can and want to change, you can take steps to make those changes. Depending on the situation, you might make some changes in yourself, in your relationships with others, in the environment, or in a combination of areas, for you can change the future on many different levels.

In turn, looking ahead and perceiving the probable future can help you influence what happens. The process operates much like the Heisenberg principle, whereby your own observations and awareness impact on the object of your observations and awareness. By announcing the future you observe, you can make that future more likely to happen, because you may act in a way that will make it happen. On the other hand, the process of observation can have the opposite effect, because it may make you conscious of what is likely to happen if you continue the way you are going. And then, having this awareness, you may act to make the change.

So, your awareness of the probable future can work both ways, because it provides you with certain choices, once you are aware of what is likely to happen in the future, if things progress in their present manner. To develop this awareness, use a meditation in which you ask yourself, If everything keeps going the way it's going now, what is likely to happen? Then, after you see the probable future, ask yourself, What might I do to change that future if I want to change it? Or, What might I do to make that future even more probable, because I would like to see it happen?

When you do think about influencing the future, keep in mind that the distance of that future in time influences the probabilities as well. Future events that are close in time are more likely to happen than those that are distant, because, as time passes, there are many intervening events that may change the future.

Then too, your own goals can impact upon future outcomes. A good approach is to set your own goals based on what you would like to see happen, but be ready to adjust them based on what you see happening in the future. For example, set a long-term goal for five to ten years hence. But then break that goal into smaller goals: What do you want to happen in four years, in three years, in two years, in one year? Then, break the goals for each year into subgoals as well. However, in deciding how far ahead to look use the approach that feels most comfortable. While some people like to plan far ahead, others prefer to think about next month or next year. So use the time frame you like best, or perhaps use different frames in different situations (like a long-term frame for a career and a shorter time frame for entering a relationship or a marriage).

Finally, recognize that your own attitude toward life and the future in general can influence future outcomes. Approaching the future with a positive, upbeat attitude will to some extent help you create a positive future. Yet your positive attitude is only one factor affecting your life. Other people with whom you interact are also thinking positive and negative thoughts, and there are environmental, social, and political events that are affecting you too. So you can't praise or blame yourself for everything that happens in your life.

Thus, when something that seems negative happens, it may be due to one of these random events, a result of the thoughts and actions of many other people, not something you have caused yourself.

Nevertheless, you can still affect the outcome of this event by your attitude. Thus if you have a positive, constructive attitude and something goes wrong, you can ask yourself how you can learn from this negative event, or ask, What is this event telling me about what I should do now?

For instance, when I encounter problems, instead of blaming myself, I try to see what I can learn from them or what they are telling me about where to go next. For example, a few years ago, I had an experience in direct sales that ended up with a lot of people owing me money. But rather than feeling discouraged and bitter I found some insights about my next move, which included going to law school and writing books about collecting money and other legal issues, which more than paid back the money I had lost, as well as opening up new career directions.

In the same way, you can look at your past experiences and from them learn how to change and improve the future. In turn, your projection can help you transmute bad past experiences so that you reexperience them positively in the future. Then, when the future arrives, you will be more likely to have a positive experience.

GETTING IN TOUCH WITH YOUR INNER VOICE

Another major tool is the ability to listen to your inner voice or self. You must be able to know when to trust it, which brings up questions of how you know what you know. To start, you must learn how to feel when that voice is true, which can take practice in picking up inner signals. Then, once you feel certain you know, the issue becomes whether or not you want to act on that information.

In some cases, you may feel this certainty of knowing, but it may not be appropriate to act, or you may not want to act because you may not be ready to deal with the consequences right now. I had this experience with a customer I had worked with about a year. I positively knew he was lying when he claimed he had forgotten his wallet, because he did not want to pay me for some work I did for him which had to be done over, since he had given me the wrong instructions originally. However, I did not want to confront him. I felt this would only lead to an angry scene at a time when I was rushing to make a deadline, and I was certain he would deny the accusation. So I remained silent about what I knew, and subsequent events confirmed my inner knowing. In fact, I had further conversations with him, in which he agreed he owed me the money, promised to pay, and even thanked me profusely at one point. But all along I knew he was lying, and when he later moved, still owing me the money, and I spoke to some of his friends about the incident, my own knowing was confirmed. However, I still feel it would not have been appropriate to act on this at the time.

Describing exactly how this knowing feels can be very difficult because it is really just a sense of certainty about something being a particular way.

People experience this knowing in different ways. Some people may be more likely to have a gut-level feeling; some may be more prone to experience a tingling sensation; some may be more apt to see an inner light going on. Or there may be other manifestations of the signal that you know something or have experienced an inner or certain truth—like having some teacher or power animal come and tell you, Yes, this is correct. Thus, to get in closer touch with your own knowing, be aware of how your knowing manifests itself. Then you can better know whether or not to trust your impressions or feelings about something.

This insight can, in turn, help you make everyday decisions. It can let you know whether to trust or deal with someone. It can tell you whether or not to do something or go somewhere. It may even save your life, as policemen and other people in dangerous positions who use this information have reported. For example, when Michael worked on an ambulance, a number of times, he suddenly got a sense of knowing that he was in a potentially dangerous situation. There would be no logical reason, but this voice would tell him, You'd better leave this place, because something bad is going to happen, and then he would leave. In one case, this quick response saved his life. He was in front of a newsstand when he suddenly got the feeling that he had better move immediately. He did, and in moments, another man stepped into the spot where Michael had been and the man was shot. So it can be critically important to pay attention to your inner voice.

In order to do this, you must be able to distinguish this voice inside you from your other inner talk, which can be relaying all kinds of information to you, some of it accurate, some of it not. So you have to be able to sort through these many messages to pick up what is truly accurate, what you really know.

After you do sort through these to tap into that truth, you will feel a close inner connection and certainty that come from communicating directly with your inner voice or vision. You may interpret this communication in different ways. Some people see this inner voice or vision as coming from their inner or higher self. Others believe they may be getting in touch with their spiritual guides, who may exist inside them, or who may be energies or entities communicating with them from the outside.

However you experience this inner voice—as yourself speaking to you or as outer beings or spiritual guides—the point is to open up the channels of communication, keep them clear, understand how your voice communicates with you, listen, and develop that feeling of absolutely and certainly knowing that you know. By getting in tune with this inner voice, you will develop this strong feeling of certainty, and once you do it is important to trust these feelings and follow them, if appropriate. For when you listen, you will find your inner voice is giving you important information. Then use your common sense to decide whether or not it is appropriate to act in response to this information. If so, go ahead and act, guided by your inner voice.

TAKING SOME TIME TO GET IN TOUCH WITH YOURSELF

One way to get in closer touch with your inner self is to spend some time alone, where you can focus on opening up and being receptive. This is called *taking a solo*. In the solo, you go off to be alone for a while in a quiet place. One good place to do this is outdoors in nature, but you can do it in any quiet place, such as in your own room.

Once you are in this quiet place, you should be open, receptive, and aware of any perceptions, sounds, or feelings you experience from whatever source—from within you or from outside natural or spiritual sources, and in response, you may get answers or advice. A natural setting is particularly good for the solo because it will help you to get in touch with the forces of nature which are also within ourselves. These include the common elements of nature—air, earth, fire, and water, which correspond to our personal qualities. For example, air is light and expansive; earth is solid and stable; fire, aggressive and powerful; water, smooth and flowing. A solo in nature can help you get in touch with those qualities, so you can later work on controlling and directing them.

One good approach to taking the solo is to spend about a half hour or forty-five minutes in this quiet place, trying to attain an altered state by whatever technique works for you—meditation, relaxation, or focusing on your breathing. Now as you move into this altered state, try not to ask questions consciously. Rather, just open yourself up and let the questions come into your mind. Likewise, let the answers come in response to the questions.

The key is not to preprogram your response. Instead, let your conscious mind go and be very receptive to whatever comes.

For most people this is a very peaceful experience. However, you may also find that it is a reflection of your usual personality or current mental state, so if you are a usually hyper or high-strung person, or are going through a period of uncertainty or turmoil, you may experience these feelings during the solo too. This is what happened to some people I know who felt spiritual beings tempting them. One woman, who was going through a personal crisis at the time, was doing her first solo on a cliff when, she reported, a spiritual being tempted her to walk off the cliff. At that point, Michael appeared and guided her back. Another man who was having problems with relationships heard the voices of children crying, and he felt some beings were tempting him into a zone of danger. But he stayed firm and overcame the temptation.

For most people, though, the solo is a nice, quiet experience. When I did my first solo, in a meadow, I imagined putting a protective circle of white light around myself. Then I experienced myself just being there, asking questions, and getting answers, as I listened with a separate part of myself. In fact, the questions I asked and the answers I got were quite mundane, like what I should do to lose weight. But even so, the answers I got turned out to be on target. For example, about a month after the solo, I dropped to the lowest weight I had been for several years, because the answer I got gave me an effective technique to lose weight.

So for some people, the solo can be a time simply to relax and meditate; for others, a time to gain deep spiritual insights or information on dealing with personal issues; and for still others, an opportunity to learn how to respond to mundane, practical matters. The nature of your solo depends on you, though you should not preprogram—just let it happen and be receptive.

DEVELOPING BALANCE AND CONTROL

Finally, it is important to develop balance and control in using these techniques and in all areas of your life.

First, you need balance and control in working with these techniques for contacting other realities. You don't want to spend so much time doing this that you lose touch with everyday reality. At the same time, if you are in such close touch with the everyday world, you might fail to pay sufficient attention to the insights possible through other levels of awareness. Thus your goal should be to find that appropriate balance in yourself by deciding how much time you want to spend with these techniques every day. Generally, twenty to thirty minutes a day is fine, at least at first.

After a while, as you continue to work with these techniques, they will become second nature to you, so a formal practice time may be less necessary. I find that although I may not use a specific meditative technique, I can enter this meditative state whenever I want. For example, I use meditation for game designing, for I can quickly get into an altered consciousness state to come up with ideas for games. Similarly, at times when I sit down to write, I enter what feels like an altered state where ideas just come to me, as if I am just typing down a message that has been dictated to me from another source. When I first started writing, I did meditative exercises to get in the mood to write, but now that I have been writing for so long, I don't need to do anything formal. The ideas usually just flow into me whenever I sit down at the typewriter.

I have also used this technique in making everyday decisions, such as renting a place or furnishing a room. In the case of renting, I have just projected myself into the place in the future and have imagined what it might be like to live there. As for selecting furniture, I have visualized the room with different pieces of furniture in different places, to get a sense of how the room looks from a distance, and then I have projected myself into the room, to get a sense of being in the room myself, which helps me to decide what personally feels right for the room.

Also, it is important to stay balanced on your various levels—physical, emotional, and intellectual. For instance, finding a good balance between physical exertion and a sedentary life-style will help you feel healthier. On the emotional level, you should be balanced in your degree of openness to others, so you can be warm and receptive, yet protect yourself from being too vulnerable. Also, balance using your intellectual skills with expressing yourself emotionally or physically.

There are various ways to find this balance on all your levels. You can meditate to get insights on your possible imbalances, so you can change. Or once you know on which levels you want to develop better balance, you can do visualization exercises to determine how you can achieve this balance.

You should also work on balancing your various personality attributes. These attributes tend to come in opposites, like masculine-feminine, active-passive, receptive-directive, and you should find a balance that feels comfortable for you. For example, balance your nurturing, tender, and intuitive aspects with your more aggressive, masculine, and directive side.

Another aspect of being balanced is being able to adapt and be flexible, so that as situations come up in your life, you can respond appropriately. Then negative situations won't throw you, or you will be better able to accept the unexpected. Yet at the same time, for complete balance, you need to have a sense of direction or purpose, so you can stay on course. In other words, you are balanced because you are both directed yet ready to change as circumstances arise. You have created a practical blend of the two.

Often it is easy to stay in balance when good things occur, because you can generally stay on the course you have already set and, if that is balanced, remain on an even keel. Yet sometimes, if people forget about keeping this balance, they can become overwhelmed by good fortune. A prime example is people who win the lottery and suddenly cannot deal with their success and the resulting changes in their lives. As a result, they may lose friends, alienate relatives, and find themselves no longer in touch with who they really are, so while they should be happy with all this new-found money, in fact they are lonely and lost.

Still another part of being in balance is knowing your purpose and keeping that commitment and direction, so you can stay centered when any difficulties arise. Then, having this sense of purpose, you can overcome any problems quickly and move on, so you don't get stuck or obsessed with something. Or if you do start to feel stuck, then maybe you need to take steps to push away the negative experience. For instance, you can write a description of the experience and burn it up, or perform a release ritual. In doing so, you can use whatever methods work for you, since different people feel comfortable with different systems. For example, some people might use chanting or breathing exhalation exercises to let go of some negativity; others might prefer to visualize what they don't want in their life disappearing or being destroyed. Try out different approaches until you find what works best for you.

Then too, being balanced means having this inner sense of self-control, at the same time that you remain open and flexible about new experiences. It's like maintaining an internal monitor that tells you when you have let go enough, so you can pull back as necessary. Also, this state of balance includes the balance between your rational, logical side and your intuitive, spontaneous nature. If you do not keep yourself in control, you can go too far in that intuitive, spontaneous direction, and you may find it hard to come back, like the person who goes into a trance without making the necessary arrangements for coming back, either through personal cues or the assistance of a willing guide.

I had this experience of losing control when I first started exploring spiritual and magical traditions in a spiritual-growth group in the early 1970s. I had always been very logical; in fact, I came to this exploration after many years of academic study in sociology. So I approached everything in an analytical way.

However, without realizing it, I gradually dropped these logical controls, and the experience became very scary. I started experimenting with many techniques for altered states of consciousness and worked with meditations. To do this, I gradually learned to let go of my logical mind, which is perfectly fine. You need to suspend your logic to respond intuitively. But I failed to keep a part of my logical mind as a kind of monitor which remained aware and ready to step in to take control as well, much like a teacher might passively supervise a well-functioning class, but then intervene as necessary to keep students from straying from the purpose of the class. As a result, I did not realize that this was happening until about a year into my project.

I only became aware of how much I had let go of the logical when I wrote the first draft of my doctoral dissertation, based on my research on this group and another spiritual-growth group. I turned my paper in, thinking it was fine. But when my professor pointed out how bad it was, I suddenly realized the problem. For when I read the draft again, with my professor's comments in mind, I saw that it was scattered and rambling. It was as if I had unwittingly written it from my stream of consciousness. Instead, I thought I was using my logical mind, just as I had always done before.

I suddenly felt very scared. I thought, What is happening to my head? I felt as if I could not think in an organized and logical way anymore. And I was very anxious for a while, as I concentrated on thinking logically again and getting back that logical control in my mind.

Gradually, after about a year I did, and was now able to balance both the rational and intuitive. I realized that when I started on the project I had been too intellectually oriented, so that I was not in touch with my intuitive abilities at all. But then, caught up in the activities of this spiritual group I was studying, I let this rational part of me go, so I felt as if my thinking abilities had atrophied. Yet the experience was what I needed to trigger a synthesis. I took about a year to achieve it, but the result was a feeling of complete rational control when I wanted it. But at other times, I could completely let that go to give full play to my creativity and intuition, until I was ready to call back that rationality.

So, to achieve balance, seek to have both the rational and intuitive working together. Then, your rational mind can be in control when you want it to be, and at other times, you can release this inner monitor to let your intuition go free. This is like having a stage director watching in the wings. He is there to give directions when he thinks the players need it, but afterward steps back to let them perform freely. And when he is ready, he comes back and gives more directions, for he is fully in charge of the play. This is the kind of balance you want to achieve—a perfect melding of the rational and the intuitive, so you can explore other realities as far and as deeply as you want. Later, you can always come back and apply those insights, as needed, to your everyday life.

THE COSMIC CONNECTION

Lastly, having a sense of connection with the cosmos will help to empower you, because you can experience a unity with all things, which will give you a feeling of support and strength. It is as if you are drawing upon the strength of the universe in doing whatever you do. When you do a solo or work with nature, this is an excellent time to tune in to that power and open yourself to it.

2
•

Achieving
Right Action and
Self-Control

There are ten major principles to keep in mind as you seek power and mastery through shamanism —right action, self-control, courage, service, compassion, honor, awareness, persistence, purpose, and patience. These are important guidelines which will help you stay on course and use the powers you develop to good ends. Otherwise, you may find yourself, as some who gain power do, taking your power for granted and using it for egotistical, selfish, or negative ends, and the kinds of thoughts and actions you put out will ultimately come back in kind, bringing this negativity back to you. By contrast, these principles will help you avoid such problems and move ahead to gain and retain the power and mastery you seek.

These principles derive from a number of spiritual traditions, including the Japanese warrior schools, the teaching of Zen Buddhism, and shamanism. They represent a blend or synthesis, adapted in light of modern conditions. This chapter and the two following discuss each of these principles and how you can apply them in your own life.

EMPLOYING THE PRINCIPLE OF RIGHT ACTION

The principle of right action means doing the right thing at the right time. To do this, you need to listen to your heart, inner voice, or intuition, and when you sense that it is telling you to act in a certain way, you should act quickly and decisively. In other words, you should come to a quick decision about whether or not it is appropriate to take a particular action, and then either do so or not. You want to avoid indecision that will cause you to act too late or halfheartedly, nullifying your action. Or if you don't act at all, you may miss an important opportunity. Thus you must be decisive when you experience that call to act.

So the key question becomes, how do you *know* what the appropriate action is? This is another of these questions you ultimately can not answer logically. You just have to feel that intense sense of certainty and rightness which comes from working with your inner voice over time. It's like opening a door and knowing you are in the right place when you see the intensity of light in the room. All the fog of uncertainty has been swept away, and you just see that warm, pristine glow. Similarly, the techniques in this book are designed to help you push away that mist so that you experience that intense and certain glow.

ACTING WITHIN THE WINDOW OF ACTION

At times, you need to choose and act quickly, because time is of the essence. It is as if a window opens and there is a certain opportunity available at that time. But you need to take advantage of that opportunity while the window is open.

People who are in certain businesses, like publicity, advertising, and marketing, know that very well. If they don't have, say, publicity ready on the due date, they lose the newspaper coverage or television exposure.

There can also be crucial windows in personal relationships that affect one's future. For instance, one woman told me how she had met and fallen head over heels for an Australian man who was visiting the U.S. for a few weeks. They were together almost every day, and when he was planning to leave, he invited her to come to his ranch and marry him. There were a few details to work out, since his divorce from his first wife was still in progress. But he desperately wanted her to come with him. And he said her presence would give him strength to go through with the divorce he truly wanted.

But should she? Every part of her being urged her to go. She felt it was absolutely the right thing, and she felt certain he was just the right man for her. And yet she kept holding back, fighting against her feeling of certainty with little fears and doubts. Maybe he would not go through with the divorce. Maybe she would have difficulty finding a job. And on and on. Thus she did not leave with him, and she kept hesitating over the next month, despite his calls and letters asking her to come. Finally, about six months later, after the calls and letters had ceased, she decided that she did in fact want to make the move, and she called the man, saying she would be willing. But now, as his divorce was proceeding, he had started seeing someone else and his ardor for her had cooled. So the relationship was no longer possible. She had in effect missed the window that had been open for a while and that could have changed her life, and for months afterward, she looked back sadly, regretting her failure to act quickly enough.

Accordingly, in whatever you do, it is crucial to look for windows of action, which are the optimal times to act. Otherwise, if you wait too long, the window may close, and then it may not be possible, or may be less advantageous, to act.

ACTING WHEN YOU HAVE THE INSPIRATION

Right action also means acting when you feel the inspiration, because if you wait too long, you or others involved in the action can lose enthusiasm. In other words, you should act when your interest in doing something is high.

Let's say you have a job offer. You will normally have only a limited time in which to accept the job or not. As a result, if your initial impression is to take it, act right away. On the other hand, if the situation is unclear or in flux, and you get a sense that it is not appropriate to make a decision now, wait. But also recognize that when the time comes be ready to make a decision and very quickly follow up on this decision with the indicated action.

Now this may seem like good common-sense advice that might be useful to anyone, apart from any connection with shamanism. Yet the advantage shamanism provides is in helping you have that sense of knowing or rightness about your decision, and the confidence to act on it. By tapping into the sense of certainty or intensity of that inner voice described earlier, you help yourself gain that power to move ahead quickly when that window for action is still open and inviting you to act.

Some other examples of deciding, then acting when you feel the inspiration include the decisions to form a business partnership, accept a marriage offer, or move in with someone. Whatever it is, when you feel the time is right and feel inspired to do something, follow through quickly, while you still feel inspired and enthused, and any others involved do too.

As you will find, this decisive, inspired action is one key to success, for one of the characteristics that distinguish people who become very successful from those who do not is this decisiveness and ability to follow through. Many people have good ideas, but never realize them because of the failure to act on them. Thus, after you start with an ounce of inspiration, you need your pound of quick, decisive action to make that inspiration work.

ACTING IN TUNE WITH YOUR OWN VALUE SYSTEM OR MORALITY

Another aspect of right action is acting in a way that conforms with your own value system or morality, so you feel comfortable with that action. In turn, having the contemplated action fit with your own morality will help you to act decisively because you will not have reservations standing in the way.

Generally, when you do trust your inner voice, your guide will suggest an ethical action, as long as you seek to act with a benevolent intention. But if a little warning bell rings in your mind when you feel inspired to act, then look at this inspiration more closely. Maybe you are getting a confused or mixed message, and you should review your inner message in light of your own moral or value system, so that you act consistently with it. Otherwise, your action may leave you with recriminations, no matter how inspired to act you thought you were.

At the same time, be aware that value systems differ, so what one person considers ethical, another may not. Ethics can depend on your relative priorities, and as long as your overall intention is good, such differences are generally fine. For example, in one workshop, a woman described being asked to cover for a coworker who needed to spend time with a sick relative, but whose boss did not want her to take the time. The woman agreed to cover because she wanted to keep peace in the office and she felt that if the boss found out about the employee's action, he might fire the employee, and the woman knew her coworker needed the job. So you may ask, What is ethical? The woman felt her action was right in terms of her own ethics, and so she felt comfortable doing it. Her overall intention was benevolent, and her decision to cover for the woman worked out. Others might have preferred a different option; they might have considered another action more ethical; but in this case, this choice felt ethical for the woman and worked for her.

Thus, in making your choices for action, it is important to follow your inner knowing about what is ethical, based on your own morals or values. At first, you may want to ask yourself about the ethics of something consciously, when you are feeling drawn to do something. But after a while, you will find this ethical judging happening automatically as you look within, and it will become part of your overall feeling of rightness and certainty because you have that inner knowing. As a result, normally, when you feel this intense pull to take some action, the ethical judgment will occur naturally because this inner part of you has intuitively considered all things. Accordingly, if you do get the signal that the action you want to take may be wrong, take another look. For right action is not only quick and decisive action; it means taking the ethical action too, in light of your own system of values.

COMBINING YOUR FEELING AND INTELLECT TO ACHIEVE RIGHT ACTION

Right action also involves combining the feelings of your heart and the insights of your mind. Certainly, you should trust that inner voice or vision, when it feels appropriate. But you also have to combine those insights with common sense, so you are both aware of your feelings and act intelligently. Then too, your intellect can help to work out the details of implementing an action, when you have the inspiration to do it.

Suppose you are experiencing a conflict in a relationship. When you look within, your heart may tell you, resolve it now. But then your intellect may suggest various ways to do it. So you can draw on both aspects of yourself to help find a solution. Then, once you see the solution, you can put it into practice.

Taking the relationship conflict as an example, you might realize that the way to resolve it is to work out a compromise. If keeping the relationship together is a priority for both of you, then that might be the thing to do. One or both of you may have to give in a bit. But how? To find out, you might seek and listen to your inner voice, and it might say OK, you need to give in now. If that seems like a rational step to preserving the relationship, go ahead and do it. In other words, you are getting insights and feelings about what you should do, then reviewing and assessing the value of those responses with your logical mind. If the ideas make sense, you can put them into practice.

Thus you have your own system of checks and balances, in the same way that the government's executive, judicial, and legislative branches check each other. You can let your more intuitive self, like the legislature, decide what to do, so you can implement the decision, like the executive. But then you employ your logical or rational mind, like the judiciary, to check yourself from time to time, to make sure what you want to do is appropriate, makes sense, is ethical, and is something you feel comfortable with and really want. In most cases, you can assume your intuition will be valid—just as you can assume that most laws of the legislature are constitutional. But occasionally your intuition may be off, just as a law may turn out to be wrong; that is why it's good to have your logic right there as necessary, ready to review and check.

KNOW WHEN YOU KNOW AND THEN ACT

Finally, pay attention to when you know that you know, because that is generally a clear sign to act immediately. In fact, this sense of clear knowing distinguishes the master from the student.

For example, Michael was on a trip to Death Valley with some of his friends, and although the night was clear, they suddenly had a strong feeling that a blizzard was coming. The thought made no sense because the weather seemed nice and there had been no forecasts of a blizzard. But they followed the powerful feeling anyway and turned around. When a sudden blizzard hit a few hours later, they managed to get out just in time.

In a number of similar cases, people planning plane or train trips have had strong feelings that they should not go, and did not. And sometimes, they report, they narrowly missed a plane crash or other serious problem. At a convention several years ago, some people described how they nearly lost their lives on the way to the convention when their plane almost crashed in a storm, and afterward, they lost their luggage. Before the flight, they reported feeling strongly that they should not take that plane. But they did anyway, because they so wanted to attend the convention. Perhaps their misadventure might be explained away as a coincidence, though they did not think so. They felt very strongly that the near crash and lost luggage were proof that their intuition had been right. Likewise, other people who have changed their travel plans because of a danger signal have felt there was no coincidence when they subsequently learned the plane or train had crashed. They were more convinced than ever that their inner knowing had been very clearly telling them what to do.

I have used this sense of "knowing when I know" to make quick decisions about prospective roommates. I chose about a half-dozen roommates over a period of four years, and each time, I decided by getting an intuitive sense of the person. This was what mattered to me, not any routine checking of references or credit. So I never really asked for details—just took a few minutes to get a feel for the person. Once I had a positive feeling I felt ready to act right away, to invite the person to move in. And each time it worked. I never had problems with roommates.

Likewise, you can look to your intuition to make quick decisions about almost anything, including major changes in your life, like where to live next or whether to take a new job. Then, once you make that intuitive leap and feel this strong sense of certainty that you are right, put your decision into action right away, for the reasons previously discussed.

THE SIGNS OF RIGHT ACTION

When you do act from the principle of right action, you will notice that things tend to fall into place and go smoothly. Also, if you have made a good decision, you will find that the natural turn of events will help to implement that decision. It is as if the new happenings serve to reinforce the decision you have made.

I had this experience when I decided I wanted to research conflict resolution. After I announced my decision to a monthly inspirational breakfast group, one group member told me about a neighborhood conflict-resolution group which had a forty-hour training program. Once I participated in the program, I could serve on community conflict-resolution panels—which would provide exactly the kind of material I needed for my book. Later, another woman asked me to lead a discussion on the topic with her group. Experiences like this suggested my decision was right.

Conversely, if after you make a decision and start to implement it, everything seems to go wrong, that may be a sign you should take another look. Does this mean you should try harder to make things work, or should you modify or drop the decision and start again? Circumstances change, or you might have been mistaken in your original choice, so look to your inner knowing again to figure out the best course of action now.

EMPLOYING THE PRINCIPLE OF SELF-CONTROL

The principle of self-control prescribes that you should have the discipline and the detachment to take a step back and assess any situation you experience or intuition you sense in a cool, calm, and rational way. After you get some insight, pause to examine carefully what is happening and determine the best way to handle it. For example, if you are feeling anxious, breathe deeply to calm down, rather than acting on impulse.

Self-control enables you to look at any situation with detachment so you can assess your options. You want to listen and respond to your feelings, but you don't want to act impulsively and inappropriately. So you need that sense of control to check and assess your actions. Self-control helps you stay in balance.

Take, for example, a problem at work. Suppose you feel very angry at your boss. You have a strong impulse to tell off your boss and you think doing so will make you feel good. But your self-control may urge you to wait, because it is generally best to avoid a direct attack on someone when you feel angry. Rather, you can usually get further with someone if you express some of your anger in a calm, collected way. Then you can talk about the cause of this anger and how you can improve the situation now.

In the case of your boss, you may very well be justified in your anger. Intuitively, emotionally, you feel he or she is behaving terribly. He is being too demanding; making you put in more hours than you should; giving you an assignment you are not ready for. Your anger may be quite justified because your boss is completely out of line. If you simply blow up at him or her and let off steam, you may beel better for the moment, but then you may be out of a job. By contrast, if you mentally step back from the situation for a few minutes and try to find a good way to present this problem, and then sit down and talk with him or her, you might be able to get him or her to understand your point of view. Then your boss may recognize that the changes you seek may benefit him or her as well, and he or she may implement the changes.

I remember encountering such a situation when I worked for an advertising agency. I was working on a few long-term research projects and I found I was more productive working at home on my own schedule. At first, my boss disapproved, because this was against office policy, and when he initially asked me to come in at 9:00 A.M. like everybody else, I was very angry. I felt like arguing with him, pointing out that I had turned in much more work than ever and that I felt unappreciated for the extra work I had done on my own. But instead, I held back my feelings, and subsequently, in a calm, cool way, I made an appointment with him to discuss the situation. When we did, I logically went over the benefits he could obtain by having me work at home, and when he saw it made sense, he agreed. As a result, I got to do what I wanted to do, and this arrangement continued until my boss received requests from others in the office for the same treatment. Shortly after this ideal situation ended I found another job. What made this perfect arrangement possible while it lasted was my use of self-control to work out this alternative, rather than impulsively expressing my anger and alienating my boss, or keeping silent in a situation that would continue to make me angry.

ASSESSING YOUR IDEAS AND RISKS

Your self-control can be especially valuable in assessing a new idea and weighing the possible risks. You may think a particular idea is terrific, but you are so emotionally attached to it that it is hard to judge it. That is when your self-control can come in to help you examine the idea with dispassion and perhaps come up with an alternative that might be even better.

Similarly, your self-control can help you determine the risks of some action, so you can decide if you want to take it. Successful people do this all the time. They regularly take risks, but they assess the risks they take first, so they are actually conservative risk takers. They balance the likely danger with the potential for gain, and they take the risk if the benefit seems substantially higher than the cost.

You can use a similar process for any venture that seems uncertain or risky. At first, you may want to think of the various risks and benefits. But after a while, the process becomes more and more automatic, so you will respond intuitively at the same time that you are exercising your self-control. Your intuition and self-control will just operate together in tandem—like an automatic fact checker and reviewer that will come into play as soon as your intuition speaks to you. Your intuition may say, Let's go! but at the same moment your self-control will take a quick look, and if everything seems fine, it will say Go ahead. But if not, it will tell you, Forget it, or perhaps, Get some more information and then decide how to proceed.

FINDING SOLUTIONS TO PERSONAL PROBLEMS

Self-control can also help with resolving a personal dilemma. Your heart may tell you one thing but your self-control serves as a useful check, much like getting a second opinion from a third party. Using this approach, you can draw on your logic to resolve a problem at the same time that you listen to your heart. You might compare this optimum combination to a perfectly balanced equation, in which A is your emotions and B is your intellect. If A and B are balanced, your choices for action will be balanced. Or perhaps imagine the process to be like driving a car. Your emotions give you the gas you need to go, but your intellect acts as the necessary brake at times. You won't get anywhere without any gas, but if you have all gas and no brakes you're bound to crash. You need the two of them together, and when you have them operating in harmony, the car will run smoothly. You will get where you're going quickly, and you'll be able to avoid the dangers that pop up in front of you as you go.

RESOLVING CONFLICTS WITH OTHERS

Your self-control combined with your insight can also help you resolve conflicts with others. Both can help you in identifying the basis of the problem and figuring the best way to deal with it. For instance, if someone is upset, you can know how best to calm that person.

The following example illustrates a case of communication breakdown that occurred because emotions got out of hand. Had the people involved been able to get insight through shamanic exercises, a peaceful resolution might have been achieved much sooner. Specifically, while I was serving on a local community conflict-resolution panel for a group called Community Boards, we were asked to help two neighbors settle their dispute over a tree. This tree had been growing in the back yard of one woman, whom I'll call Anita, for fifteen years. The problem was that this tree grew so tall that it was damaging the roof of the house owned by Anita's next door neighbor, whom I'll call Alice. In fact, it had already caused about fourteen hundred dollars' worth of damage, and now that the rainy season had arrived, the situation would get worse.

Unfortunately, there was a breakdown in communication and trust between the two women, because Anita, the only Hispanic on the block, thought Alice was picking on her, perhaps because of her ethnic background. Also, Anita believed Alice was making up the complaints about the tree's damage to get Anita to pay for some long-needed repairs. On the other hand, Alice felt that Anita was unwilling to take the responsibility for the damage, and Alice's insurance company had already agreed that Anita's tree was responsible for the damage.

Thus there was a gap of misunderstanding, and the two women kept leveling accusations at each other. At one point, the resolution panel was able to calm them down and consider some ways they might resolve the problem. For example, Anita agreed to get some relatives to cut down the branches, and she said she would check with the legal aid society for the elderly for some financial help in reimbursing Alice. Also, Alice agreed to see if her insurance company could cover the damage, since Anita had no insurance. So for a moment, everything seemed under control.

But then Anita suddenly lashed out again with more accusations. Even if they had agreed to all these things, she still wanted to tell off Alice. "I still think she's making it all up about my tree causing the damage," she cried out. "She just wants me to pay to fix her house."

Suddenly chaos reigned again, and Alice walked out, saying that she was going to get a lawyer and after winning her suit, put a lien on Anita's house. The two had been so close to a settlement, but because one of the women hadn't been able to stay in charge of her feelings, had let go of her self-control, the tenuous truce had fallen apart, and there was no way of bringing it back.

So having this self-control can be critical in a conflict, to calm things down and keep them calm. Without self-control, it may be impossible to resolve the conflict.

In the Community Board's conflict resolution situation, that push for self-control comes from a neutral panel. But you can develop that self-control mechanism in yourself, so you can observe what is going on much like a neutral third party, and then intervene to take control, if matters seem to be getting out of hand.

For example, if you are in a confrontation and you see emotions rising, take a moment to call for time-out and suggest you both calm down before you try to deal with the conflict yourself. In the case of an internal conflict, in which different parts of you seem to be pulling in opposite directions, you might call on your self-control mechanism to try to calm the different parts of yourself and get them to talk to each other. In this manner, you can seek to moderate a conversation within yourself and let the different parts share their views. Then your neutral, self-controlling part can act as both moderator and judge to get these parts to work out a resolution, much like the panel just described might try to get two disputants to come to terms.

Another technique for calming someone who is upset (at you or about anything else) is simply to listen and agree with whatever he or she is saying. You can do this in such a way that you validate having heard the argument, rather than trying to show you agree. Later, when he or she has calmed down, you can go over your own position more clearly.

Suppose someone is very angry and wants you to take a certain action. To restore peace, you might agree that you could do that, even if you do not want to or do not think it is practical. By saying "could," you are phrasing your agreement in the conditional, yet at the same time making a positive statement that sounds like agreement. As a result, you might calm this irate person. This approach works because you are telling the person what he or she wants to hear at a time when he or she is very emotional and is not apt to respond rationally to any resistance. But a yes or other words of agreement will support his or her own position and will therefore have a calming effect. Later, when the emotion is defused, you can sit down, rationally explain your position, and seek to work out a mutually satisfying agreement.

A good example of when to do this might be in a family battle. A mother is yelling "I want you to do this," or is saying without any good reason, "No, you can't do this." What often leads to uproar is a child's defiant no, which makes the mother even angrier. It may be better if the child says a provisional yes, in the spirit of saying, "I heard you," though the mother is likely to hear this as "Yes, I agree," or "Yes, I will."

The technique is not really a lie, because at some point you have to sit down and deal with the situation. If you constantly say you will do something, and then don't (or if you promise not to do something and then do), that can create even more problems. But as long as you express your agreement in the heat of the moment, and then clarify your real position and reasons later, this ploy can be effective. It is essentially a temporizing device, designed to buy time while you get the person to calm down, so he or she is ready to listen to your point of view or version of the facts. However, this technique should not be used as a method for evading one's responsibility.

Another good technique is simply to be willing to listen while a person lets out anger for a while, whether directed at you or not. This listening can be very helpful to someone, even when you do nothing more than acknowledge that you have heard, because it serves as a release and lets the person know that someone cares enough to listen.

People who are very emotional often need this release, because otherwise they can get so caught up in their feelings that they can not think about or move on to anything else. This kind of blockage can be quite common, because most people tend to be fairly emotional when they get into a conflict. There are relatively few people who can stay in a neutral state when they encounter something that hurts or defies them. Typically, they will find it hard to put the experience aside, because although people may want to think they are logical, they will normally react emotionally to such things, particularly if they unexpectedly encounter something negative or are disappointed in a close relationship.

You can help people get out the emotion if you just listen, and this may mean listening several times, until they feel you have really heard them or that you accept what they have to say. That is one thing I learned from sitting on panels in the Community Board's conflict-resolution program. I really had to learn to listen, and sometimes an hour could go by with people saying the same thing over and over again. Nevertheless, I find it is important not to lose patience because when people repeat themselves, it usually means they simply want to be heard and want you to show you have both heard and understood.

To do this, you can feed back to people the gist of what they have said. You don't want to repeat their exact words because that tends to stall the conversation, and they might think, But I just said that. However, if you feed back some related ideas or an interpretation of what the person has said, then he or she can feel not only that you understand, but also that he or she has gained a bit, for you have pushed the conversation along. For example, if a person complains about someone, listing a number of unpleasant traits, you might respond with a summary of this position and say something like, "It sounds like you have been having a great deal of trouble in your relationship with this person, and you are feeling very frustrated with her right now."

After the person releases these feelings, he or she will be ready to move beyond the bad experience causing those negative feelings and perhaps try to work out a solution to the problem. By contrast, if the person does not vent, he or she can remain stuck, because until someone has been heard, he or she can not release.

At times you may have to use a great deal of self-control, because you may find it very difficult to listen to all of these negative outpourings, especially if the person is speaking negatively about you. But sometimes you just have to sit there and take it for a while, because if you try to shut the person up or counterattack, you can make the person even angrier, and the situation can escalate, to the point of trading blows. The process is like trying to shut off a pipe that is spurting water. If you try to dam it up, the pressure will accumulate until it spurts out even more forcefully. Or if you try to force the water back into the pipe, you may be attempting the impossible. But if you just let the excess water drain off, at a certain point, you can either shut off the faucet or turn it down so you get a smooth and even flow.

USING YOUR SELF-CONTROL TO STAY CENTERED

One of the advantages of being in closer touch with and developing this controlling part of yourself is it will help you feel more centered and in charge generally. In a difficult situation, of course, this ability will help you stay calm, examine or accept the situation objectively, and put emotions aside. But beyond that, this sense of self-control will carry over into other areas of your life.

For example, feeling in control will help you feel stronger in dealing with the world around you. You will be more self-assured and certain in your speech and actions. Then too, this sense of control can help to reinforce your ideas about your direction in life and help to still any doubts. Your sense of control can help you assess what you are doing objectively, as a neutral third party, which will make you clearer about yourself and your directions, so you can reaffirm the path you have chosen.

In short, your ability to stay in control and take charge as needed is like a keel on a ship which helps you steer by keeping you balanced and stabilized so you can better negotiate the course. Your control may not tell you where to go, but it helps you to keep centered so you can get there. And at times, like the conflict-resolution panel described above, it can act as a peacekeeper within yourself or in your interactions with others, to calm the situations, defuse any emotions, and lay the firm foundations for a resolution.

Exercise 1: **USING YOUR SELF-CONTROL TO TAKE THE RIGHT ACTION**

The following exercise is designed to help you apply the principles of self-control to choose the right course of action in a conflict.

Although the approach is similar to that of many popular psychologists and self-help groups, it draws on the shamanic tradition of calling on wise people, spiritual teachers, and others. Also, it is like a shamanic journey into another world in that you can leave behind your everyday awareness and feel yourself in another place or reality. You can also add more elements of traditional shamanism, if you like, by including the prelude, whereby you go to an upper or lower world of reality for information.

This idea of an upper and lower world comes from traditional shamanic practice, where the world is thought of as divided into three levels—the earth's surface called the middle world, the sky or upper world, and the area beneath the earth or lower world. Commonly, the lower world is that place where the shaman or other person on a shamanic journey goes to primarily contact power animals as teachers while the upper world is commonly visited to contact spiritual guides and teachers in human or spirit form, but different types of beings can be contacted in these areas.

For some people, these added elements may intensify the experience, but they are not essential, and I have found after working with these techniques for over twenty years, that there are many routes to the same altered state. The metaphors of traditional shamanism are one way, but other imagery can work too, for the essence is tuning in to that inner source, and the particular road you take is less important. In fact, the more you work with this material, the shorter the road, the less need for imagery, and the more immediately you can enter that altered state.

And now for the exercise on self-control and right action: Start by just concentrating on your breathing. Experience it going in and out. In and out. You're feeling very, very relaxed, very calm, and very comfortable.

Optional prelude

Now, feeling this sense of relaxation and comfort, imagine yourself starting on a journey, where you will be going to the upper world or the lower world of the shaman. You can go to either place and enter this other reality. When you get there, you will meet various teachers or power animals whom you will find helpful as sources of wisdom and information.

So now you can start on your journey. Just imagine yourself on a trail in the woods, and if you want to go to the upper world, you notice that the trail is going up, up, up, toward a high place. Or if you want to go to the lower world, you experience the trail going down, down, down into a valley. And then you enter a cloud or a cave, and you experience yourself wandering about, exploring this other world. As you do, you may see some teachers or animals. But for the moment, just look and wander about, getting a sense of this new world.

And now notice how one of these teachers or animals may start to approach you. Then, ask, Are you my teacher? If the answer is no, just thank the being and walk on. But if the answer is yes, just take some time to get to know your teacher. Meanwhile, if you are still looking, notice that others approach you, and ask your question again, until finally you receive a positive response. Then, take some time to get to know your teacher. Then tell your teacher you may be back shortly with some questions.

But for now, just find a very calm, quiet place where you can relax and think about the questions you will want to ask.

Now, from this very calm, centered place of mind, think of some problem or conflict you want to resolve. It could be something involving a relationship or something at work. It could be something that doesn't involve anybody else. It may be a decision you're trying to make that you feel in conflict or are upset about.

Once you have thought of some situation, focus on feeling that emotion, feeling that situation. Experience this situation as if it is happening to you now.

Then, as you see this situation, if you feel emotionally involved in it or upset by it, be aware that you also have a part of yourself that can be detached from this. So you might see yourself stepping away from the situation, as if you're leaving that situation in a pile somewhere, turning around, and walking away. Then you can ask that intellectual or self-controlling part of yourself to step aside and look at the situation.

Now, as you look at the situation from a detached point of view, start thinking of other ways you could resolve this situation.

If you wish, call on some advisers to help you. These advisers can be anyone you feel would be helpful: wise people you know, a religious or spiritual teacher, or a knowledgeable political figure or leader. You might think of these advisers as a cabinet of wise people who are there with good and powerful advice when you need them.

You might also look at the situation from different sides. Perhaps imagine it surrounded by glass, experience yourself walking around the glass, looking at the problem or conflict. So you're separate from it, and you feel very safe, because you are outside of it and looking at it. It's separate and apart from you.

In fact, now you can imagine that this is somebody else's problem and you're trying to help solve it. So use your thinking to come up with possible solutions. Come up with as many as you can. It doesn't matter what they are. Some of them you will find really good to use. Some of them may not seem to be appropriate. And then there may be others which you may feel unsure or neutral about. Just come up with all of these solutions first, no matter how you feel about each one. Don't try to censor the ideas as they come into your head.

As you get these ideas for solutions, see what you think of them. Let your inner self, your heart respond. And see if you can pull out, from all those solutions you have come up with, one that is particularly right for you.

Now take a minute or two to pull out these solutions, and perhaps see yourself putting one or two into practice and see the favorable results. Then, when you feel ready, you can come back into the room and open your eyes.

THE ADVANTAGES OF OBJECTIFYING CONFLICTS

The approach described above essentially objectifies a conflict or emotionally loaded situation, so you make it separate from yourself and neutral. Then you can think about solutions more objectively, without your emotions getting in the way. At the same time, while you are being objective, you are tapping into your inner knowing to take advantage of its wisdom and advice.

For example, at a workshop on this technique, one woman reported that she was able to take a conflict that she had dealt with before but had not solved, and come up with a more organized plan for resolving it.

> The problem I looked at wasn't anything new to me. But I found the process of objectifying the conflict a clear and logical way to deal with it. I tend to deal with problems in a scattered way. But this seemed to be a more step-by-step way to deal with it.
>
> I found it helpful to get inside of the problem and come up with different ways to solve it and approach it. And then I found it helpful to pull away from it, because it's such an emotional issue that I have found it hard to deal with it head-on in the past.

Another workshop participant found coming up with different alternatives and options especially helpful in opening up possibilities, so the problem seemed more manageable. As he stated:

> It's a problem I've been trying to deal with myself, and I was feeling stuck. But in meditating on it, in objectifying it, I saw different options. For me the solution came by just thinking about the options more. I saw more options than I had in the past, and then the solution became clearer to me.

Still another participant found the key in being able to look at the problem by dispassionately detaching himself from it. Before he had been so caught up in his emotion that he had not been able to come up with a good, workable solution. As he put it:

> I have been feeling so much stress in the relationship, it was good to just detach. The problem with feeling stress in a relationship while it is happen-

ing, is that it is hard to get out of that bind without getting even more upset and walking away. But I found I could disconnect, and part of me pulled away from the conflict situation, so I could look at it calmly. Then I could think about what to do.

THREE KEYS TO OBJECTIFYING AND RESOLVING CONFLICTS

These three comments reflect the three keys to resolving your conflicts by objectifying them. First, you separate yourself from them so you can defuse the emotion and look at the situation clearly. Second, you think of various alternatives and options, using a shamanic journey or other method to generate these, so you can choose among them. And finally, you assess those choices in a clear and logical way to work out a step-by-step plan for achieving the resolution.

The self-controlling part of you does all this. Once you know what to do, you can put into practice this right action you have come up with through this objectifying process. Or perhaps think of the process this way: after you are able to separate yourself from the situation, you intellectually or rationally come up with all these different ideas. It's like brainstorming. Then you let your heart respond to those ideas which you feel really good about or which you feel are the most appropriate. Your inner knowing then takes over and decides which are the best.

3

•

Tapping Your
Inner Courage

The third major principle for achieving personal power and mastery is having courage and this chapter is designed to help you tap the courage within you. Courage involves the ability to recognize that you must move forward once your heart says you should do so, and this can mean pressing ahead despite the difficulties on the way. The process can be hard and painful, the way may be long and steep, and the goal of success may seem far away. But if you believe in a goal, if you really want something for yourself, you have to be willing to push through the barriers or pick yourself up if you trip and stumble. For ultimately, that kind of endurance or courage in the face of difficult odds will allow you to prevail.

I know a woman in the toy industry who had her lifework collected in a large flat where she both lived and worked in an industrial part of San Francisco. Harriet had lived in the flat for about twenty years, and used it for regular weekly gatherings, as well as for a growing collection of toys, publishing projects, posters, and special activities. One night when she was out of town, a fire burned through her flat and devastated everything. She lost almost all her possessions and the destruction was so great that she could not reoccupy the flat.

For a few days, she was in total shock. But then she began to return to the flat every day, and soon she decided she was going to recreate what she had had at another location. And so she plunged in again and began to rebuild her life. She reached out to her friends and associates, which was hard to do, and she gained the support of many people. They helped her build up her toy collection again, so she was able to realize her dream of having a toy museum. And once again she began working on her writing and other projects.

Thus, despite her devastating loss, Harriet recovered and moved on. She had the will and strength to do it, and as a result, she came out of her crisis even stronger. In turn, people saw her determination, her conviction to pull herself back together and keep going, and they rallied around her.

By contrast, other people who do not have this personal courage can encounter a disastrous experience and become paralyzed. They feel helpless or pity themselves, and instead of putting the event behind them and moving on, they wallow in their unhappiness and self-pity. They feel there is nothing they can do and so they do nothing. Or they see themselves as powerless victims who must await a rescuer, never realizing that they hold the inner power to rescue themselves.

The plight of one such couple from New York was featured in a public-television program about the victims of city life. The couple, in their late twenties, lived in a small flat in Brooklyn with their three children, and one day while they were out, a fire started and consumed everything they had. But instead of showing the courage to move on, as Harriet did, they felt powerless to do so, and were mired in self-pity. They moved into a hotel and began to collect welfare. The husband, who had worked as a carpenter, had lost his tools in the fire, so now he believed he could no longer work in his chosen occupation. And the wife insisted she could not work, because she had to look after the children.

So the couple ended up living on welfare in a depressing, rat-infested hotel subsidized by city funds. And when the program was aired, two years after their experience, they were still there, remembering how they had lost everything and feeling as if their lives had come to a screeching halt at that point. And, the wife explained, crying profusely, there was nothing else they could do to get out of their predicament because "We've got to keep the family together. It's all we've got. So we can't move. We just have to endure."

Now this may sound like a common situation for any family on welfare—this sense of despair, futility, and misery in what seems like an impossible trap. And that may be true for many people.

But the important point to remember is that some people do get out of such traps, and a key factor in doing so is the element of personal choice, will, determination, and vision that there is another way. And this is where the techniques of shamanism and the principle of courage come in. By employing these one can see other ways and then one can have the determination and commitment to pursue a path to get out.

And that could have been true for this couple. They had wallowed in their misery and poverty because of their attitude of resignation. Yet had they only been willing to look, had they had the courage to open up to new possibilities and alternatives, they would have discovered they did have options and they could move on and out. Perhaps they might have temporarily split up the family while they both found jobs. The man might have asked friends to loan him money for new tools. He could have taken a job with a company which provided tools, until he saved up enough money to buy his own. The couple could have found a rentfree situation, managing an apartment for someone else. And so on.

In short, the difference between wallowing in a problem or an unproductive approach and moving on to new opportunities for a better life can simply be having the courage to confront the unknown and try something new. In turn, having this courage can require imagining the alternatives and creating a new future. For there is no need to get stuck in the past. That is over and done. Instead, one should always look toward the future and be willing to take on the risks and challenges that lie ahead, after learning from the past, so that one can better confront these risks and challenges in order to move on successfully.

FACING AND OVERCOMING YOUR FEARS

One key element of courage is having the strength to confront your greatest and deepest fears, because by facing and overcoming these, you move closer to mastery. In a sense, this process is like overcoming the dragons in your life—each fear threatens you with its fiery breath, and you have the choice of turning and running away or facing the heat and learning to control and direct it or extinguish it. If you run, the fear remains and continues to rule your life. But if you face and master that challenge, you have slain that particular dragon; you have won that conquest.

The key to doing so is to confront that fear or dragon directly. Then, once you master it, the fear is gone, and you have moved up to a higher level of self-awareness and mastery. For example, when I was younger I used to be terrified of speaking to groups, and in elementary school, I barely spoke to anyone at all, since I was so afraid of saying the wrong thing. But I got over that fear by forcing myself to speak, although I was afraid. I started off by volunteering in class, and when I got used to that, I knew I wanted to move to the next step, speaking in front of a group. So I volunteered to be a teaching assistant in graduate school, though the thought terrified me. But by throwing myself into it, and by doing the same in a Toastmaster's Program, eventually I became accustomed to public speaking and the fear subsided.

Similarly, when I first entered the game business, the prospect of showing my game ideas to company presidents and directors of research and development frightened me. But there was no one else to do this, and I knew I had to make these presentations myself if they were going to be made at all. So I started out feeling very unsure and frightened, and I even introduced myself as the secretary of my company (actually, a company name—I used to appear like I was part of a large organization, not just acting as myself), because I felt as if people would take me more seriously if they thought I was working for someone else. Then, gradually, as I became more knowledgeable about the field and more confident of what I was doing, I "promoted" myself by taking on a higher "position" or title in this company. So my status in my own company was like an indicator of my own feelings of confidence, personal mastery, and self-worth. Thus, as I continued to make presentations, my confidence grew and my fears subsided, and I worked my way up from secretary to director of research and development, and finally to president. So once again, by doing something, I learned I could do it successfully, and my fears faded away. Similarly, consider your own courage like a warrior who goes out in battle to meet a challenge, and as you do this successfully, your courage or warrior kills your fear.

ACTING TO ELIMINATE YOUR FEARS

Some people have had these encounters with the dragons of fear in somewhat more dramatic ways and have overcome them using specific shamanic or magical rituals. One woman described to me how she had once been very shy and frightened of people generally, and was quite reticent and withdrawn in a group. She also felt that she let herself be walked over by the men in her life, rather than standing up for herself. But when she joined a group working with shamanism and magic, she felt herself powerfully drawn to the image of a cat, and one night she performed a ritual with incense, candles, a small chalice of water, and a small ritual knife to focus her power: alone in the darkness, she evoked the spirit and strength of the cat and imagined it drawn into her. As she watched in her mirror, in the smoky darkness, for a few moments, she actually saw herself become that powerful cat, and thereafter she felt a new sense of strength surrounding her. Soon after, she broke up with her boyfriend and experienced a new sense of freedom, independence, and power, and then she gradually became more outgoing at social gatherings. Although there might have been other ways to achieve this new, more powerful sense of selfhood, this woman found the tools of magic and shamanism a forceful way to break symbolically from her past self and create a new image for herself. Then, with this new symbol of self, she could act accordingly, until she eventually felt this new, self-created being had truly become herself. Using shamanic techniques, she had made real the persona she wanted.

Your courage can often quell your fears, because many times your fear lies in your *anticipation* of attempting something you feel you can not handle, rather than in the activity itself. As a result, if you just muster your courage to do whatever it is you fear, you may find yourself so caught up in the act that you are not scared any more.

Furthermore, ironically, it is sometimes your very fear or nervous anticipation that may enable you to do this activity well, because this anxiety gives you the charge of energy or stimulation you need to perform at top capacity. Actors commonly report feeling very nervous when they go onstage, even when they excel. Yet they find that this nervousness helps them perform better. In fact, they may not be able to play their role as well as usual if they do not feel this jolt of nervousness just before they go onstage.

The extra adrenaline released by this mild nervousness gives a ''rush'' which helps them perform well.

Also, your courage can kill your fears, because you may find, in performing an activity you fear, that you can handle it after all, even though your fear of a certain negative outcome might be justified to some extent. You may be justifiably worried that a situation may turn out difficult, but when those difficulties materialize, you find out you can deal with them, so you no longer feel afraid.

For example, one woman I know had much difficulty dealing with her overbearing, domineering, and oppressive mother. When she was younger, she would simply return her mother's screams and yells, almost enjoying the spirit of combat. In fact, she began to think of this kind of interaction as quite normal, and she developed as a survival mechanism a very unfeeling, thick-skinned nature. However, this disposition also prevented her from fully experiencing and enjoying the more pleasant sensations and gentler things of life.

Thus, she was drawn into personal-growth activities to try to change her attitude so she could get more out of life. But, at the same time, as she opened up, she also started feeling more vulnerable to the aggressions of her mother, for, now, instead of fighting back, she tended to feel overwhelmed, tense, and depressed, and accordingly tried to avoid her mother. Since they lived about five hundred miles apart, this was fairly easy. But after she had managed to avoid seeing her mother for a year, the holidays arrived and her mother was extremely insistent. Finally, feeling very guilty, she agreed to visit her mother for a couple of days, although she trembled at the thought.

However, shamanism helped her get through the encounter successfully. Using some of these techniques before her trip, she imagined herself going into this other world, asking her power animals and teachers for advice, and asking them to give her strength to deal with her mother. Then, at their suggestion, she imagined herself clothed in a suit of armor and surrounded by a glow of white light as she went on her visit.

Thus, when she arrived for her visit, she experienced a sense of detachment, rather than her old readiness for battle or her more recent sense of openness and vulnerability. As a result, she let many of her mother's hostile comments go by without any emotional response, and sometimes, when her mother said things that bothered her, she just imagined she was shutting the visor and flaps of her armor, so that she could not hear her mother's words. At the same time, at her guides' advice, she acted gently and calmly toward her mother and avoided criticizing her or doing things that tended to upset her mother.

As a result, the visit went quite smoothly—in fact, she had not experienced such a calm visit with her mother in years; her mother even called her afterward to comment on the change. The woman did not tell her mother exactly what she had done, since she did not think her mother would understand and she might have been offended at the idea that her daughter had to steel herself for the visit. She simply thanked her mother for the pleasant time, and this marked the beginning of a change in their relationship. Future visits continued to be more peaceful and pleasant, and thereafter, the woman could discard the armor she had used.

GETTING INVOLVED AND THINKING OF OTHERS

When you have the courage to act, you can also overcome your fears, because by getting involved, you turn your attention toward your actions, toward others, and away from yourself. This process of looking outward can work to still any fears you have, because when you think about yourself too much, you start to question your own abilities ("Can I do it?" or "Will I have the resources?"), thereby escalating your fears.

By contrast, if you project your attention outward and simply act, you can short-circuit the inner fears you may have. Your external orientation makes you more goal directed and more responsive to others and their needs, so you can act appropriately without thinking about it. By simply acting in response to what is happening around you, you are more likely to act correctly. In turn, this kind of action can help you achieve your goals. This approach is like putting yourself on automatic pilot. By looking outside yourself and getting involved, you trigger that automatic pilot to point you in the right direction. The process starts with an act of courage—to look outside yourself and be ready to act. But then this right action produces the right result—which helps to bring you a feeling of personal mastery too.

HAVING THE COURAGE TO LOOK AT YOURSELF

To develop personal mastery, you need courage not only to move through your fears, but also to confront and really know yourself. Thus you have a clear picture of who you are, what you want, and where you are going, and can move forward accordingly.

Some of the ways you might examine yourself include doing a solo or a ritual in which you take a close look within. These are times when you need courage, for when you are looking honestly within, you may discover things about yourself that bother you, things you need to confront and perhaps change so you can move on.

You may need to confront painful thoughts, feelings, or memories in order to eliminate a block. If you push them down or ignore them, the emotions triggered by these repressed thoughts, feelings, or memories will keep bothering you. By contrast, a direct confrontation can help you move on, for this confrontation can help you to understand yourself better. Or perhaps you may need to do a releasing ritual to let the thoughts, feelings, or memories go. (An example of this might be finding a quiet place, writing down the experience you want to release on a piece of paper, and then burning that piece of paper, as you chant or repeat to yourself the thought that the source of this experience holds over you is going away.) Then, with these pent-up energies or symbols released, you can feel psychologically or spiritually freer, which can help you advance and feel more personal power.

LISTENING TO YOUR HEART

Finally, you need courage to listen to your heart and act accordingly. At times it may seem like such courage is not necessary, since your heart is telling you to do something which seems easy or comfortable. But at other times, your heart may pull at you to take on a real challenge, and self-doubts and fears stand in your way.

At times like this, when you get a strong feeling in your heart that an action is good and right, just move ahead to do it. It may take courage to make that step, for while your heart is telling you to go ahead, your rational mind may be raising all kinds of uncertainties.

However, in such cases, when you do have the courage to take a right action, you may find that events facilitate that action. For instance, if you decide you want to do a particular project, you will often find that the people or resources you need will suddenly start coming into your life. Just notice what happens when you announce your intention to yourself or to others. People commonly will respond in kind, and it will seem as if the universe is responding to fill your needs and wants. Whether you are planning a trip, looking for a new job, or trying to find a relationship, when you clarify your goal and relay that message, you will find that others respond. So in this way you can create your own reality—but it begins with deciding to act in response to the proddings of your heart—and at times, it can take courage to choose to act. But once you do, the events you want to happen and the things you need to make them happen will likely occur. This may be for several reasons: perhaps you are more alert to opportunities; perhaps you are devoting more energy to a particular goal; or perhaps you have changed your life in certain ways as a result of your decision or action. But whatever the reason, just notice the connections between what you need and want and what happens, and you will likely find that this connection seems very real, as the things you want and need repeatedly appear.

Exercise 2: **CALLING ON YOUR COURAGE TO OVERCOME A CHALLENGE**
When you do face a challenge, it may loom large in front of you. You may feel discouraged and dismayed by the potential difficulties. But if you draw on the courage within you, you will gain the power for action, which will help you overcome the barrier.

The following exercise is designed to help you call on your courage to overcome a challenge confronting you.

In the following visualization, you'll focus on a challenge and see yourself being very strong in overcoming it.

So start by getting relaxed and concentrate on your breathing. Just notice your breath going in and out. In and out. As you do, you're going to get very relaxed, but at the same time, you'll be able to stay alert. And you'll be able to look at yourself being relaxed. So you feel very comfortable, but you also are very aware of what is happening.

Start by thinking of some situation, maybe something happening in your life now, maybe in the recent past, maybe something you will be confronting in the next few days or a week. It's a situation you might feel a bit insecure about, a situation which makes you concerned, because you're not sure what to do about it, or perhaps you fear it.

So just look at that situation for a moment. Note any fears you feel. Get a sense of what these feel like, and perhaps look at why you fear that situation.

As you look at these fears, you can see them getting smaller and smaller. Perhaps you can squeeze them into a ball, and watch them get smaller and smaller within it.

Now, put the ball in a bag and close it up, so you make the fears disappear. For with the bag closed, you can't see them anymore. Then throw the bag away, bury it, or destroy it in any way you want.

Then, if you wish, repeat the process for any remaining fears. Capture them in a ball, watch them get smaller, put them in a bag, close the bag, and throw it away.

Meanwhile, as your fears get smaller and smaller and disappear, you also see yourself being very strong and very competent in whatever situation you face.

Now, focus on that feeling of strength. Think of any images or symbols that suggest strength to you and see those images or symbols around you giving you strength. Maybe see yourself in a suit of armor. Perhaps notice that you are holding something powerful, some object that represents strength for you, like a stick or a staff.

Then see yourself striding forward, having the strength and power that you need to confront the situation you face. For you are empowered by this feeling of strength, by these images and symbols of strength around you.

Now, see yourself doing whatever you need to do in that situation and mastering it. For you have all the strength you need to do it, and you know your fears are very far away. You've been able to put them behind you. You've made them smaller. You've made them disappear.

And now there's only you, standing there without any fear, being strong, powerful, ready to confront whatever it is. So as you do whatever you need to do in this situation, you are totally in control. You feel powerful and you have the courage to confront it. You have the confidence that comes with mastery.

So just feel that strength and power that comes from you like a beam of energy. For it comes out of you, like a beam of strong white light or flashing red sparks.

Yes, bask in that feeling of power. And now see yourself walking through a room, experiencing that sense of power, as if you have mastery of the whole world. And know that you can take that image with you whenever you want to get that sense of power wherever you go.

For it is something that radiates from you, as you walk down the street, as you talk to other people, as you go to work. Whatever you do, the source of that power comes from you. For it comes from your courage in overcoming past fears, in making them smaller, and making them go away. And each time you do this, each time you overcome more fears and more challenges, this heals you and creates more power, more energy within you, so you can move on to new and greater challenges with even more power.

Just bask in that feeling of powerful energy for a while.

And, now, with that feeling of power, look again and see if there is anything else you would like to confront, maybe something further in the future. Then see yourself with this feeling of power, going to confront that, meeting the challenge, and overcoming it.

Then, when you feel ready, let go of that image and start returning to normal consciousness, as you count backward from five to one. Five, four, becoming more and more alert. Three, two, becoming more and more awake. And, now, one. Come back into the room, back to your normal state of consciousness, and when you're ready, open your eyes.

Once you have stirred your courage, as in the above exercise, the next step is to go out and apply it. For example, one man in a workshop described the problems he had faced with the inefficiencies of the city bureaucracy: an antiquated billing system at the water department and a parking system which wasted a great deal of space. He claimed that he had once used his computer to figure out how he could save the city thousands of dollars by making its billing system more efficient and redesigning the parking arrangements to create roughly about 40 percent more space per block. But he had never done anything more than think about the possible solutions and feel angry about the hassles he encountered in paying

his bills or parking his car. After a courage-raising exercise, however, he suddenly felt empowered to go to the city with his solutions, stating:

> Well, I have these ideas, and I think I can make some changes. . . . I don't
> really want to just be coming from an angry place. . . . Now if I notice a
> problem, I can think about creating solutions and making them happen. I
> feel empowered to pursue this and help find an effective solution now.

Another man talked of how he felt ready to confront a person who
had owed him money for several years. He had felt angry about all
of the man's excuses, but had continued to accept them, feeling he
had little choice because he was afraid to accuse the man of bad
faith. Instead, he had wanted to keep the peace and feared the
results of exerting more pressure. As a result, the borrower kept
putting him off and he felt angrier and angrier. However, once he
felt his courage raised, he felt empowered to confront the man
directly and insist on working out a payment schedule. He explained:

> I was feeling my energy with this man blocked before. I felt he was just
> giving me empty excuses. But I accepted them, feeling if I waited, maybe
> eventually he would pay.
>
> Yet now I want to go back to him and stir him up. I want to get that
> energy flowing again, and I feel confident that the tools I need will be
> available now to get him to respond. I didn't think I would have them
> before. But now I feel I have the strength to get him to respond.
>
> For example, I have an old promissory note from him, and I want to
> bring it up to date. I want to let him know that I need to make new terms
> on it, because the old payment schedule has gone past due. I also want him
> to agree to a payment plan now. The main problem is that he doesn't have
> a lot of money now. But I feel ready to insist that he start to pay something.
> And I feel confident now he won't refuse. I'll insist on working out some-
> thing now, whereas before I was too ready to back down, and I'm sure he
> sensed that.
>
> But now I feel ready to turn the anger I have been feeling into some
> positive action. I realize it's time to do something to make a change, to get
> some results, and I feel I have the power I need to do it now.

A third participant talked about feeling the power to take on two
challenges. She felt ready to change careers and to sue a bank on

her own, since the lawyers she contacted either did not have time or felt the case was not lucrative enough. She stated:

I've been wanting to be a speaker for some time, but it's a totally different thing from consulting with small groups, as I am doing now. But what came to me is that I have to keep getting out there and doing it, and each time have a more powerful feeling as I do it. It has been a little scary for me to get up and talk, but I know I can get better the more I do it, and I feel I can really do it by seeing myself doing it in the future even more powerfully.

Secondly, when I thought about this problem I have been having with my bank, it came to me what to do. The bank put a hold on some of my funds and they shouldn't have done it. And I've had some correspondence back and forth with them, and then, when they weren't willing to compensate me for my damages, I had a lawyer who was going to represent me in following up. But for about a month I have been unable to reach him, and I know I have to do something soon, before it is too late.

So what I realize now is I have to take on the confrontation myself, and I can't let the lawyer do it for me. And I realize I can, with the assistance of another lawyer, who said he would help me do this action. I was resisting doing this before, because I kept thinking I couldn't do it. But now I feel I have the strength to do it.

USING YOUR ABILITY TO EXPAND YOUR POWER CONTINUALLY

As these examples show, you can raise your courage to confront obstacles and difficulties by increasing your feelings of strength and power. In turn, you can use this process to encounter ever more difficult obstacles and challenges, because the more you expand and express your power, the more strength and power you will feel.

This is true because you are working with an endless stream of energy that can continually be refilled, the way you fill up a glass of water. As long as you keep pouring out the water, you can fill up the glass again. And in order to fill up the glass with more water, you have to pour out the water.

You can imagine energy in much the same way. As you release the energy, you leave room for more energy to come in. And so it is with your inner strength and power. As you express these feelings and engage in acts that take courage, you open yourself up for more of these feelings to pour in. Just like the glass of water, the more you pour out, the more you can pour in.

In turn, you can continue to do this because you have an unlimited supply of empowering energy to draw from; you merely have to use your imagination or mental powers to envision drawing it from different sources. For instance, you can imagine drawing the energy from the earth or from the air. The technique is to simply visualize drawing this energy from this other source, or do a ritual along with the visualization, to intensify the visualization with the physical action of a ritual. Then, as you pour out this powerful energy, you have room for even more energy, as long as you want to draw it into you.

So you are like an energy machine, empowered by energy. As you use energy and need more, you can keep pulling in more, so you get refueled en route, much like a car has a gas tank to pick up more gas continually.

Thus, anytime you encounter a challenge, anytime you experience a fear you want to overcome, you can simply draw on the energy within you, your courage, to empower you to move through it. And you can always draw in more energy and courage because the energy is all around you. You just need to draw on it, using your powers of visualization and intention, and the more you do, the more you will feel empowered and able to confront any challenges you meet.

4

•

Giving True Service to Others

The next series of principles for achieving personal power and mastery related to the type of relationships you should cultivate with others. Such relationships should be based on three key principles: service, compassion, and honor. These principles work because they help to produce smooth, equitable relationships, and you will find that when you work with others in a spirit of offering true help, treating people with understanding, and acting from integrity, others will generally act toward you in kind. So as you give, you will also gain, in accordance with an overall process of balance, harmony, and justice in the universe. The following two chapters detail how you can apply these basic principles in your own life.

THE PRINCIPLE OF SERVICE

The principle of service to others is an important one to keep in mind, because it helps to provide you with balance as you seek to attain personal power, maintain control, stay in touch with your inner voice, and otherwise help yourself. You need to balance all you do to help yourself with a sense of reaching out and helping others. This way, you balance being a giver with a receiver, which helps you stay balanced in the various aspects of your life. This more general balance is provided by keeping the balance between being a giver or receiver, since giving to others can motivate them to give back to you in a spirit of reciprocity. Then, too, there is a state of internal balance produced much as there is a need for an equilibrium in inflow and outflow in nature. When too much comes in, a system can be overloaded, much like a body of water overflows when there is too much rain. Conversely, when too much goes out the system can be drained of its energy, like a stream running dry. In other words, you need to balance your desire to develop yourself with offering benevolent, unselfish service to others.

When you engage in such true service, you are giving to others without expecting any reward. The thoroughly altruistic act should be complete in itself, so that performing the service becomes its own reward. You could, for example, find things of value to give to others. For some people, these may be material offerings, but different people may prefer to give different things, such as people with special gifts or talents might choose to give something of themselves to others directly. As an example, people with fine voices might offer to sing for hospitals and charitable groups.

When you give in this manner, your focus should be on the giving, although you may also get paybacks from the people you are working with or from other incidental experiences. For when you act in a spirit of true altruism, you tend to trigger a positive response in others. Also, an act of service generally leads to other rewards, because there is a kind of exchange process in the universe. Somehow the benefit proffered will come back to you. It may not return directly from the person you have helped. But you may get the help you need later from someone else. It is as if the spirit of help and compassion or service you have expressed is destined to come back to you in some way.

GIVING SERVICE WITHOUT EXPECTING A RETURN

This notion of true service goes beyond working in return for some monetary gain, which is an important principle of success in business. In contrast, after you have given true service, it is time to move on, without expecting the recipient of your service to feel obligated in any way.

Michael described how he helped a woman without making her feel obligated. He was in a bus station when he saw a woman of about seventy, who seemed on the verge of tears. So Michael sat down beside her and listened to her problems.

She told him that she was in a convalescent hospital and was scared of dying alone in this stark impersonal setting. Yet she feared leaving the hospital and moving into her own apartment, which would provide a more homey setting, though she was physically able to do so, because she felt too old. However, as they spoke, it appeared obvious that she really did want to leave, for she felt trapped in the hospital; yet she was afraid to go. Thus Michael urged her to have the courage to leave. She should imagine the move as a new, invigorating adventure, and she should not feel that her age held her back.

After she did leave, she wrote to thank Michael and she asked him to write back. But Michael decided not to, for he did not want her to feel obligated to him in any way. As he stated, "I had helped her at one point, and my help had been instrumental in getting her to leave. But then I felt that was the end of the connection. I had offered her my service expecting nothing more, and afterward the service was over and done with. For in true service, you want to give the help someone needs. But then you don't expect anything, and don't feel a need to continue the connection, so you move on."

THE ADVANTAGES OF SERVICE

While your focus in providing true service should be on others' needs, the act of doing so will provide you with many benefits. This is part of the process of balance and exchange. When you give something, you get back something of equivalent or even greater value. The following are just some of the benefits you may experience.

Pulling Yourself Out of Yourself Since service involves orienting yourself toward others, it helps to pull you out of yourself, so that you are less centered on yourself and more externally oriented. As a result, if you are feeling stuck in any way, this can help you move along. For example, if you are agonizing over a decision or feeling uncertain about your next step, aiding others can help you put your own difficulties aside. Then your problem may solve itself, or you may return to it refreshed, with another point of view.

Helping You Feel Connected to Others Helping others can also make you feel in touch and part of a larger network, so you have more social support. For when you reach out, others reach back, and that feeling of connection brings with it warmth and overall happiness.

Recharging Yourself Being of service can also help to recharge you, for as you pull yourself out of yourself, orient yourself to others, and connect with them, you experience that energy from them flowing in. As you give to people, you get back their good feelings and appreciation which provide a charge of new energy. Their expression of satisfaction is like a beam of light that makes you feel warm and happy inside. For example, while doing volunteer work for the community boards, I felt a great satisfaction in seeing people resolve a conflict. And when the people who were in conflict thanked us for helping them, it was heartwarming, like a jolt of energy that stayed with me for several hours.

Then too, you may feel this recharge in serving others for much the same reason that an actor gets energized while playing before a receptive audience. In a sense, the people you are serving are your audience, and if you give a good performance in which you are in tune and empathic, you have made a connection and opened up a channel for their energy to come back to you. Then, if you have served them appropriately so that they have received what they needed, their satisfaction is like applause to you, and as they feel good, you will feel good too.

Getting a Rewarding Return Though you should not look for a specific return when you are offering true service, you will generally get a reward. Some people may be afraid to go out of their way for others, because they fear someone will take advantage of them, and occasionally this may happen. But generally, when people see you are relating to them in a positive, helpful way, they will want to be just as positive and helpful, so you will find your efforts to provide true service returned. Yet the paradox is, in order to benefit from true service, you must truly give of yourself without being concerned about what you will get in return. In due time, however, the reward will come, and often in unexpected ways, since you are not seeking a particular benefit.

Learning More about Yourself Serving others is also a way you can learn more about your abilities and interests. Volunteering can open doors to activities and connections with people that might not open otherwise, and then, in the course of volunteering, you may discover skills that you have not yet developed. You can also practice a skill you want to develop. Initially, you may not feel it valuable enough to charge for your time, but as you get more experience, you may develop a salable skill. When I was evaluating crime-prevention projects, I met many women on committees who did a great deal of volunteer work in the community. Some of them had started doing this only in their spare time. But then, as a result of their work, some developed credentials that helped them obtain future paid work in social service or counseling. So, through service, you may discover these interests and abilities, and sometimes, if you want to develop them, you can turn them into marketable skills.

Getting More Balance in Your Life Providing true service also leads to balance, since you must give as well as get to stay in balance. This is because there is energy flowing in and out between you and others in the universe, and if you concentrate on taking in too much energy, you can be overstuffed, just like a greedy overeater. So, at times, you must release the extra energy to achieve a comfortable equilibrium. Wealthy individuals typically do this by giving to the needy, and many charitable organizations serve this need by providing an outlet for giving by the more fortunate.

In fact, this need for balance of giving and getting exists not only on the individual and interpersonal level, but also affects society as a whole. Although as an individual you may not be in a position to influence directly this overall social shift in attitudes, it is helpful to be aware of it, because as individual attitudes shift, the collective power of this shift can gradually bring about societal change. In turn, this broader social focus is actually related to one of the roles of the traditional shaman, who not only sought to help the individual overcome illnesses or personal and social problems, but also tried to help the entire community achieve more harmony and balance, perhaps through a communitywide dance or ceremony. Today our society has become too complex and large and the traditional shamanic approach is too limited in its social acceptance by the mainstream for the shaman to play a major role in societal healing. Yet, there have still been times when these inspirational or ceremonial activities traditionally associated with the shaman have helped to inspire and create a brief spiritual uplift and even an attitude shift; for example, an event like Hands Across America brought attention to poverty and hunger.

In any event, you can use possible imbalances in society as a signal to think about how you might shift your own attitude away from those things that seem unbalanced or disruptive, or perhaps dissociate yourself from disturbing settings (like those in which everyone seems to be overly greedy, because these kinds of individuals or societal focus can lead to imbalance).

It is just such an imbalance, caused by too much emphasis on getting and not enough on providing service, which operates on the social and individual level. We have recently seen many examples of the destruction wrought by the massive emphasis on greed—the insider-trading scandals, the creation of paper financial empires through takeovers and acquisitions, the savings and loan fiasco, and recently, the fiscal problems of Donald Trump. And now there seems to be a swing back to a concern for community and social problems, in order to bring society back into balance. You might consider joining this larger wave yourself, if you haven't already.

Creating Goodwill in Others Offering service can also help you create goodwill toward you or your organization, which can be quite profitable in the long run (although again, you have to start with the desire to be of service, not just to make a profit). I had a few such experiences in stores, where clerks voluntarily reduced prices in the spirit of good service, and as a result, I not only left feeling really good, but also returned and spent more than I would have otherwise, so the stores gained back more than the amount of the discount. In one case, I had several rolls of film developed. But when I was about to pay, I was informed that if I had used a special mailer when I came in originally, I would have saved about $2.50 per roll. However, since I had not known that, the clerk said, "I'll give you 10 percent off," though he did not have to do this. In the second case, I was at a copying center, and the color machine was not copying as well as usual. But I needed the material and did not have time to go elsewhere, so I told the clerk to make the copies anyway. And when he was done, though I had not asked for a discount, he took fifty cents off the price. Again, he did not have to do this, but when he did, I considered it a very nice gesture, and it made me want to go back to the store, which I did.

In short, when people act out of a spirit of fairness and giving, that helps to create goodwill. By contrast, when people act as if they do not want to be bothered, they may find a short-term saving of energy, but a long-term loss, since their unfriendly, brisk nature breeds ill will.

BALANCING THE AMOUNT OF SERVICE YOU OFFER

Just as you can get out of balance if you don't give enough, you can also feel overextended or burned out if you try to give too much. Or if you continually give to someone who does not give anything back but could do so, you could feel cheated or ripped off, which is a form of feeling out of balance in the giving and taking arena too.

To a great extent, you can listen to your heart or inner voice in deciding how much to give, because your heart helps to determine the proper balance. It helps you sense how much service you want to give to different people or groups, and it lets you know when it is time to pull back because you need to stop giving or need to receive, either from the person you are giving to or from others generally.

Besides satisfying your own need to stay in balance, balancing your giving and receiving also benefits the people you give to. If you give people too much, you may make them dependent on you and undermine their own self-sufficiency and confidence, thereby lowering their self-esteem. Then too, all your help can contribute to their obligatory desire to repay you, which can feel oppressive. So for the sake of people you help, you want to achieve a correct balance.

However, knowing when you have attained this state of balance can be difficult to perceive. You may not always know how other people feel. People you are helping might not let you know right away that they are feeling a heightened sense of obligation, but if you are sensitive to their feelings, you may be able to pick that up, perhaps if they seem to be ambivalent about taking your help.

Likewise, if you have given a great deal and the recipient hasn't given anything back, you might start to feel things are a bit off, and this might be a signal to pull back because you have given enough. On the other hand, if you ask someone for assistance, and you feel he or she is tallying up your request on a checklist, as if you now owe something in return, this might be a time to shift gears and seek help from other sources or give help yourself, to find that balance.

To some extent, this search for balance in giving and getting may seem like accounting, in which someone does a favor for you, and then you feel you owe something, or vice versa. However, you should not try to calculate this give-and-take precisely; if you do, a quid pro quo mentality forms that operates against the principle of offering true service. Rather, you need to achieve this balance in a more spontaneous way, in which you intuitively sense when you need to give or receive more in general or from a particular person. Once you have picked up such a message intuitively, from your heart, rather than keeping track precisely in your head, you can then react accordingly to give or get more, based on what you or another party needs.

This intuitive processing will lead to a natural state of balance. By contrast, for example, I've seen letters to "Dear Abby" written by people who sound as if they have bookkeepers monitoring their every move, since they complain that they have hosted so many dinners or spent so much on presents and others have not responded in kind. This approach can get very petty; sometimes people are just not able to give back in the same way that you can give, because they do not have the same resources. For instance, if you give them gifts, they may not be able to purchase equivalent ones, because they do not have as much income, but they can make an exchange by contributing their time.

Thus the ideal is to seek balance in the amount of service you offer and receive. But do not try to do this by keeping score. Rather, listen to your heart and respond intuitively. Let your heart be like your gyroscope, telling you when you are balanced between the two poles of giving and getting, or too much to one side or the other. Then, if you are out of balance, you can let your internal gyroscope push you in the right direction, and once you are in balance, you can move full steam ahead, letting the waves come in from either side, as you drift comfortably back and forth with the flow.

PROVIDING SERVICE WITH MIXED MOTIVES

One question that frequently comes up in thinking about true service is, What about mixed motives? What about wanting to give, yet also wanting to gain through that service?

It can be fine to have this desire to gain in the background, but it has to be a secondary concern. The desire to help with no expectation of an immediate gain has to come first. Let's say you would like to learn from volunteering, perhaps to gain enough knowledge to get paid work in that field. Or you think that offering some service will help you decide on your direction. It is perfectly fine to have such desires.

But your primary focus still must be wanting to give people the help they really need. Certainly, you can hope to gain. You can want to gain. You can expect to gain. But your concern to help still must be first, so you do not appear to be plotting and calculating, or bargaining your help like a chip in a negotiation, in return for a premeditated gain. As long as your desire to help comes first, your desire to act for other reasons is perfectly fine.

For example, one man at a workshop decided to volunteer to help a local church edit some tapes. He said he wanted to help because he believed in the purposes of the organization, and he saw its need. Yet he had motives besides this altruistic one:

> I said I'd do it because I wanted to help this person. . . . But I also did it for pure fun, and because here was a chance to learn editing. I saw they had this need for something, and I wanted to give all of my help, so the organization would have something to sell, which would help it survive. . . .
>
> But at the same time, I wanted to develop myself too. So I worked on the project in that fashion, and it turned out fine. . . . A real win-win situation for both of us. They got the tapes, and I got all sorts of new ideas, and I enjoyed it too.

Similarly, people who are very successful may turn to philanthropy as a way of giving something back. Yet at the same time, they may get back some prestige for their efforts, so that is a form of mixed motive too.

You can often see the same process operating in people who volunteer their time in group leadership. I belong to the National Speakers' Association, and many members speak at meetings gratis; some even fly across the country at their own expense to speak. Their motive is to give something back to the speaking profession, because they have gained so much from other speakers. So they are providing a true service for other people. Yet for some there is another motive as well, for in the long run public speaking can advance their careers because it helps them become well known.

Thus, in many cases, we do have mixed motives when we serve. We feel we may get some benefit while serving someone else. And that is perfectly fine, as long as we are genuinely putting someone else's need first. For then we are offering true service, though we may gain from it as well.

DECIDING ON HOW MUCH SERVICE TO GIVE

Part of the process of balancing the service you give is deciding how much time to commit to providing this service and being willing to say no when you have reached your limit. Imagine that the service you are offering is like a package of energy and you only want to place a certain amount in that package. The man mentioned earlier who helped a local church edit tapes described it thusly:

> To me it was like an envelope of energy, because there was a certain amount of energy that I wanted to devote to helping this group, and then I wanted to do something else. . . . I spent about two to three months working with them, videotaping their performances and making tapes for them. And then I felt my envelope of energy for them was used up. I felt like I had done what I could for them, and I felt good about it and ready to move on.
>
> At that point, the group asked me if I wanted to do more, by becoming an officer, in this case, a minister of the church. It was inviting and flattering. But I found you have to be able to say no. Because there were other things I needed to complete and I felt I couldn't spare the commitment of time to this too. I felt it was time to send out another package of energy somewhere else—I had to say no here, to be able to say yes to someone else.

Thus, to stay in balance when you do true service, be very clear about your limits. As long as you help, be totally committed. But also figure out how much of your life you want to put into it, and then, when you no longer want to do it, pull away and let go, because that is part of the process of maintaining balance.

DEALING WITH DANGEROUS SITUATIONS

Another question which sometimes comes up is whether or not to help if you are in a situation of danger. Ultimately, it is your decision though you should not feel compelled to help if you would be putting yourself in danger. In fact, sometimes your help may not be appropriate and may only make the situation more dangerous for the victim and risky for you.

One man I knew who worked in social service sometimes wanted to go beyond the call of duty for clients. But when he visited them on his own time, he sometimes feared that they might take advantage of him or even attack him. Yet if he did not go, he would berate himself for not doing enough. So he was caught in a double bind—afraid if he acted, feeling guilty if he did not. And the reality was, he continually placed himself in potentially dangerous situations unnecessarily, because of his desire to help, which was weighted down by shoulds, rather than coming free and clear from his heart.

Thus, if you see someone in need, look to your inner voice to decide if you really want to help. Then, as you look within, or if you later get the sense that helping is going to put you in danger, this may not be the time to intervene. If you feel it is not, pull back and do not feel guilty. You have a perfect right to avoid the danger and say no.

In fact, sometimes you even have to be alert to the potential danger of helping in a situation that looks benign, but is really a deliberate trap set by someone who is just posing as being in need of help. An example of this would be thieves who prey on Good Samaritans—people stopped by the side of the road with their hood up, who look like they have car trouble, when in truth they are waiting for an unsuspecting motorist to stop, so they can rob him or her or take his or her car.

Thus, in such situations where your assistance could involve danger, it is wise to check out the situation for a moment, perhaps by calling on your inner voice to avoid getting hurt. In some cases, the danger may occur because someone is lying in wait for the person who offers to help. But, at other times, the danger may not be premeditated; say because the situation involves a person who is out of control, like a mentally ill person who is acting out on the street. So unless you are trained in dealing with someone like that, it may be best to stay away, because if you step in, you may find yourself in a situation you can not handle.

In sum, then, to stay in balance, be ready to help and be fully committed when you do. But also be ready to say no when appropriate, when you feel there is some danger you want to avoid, or when you feel you have done enough.

AVOID GIVING TO PEOPLE WHO ARE NOT READY TO RECEIVE

There can also be a problem if you try to give a service to people who do not want it or are not yet ready to receive it. How can you tell if this is the case? People might resist your advice. Or they might not do whatever would enable them to make use of your service.

One man had such an experience when he offered to computerize a list of names and addresses for a church group. One official said the church wanted an easy-to-use mailing list, but then the other church members never came up with the names and addresses. At first, the man felt resentful; he was offering to help, and the church members were putting a block in his way. So he felt some personal rejection and anger because he could not follow through on his plan. But then he realized there was no point in feeling this way. He was trying to push on the group a service it was not ready to receive. So he saw that he should not keep trying to push that service and should not feel bad.

> At first, I felt angry and annoyed, because they never got the time to sit down and let me show them how to set up the proposed system. . . . Then I kept trying to push it and only got angrier. . . . But finally, I just let the project die, because I couldn't beat a dead horse. I was willing to do it, but they weren't as interested as they first appeared, and I finally concluded that was fine. They said this was something that they wanted, but I realized I'm not the one who's supposed to do it. They just were not ready to receive it. . . .

Thus, as this man came to realize there needs to be a mutual give-and-take, so that there is a balance between what people actively want and need and what someone else is willing to give.

Moreover, there are times when people may appear to want something when they really do not—or at least, not at the moment. So this is the time to back off. After all, there is no point in trying to give a service to someone who is not ready to receive.

Likewise, this principle applies to unwanted advice. There are many people who offer gratuitous advice and suggestions to others. I had a relative who did this repeatedly. She was always eager to tell people what she thought they should do, and it often made them furious. They liked neither her advice, nor the fact that she took the liberty of giving it. So her "helpful" advice did not help at all. Instead, it just made the recipients angry, though she could not understand why. "I'm just trying to help," she would say, thinking her own way of doing things should be correct for all. But again, the principle applies: do not give a service to someone who is not ready to receive it. If someone does not seek or want your advice, why give it? Unless there is a special emergency in which your advice is crucial, it is generally best not to butt in. You are not doing someone a true service if you give something he or she neither needs nor wants at the time.

AVOID GIVING SOMETHING PEOPLE DO NOT WANT

An even worse problem than trying to give to people who are not yet ready is trying to push a service on someone who does not want it at all. Thus, it is important to be sensitive to this; there is no reason to try to give what the recipient does not really want. And that goes for material goods, help, and advice.

For example, this relative I mentioned earlier always seemed eager to help people in ways they did not want. In addition to giving people unsolicited and bad advice she would righteously try to "help" people do things her way, not recognizing that they had a different point of view. For instance, she tried to manipulate her "generosity" to her daughter this way by tying it to her own view of what was right. An example of this occurred when she offered to help her daughter, who was in a financial bind, buy some clothes. But once at the store, she only wanted to buy the clothes that suited her own tastes, which were generally not the styles that her daughter liked, so these trips often deteriorated into screaming matches. Yet the mother could never understand the problem. She was trying to be so generous and helpful. Why couldn't her daughter appreciate her help? Yet, if she had only looked, the reason was very plain. She was offering to help, yet not really being helpful at all, because her help came with strings attached. So it was help her daughter did not really want.

MAKING PEOPLE FEEL INFERIOR WHEN YOU GIVE

Also problematic is offering to help someone but then making him or her feel like less of a person for accepting that help. In this case, the offer is made in order to engage in power-tripping—not to give supportive service.

And here again my relative provides an example of what not to do. She and her husband used to give their old clothes to her sister-in-law and her husband, who earned a much smaller income. Certainly, the sister-in-law and her husband could use these clothes; they had little themselves. So at first they took them. But whenever they did, they felt degraded by the woman's condescending attitude in making the gift. So the woman was offering charity, but she was not being charitable because her attitude made the recipients feel subservient and demeaned. They felt as if they were being reminded of their lower social status. And so eventually, they declined these clothes. They were aware of the woman's uncharitable attitude and so they rejected the clothes to preserve their sense of pride, and at the same time they developed hostility toward this woman.

Thus, once again, wrong giving can produce wrong results— hostility and lowered self-esteem instead of support and love.

SERVING UNWILLINGLY

You should also avoid the trap of trying to serve others when you do not really want to do it. Other people can tell when someone is helping them in a spirit of obligation, not true concern, and they will not feel very good about receiving this help. At the same time, the person who is helping will feel resentful too, because his or her help comes unwillingly.

This problem plagued my "helpful" but poorly intentioned relative. She grew up with the belief that she should help others and she preached continually about the importance of "doing for others." She also held onto the image of herself as an altruistic person. But in truth, she often pushed herself to help because she felt she should, not because she wanted to, and at such times, she would act like a martyr. Under the circumstances, much of the help she offered simply generated bad feelings. On the one hand, she put out the message that everyone should serve others. But it was obvious that she did not get any satisfaction from it most of the time. Instead, she often seemed very annoyed that she had to help. In turn, the people she was serving often did not like or want her help, because it was not what they really needed, or they could tell that she was simply going through the motions.

Thus, when you serve unwillingly, it is as if you are listening to an internal tape that says you are supposed to help others. But if you do not really believe it, you will not get any satisfaction out of giving, and the people you help will feel put-upon, not appreciative. And if they are not appreciative, you may feel resentful because they are not acknowledging or responding to all of your help.

In short, such service for the wrong reasons can set up a negative cycle. The giver can feel resentful because the recipients are not grateful. And the recipients are not grateful because they feel the help is not sufficient or is not what they need. And that is exactly the case. The person helping is neither doing enough nor giving the right type of help because he or she is acting from the wrong motives, so it is no wonder that the recipient neither needs nor wants that kind of help.

HELPING PEOPLE WHO NEED TO HELP THEMSELVES

The final type of help to avoid giving is that which makes people feel dependent or guilty for taking it because they really need to help themselves. Even if you have the best intentions in the world, you may find that the person you are trying to help has a lot of difficulty taking or benefiting from that help, and so responds strangely.

For example, alcoholics or people who feel powerless may feel guilty or experience lowered self-esteem in taking help, because they feel they should not need it. Or they feel jealous of the person giving the help, who seems so mentally healthy when they are not, and so they strike out at the very person who is there to help them. The helper, unaware of this dynamic, can get trapped in a no-win situation in which he or she continually offers help but is attacked for helping. A typical example would be the relationship between an alcoholic who is constantly in need of help and the partner who is constantly helping. This is an entrapping situation, in which the helper reinforces the other person's helplessness, while the person being helped lashes out at the helper for doing this. So both need to break out of this cycle, for what the recipient of this help really needs is to be able to help him or herself. And in this case, the helper needs to be able to stop helping.

Thus, should you find yourself in such a no-win helping situation, the key to true service is not to serve, for your help is not really beneficial. So let the person help him or herself—or help him or her to realize this is necessary, and then let go, so he or she can begin self-help.

KNOWING WHEN AND HOW TO HELP

Given all these considerations about when and how to help, how do you know when it is best to do it and what kind of help to give? Again it comes back to the same principle discussed earlier: listen to your inner voice in deciding whether and how to help. Also, your inner voice will tell you when to stop.

Your inner voice sometimes will urge you to help in a situation where you normally would not. This is often because your inner voice has a higher form of knowing. For example, Michael once passed a young woman who was hitchhiking by the side of the road. Normally, he did not pick up hitchhikers because of the potential danger, but, this time, his inner knowing began to tell him, You really do need to pick up this woman. She really needs help. So he did stop and picked her up and just as he did, a lowrider car passed and the three men inside it jeered at her. "They were about to pick her up," Michael explained, "though I didn't know it at the time. But my inner voice perhaps predicted the danger and so I picked her up and I saved her from a bad situation."

Likewise, Michael listened to his inner voice after he had helped the old woman described earlier decide to leave a nursing home. "She wanted to give me her number so we could stay in touch after I helped her, but I turned it down. My inner voice told me no. I felt I wanted my help to be its own reward, so my inner voice told me to stop and let go."

CHOOSING YOUR OWN FORM OF SERVICE

In summary, serving others at times can be a way to achieve and maintain balance in your own life by finding ways to give as well as get. The process contributes to its own homesteads, so that overall you gain by giving.

Exercise 3: **SELECTING THE FORM OF SERVICE TO GIVE**
The following exercise is designed to help you choose the best form of service to benefit you and others.

To start, just get relaxed again. Focus on your breathing. Experience it going in and out, in and out. And as it does, you can feel yourself settling down; you are getting more and more relaxed. At the same time, a little part of you is going to stay alert. So you'll be very aware of what's going on.

Now, think about the various things you feel you can do to be of service to a person or an organization. Think of the skills you have, the talents you have to offer. You might also think about how much time you'd like to commit, the interests you have, and where you would like to perform this service.

Now, see yourself in that environment, providing whatever service you are thinking of. And as you provide that service, notice that you do it very well, and you see that the person or organization feels very satisfied. For you're doing something that's very much needed. And now you're experiencing the appreciation that the person or organization feels. So just see yourself for a few moments, doing whatever it is that you're doing to serve. And you're feeling very, very good about it too.

Notice now what kinds of gains you might be getting from giving that service. Are you feeling good about helping people? Are you learning something? Are you finding out more about yourself? Just start to think of the various gains you're getting from the service.

Now, think about what this service might prepare you for doing next. Maybe it's opening up certain doors for you. Maybe it's giving you some new knowledge. Maybe it's giving you some creative ideas. So just see what might come after this service.

Also think about how long you might want to do this service. Perhaps think of this activity as a little package or envelope of service you're providing. Think about how long you want to be involved, how much time you want to commit.

Then, imagine that you are at the end of this process. You're getting ready to go on to do other things.

Now, if you like see the next service project you want to be involved in. Again imagine what it is you might do, the skills you might bring to it. Think of what kind of person or organization might use this service. Think of what you might learn from it, what kind of ideas you might gain, what kind of knowledge. Then see yourself doing this activity. And see the person or organization you are helping giving you a great deal of appreciation.

At the same time, you know that you are doing this in a spirit of true service. It's something you want to do. You feel very good about doing it.

And now also think about how long you might want to do this, what kind of time commitment you might want to give.

Then, when you feel ready, bring that image to a close; see yourself completing that service. As you do, you feel ready to move on to whatever is new, whatever your experiences might bring. And know that you have gained a great deal from your service, just as the people or organization have gained a great deal from the service you have given.

So now bring your experience to a close. Then, when you feel ready, start coming back into the room. As you do, count backward. Five, four, feeling more and more awake. Three, two, almost completely awake. Now one. You're back in the room.

5

•

Displaying Compassion
and Honor

Compassion, like service, is also a form of giving. However, the distinction is that with compassion you are not only giving to help someone, but you are giving them what they need, as opposed to what they think they want.

These wants and needs are not always the same because often people will want something that is not what they need, and, in fact, may not be the best thing for them. So part of showing people compassion is taking into consideration their true needs, which do not necessarily coincide with their expressed desires.

TRANSFORMING APPARENT NEGATIVES
INTO POSITIVES

Because of this distinction between wants and needs, sometimes a person showing compassion may seem to be doing something negative, because the recipient does not want or enjoy the intervention at the time. However, the action may turn out to be very positive, because it is really serving the person's needs.

Take, for instance, Michael's actions toward a woman who was training with him. She reported being frightened by the visions she was having when she meditated. But instead of sympathizing with her or comforting her, he came by and hit her lightly, which startled her and made her angry. But this turned out to be the best thing he could have done for her, because, as Michael explained,

> Hitting her, rather than being sympathetic to her, brought her back to reality. For now she realized she had to get rid of these scary visions herself if she didn't like them. Whereas if I had been very empathetic, supportive, and sympathetic, she might have gotten more into these scary visions, because she was getting all this supportive attention for having them. And that might have reinforced her belief that these are things to be scared about. But by [my] striking her with a light slap, she realized that she wouldn't get this kind of support for being scared; rather, she would feel a mild rebuke for it, and so that would discourage her from having these feelings she didn't want.

Hospitals and mental-health professionals have found the same technique effective in treating some types of mental patients. For example, catatonic people generally say nothing to anyone and then may suddenly throw temper tantrums. In response, the nurses usually try to be sympathetic. But as researchers found, this show of support turned out to be the worst thing they could have done, because the patients got attention for being sick. So this help was actually reinforcing the sickness. By contrast, what would really be helpful, although it might be painful for the patients and disturbing for the nurses initially, would be simply to walk away whenever these patients behaved negatively, rather than coming to their aid. And now many hospitals are using this approach.

Similarly, many psychologists have trained parents to exercise this type of restraint with their problem children, who act out because they get parental attention whenever they do something wrong. Just like the nurses, the parents may think they are being helpful, sympathetic, and supportive when they pay attention and rush over to support their problem child. But all they are doing is reinforcing their child's nasty behavior. In fact, some parents have provided so much love and attention to problem children that they have ended up encouraging sociopathic behavior, in which children think they can do virtually anything they want. Or they may be supporting their children in maintaining a catatonic, withdrawn state. By contrast, to show real compassion and give their children what they need, the parents should withhold their intimacy and attention when their children are doing something wrong, and reward them with attention for good actions, thereby encouraging this positive behavior.

In other words, to have compassion, you have to distinguish between giving others what they think they want at the time and providing something that will really benefit them. As the above illustrations have shown, people may want immediate affection and attention, but the worst thing for them can be to get that attention when they are doing something wrong or having a negative experience (like the woman who was having scary visions), since that action will only support their harmful behavior. Rather, to show real compassion in such a situation, one should hold back that affection and attention which they want and instead give them what they need—the cold, hard knowledge that they must take positive action to help themselves.

Sometimes it can be extremely difficult to meet someone's real needs when that involves withholding the sympathy and supportiveness you feel and the other person really wants. But by resisting your initial impulse to help, you can show a true understanding of that person's best interests.

For instance, one woman's mother was experiencing a very difficult adjustment to old age. One day the mother, Mrs. James, fell in her house and injured her hip. Her doctor put her in a hip cast, and for the average person, it would have taken about six weeks for the injury to heal and the cast to come off. But for Mrs. James, the incident became a major crisis.

She lost her mental balance because she was so despondent over being confined at home with her cast. Ultimately, she attempted suicide five times, more for the attention than because she really wanted to die. Each time she took just enough pills to become unconscious and require a trip to the hospital to have her stomach pumped, but not enough actually to kill herself.

Each time this happened, Mrs. James or her doctor would call her daughter Nancy to come. The first time Nancy did so. But once she arrived, she immediately recognized what was happening. Her mother, who had always been a very negative person, had as a result of her accident-induced isolation started to direct her negativity inward against herself; she was using her illness to control and manipulate others and get their sympathy and support. As Nancy told me:

> As soon as I saw her lying there in her hospital bed, I saw what was happening. It was like all her negativity was catching up to her, because she had all this time to be alone, instead of being negative toward other people and putting them down. Now instead she was suddenly directing this negativity inward and putting herself down.
>
> At the same time she was using her illness as a kind of power trip over other people. For instance, she now wanted people to cowtow to her and bring her things. But it was not like she needed these things. Rather, it was a way of showing she still had power. As an example, she would ask somebody to bring her a robe, and when they arrived with it, she would say, "Well, it's not the right robe. I wanted my robe in the other color."
>
> Whenever people did things for her, she was very critical. People could never do enough. For instance, when somebody completed all her errands, she would say something like "What took you so long?" or "You bought the wrong brand."

Thus, instead of giving her mother the sympathy and support she wanted, Nancy resisted. She felt such attention would only encourage her mother in her illness, not help her get well. Yet it was hard to do this, because Nancy appeared uncaring. Actually, she was giving her mother exactly the resistance she needed to realize she had to help herself get well. Nancy explained:

> My mother kept wanting me to come down to do errands for her and take care of her, though I knew she could do the errands herself, because physically she had the ability. She just had to get up and do it and let go of her negative attitude that she couldn't and that others now had to do it for her.
>
> That's what I saw when I went down there, so I held back, even though I had all this pressure to give in and help out. For instance, at one point, my mother asked me to come down and become her conservator and she even got one of her friends to call me to say I should do this.
>
> But even so, I decided not to. I started to feel guilty at first, because my mother and her friend made it sound like she might die if I didn't help. But I realized that she had to live for herself and not for me. So I said to myself, Well, I will help her if she is willing to help herself. But I am not going to take over her life or support her in the negative things she is doing.
>
> So initially, it might have seemed like I was not being very sympathetic

to her. But I was simply saying "Get back on your feet. You can do it. It's your attitude—you just have to change your attitude."

And at first, my mother rejected doing this. She just kept saying, "Well, you're the only person I have. You've got to come down here. I need you."

But I said, "No, I'm not going to come down there. You do it yourself."

And eventually, she came out of it. She's back on her feet now. But if I had gone down there, it would have only continued this bad situation. It would have destroyed me as an independent person, and I think it would have trapped her into this dependent-aggressive relationship, in which she was seeming to be dependent on me, but then she would still try to be in charge by using her illness as an excuse to have me at her beck and call to order me around. So the situation would have really been a mess.

At the time it might have seemed like I was not being a dutiful, caring daughter. And she said that to me; her friends said that to me. She even said at one point, "Then I don't have a daughter anymore," when I refused to come down.

But I was determined not to be drawn into her negative space, and it turned out to be the best thing after all.

According to Nancy, for a while her mother seemed to get worse. Since Nancy was not responding, and Mrs. James's other friends stopped helping, since they felt put-upon too, Mrs. James sunk deeper and deeper into depression. She stopped eating, and Nancy felt as if any day she might hear from the hospital that her mother had died. Yet even so, Nancy was determined not to give in and help her mother unless her mother was willing to help herself.

I felt she had to realize that I'm not responsible for her living or not. I felt she had to decide for herself that she wanted to live. . . .

And then from her lowest point, she made that decision. It's like when she reached the very depths of her despair, she realized that "nobody else is going to take care of me, and if I want to live, I have to do it myself, and I can do it."

So she literally picked herself up from bed and decided to go to this self-help group, and within a couple of weeks she was like a normal, happy person. In fact, she seemed even happier than she had been before, because the illness seemed to drain out all her negativity.

It had been hard on me to let her go through this, but I felt it important that I hold back. And now that I have seen the results, I am really glad I did.

In summary then, it can sometimes be very hard to show real compassion and give others what they really need when they seem to want something else and when fulfilling that want seems to be the kind and human thing to do. But in fact, this immediate kind response may actually be the wrong choice, because it will be harmful to them, say by making them more dependent or encouraging self-destructive behavior. Thus, it is important to hold back and not give in to immediate wants.

This approach can be especially important in close relationships. For sometimes people let themselves get trapped into looking at the world from someone else's point of view, and as a result they start responding to the other person's immediate wants rather than more objectively, determining the real needs of that person or the relationship. The ideal should be mutual independence, and by stepping back, you are better able to achieve this, because you can look at true needs.

For instance, one woman was able to more objectively look at the relationship she had had with her parents when she was younger. She noticed that her parents were always supportive, willing to listen and help, when her life was not going well. But when her situation improved, they became very judgmental and critical. Eventually, toward the end of her senior year in college, she realized that they wanted her to be dependent on them, so they were actually more comfortable when she had troubles, because she would turn to them for sympathy and support. That was why, when life was going smoothly, they would find ways to cut their daughter back down to size. Of course, they never admitted this; in fact, they may not even have been aware of this dynamic. But it was keeping the daughter and her parents tied together in this web of dependency when in fact what they both needed was for the daughter to break free from this mutually destructive cycle. And ultimately, the daughter did so by reducing her communication with her parents for a while and refusing to turn to them when she had problems. She realized she had to work her difficulties out for herself, and once she did, she opened the way for a much more mature and satisfying relationship, based on the needs of both herself and her parents, rather than their immediate wants. As the woman explained:

> I kept getting the same message from my parents when I was younger. Things are not going to keep working. . . . So don't expect things to work

out. . . . And then when things didn't work out, I would go back to Mother and Daddy and seek their support, which is what they wanted. So what they were doing was in a sense giving me what I wanted at the time—their love and support. But they were really plugging me into a very negative kind of pattern.

I needed to pull away, and they needed to be free of this too. So after I realized this, this is what I finally did. I started to work out my own problems, instead of turning to Mother and Daddy, and once I found I could do this, I felt free. I think they felt a little disappointed for a while because I stopped turning to them, but then they learned to appreciate what I had achieved. So it worked out better for both of us, though initially it was hard to take that first step. I missed them telling me everything would be OK when things went wrong. But I realized it was more important to struggle and learn how to make things right—rather than seeking their help when things went wrong.

THE HEALING POWER OF PAIN OR OPPOSITION

Another difficult aspect of compassion is the fact that it sometimes requires intervention that will actually cause people some physical or emotional pain or keep them from getting what they immediately want. Yet giving this pain or causing this opposition can be an act of compassion because it is necessary to the person's physical or emotional healing.

For example, Michael was once at the scene of a fire and saw a man sobbing outside his burning house. The man was limp as a rag doll, weeping on the ground. Michael went over to the man and offered to help, but the man seemed oblivious to him, shook his head, and kept sobbing. Feeling the man needed some shock to jar him out of his desperation, Michael suddenly asked him, "Did you do anything bad to someone?" It was as if Michael were suggesting the fire had resulted from divine retribution. The man immediately became very angry. "How could you say such a thing?" he yelled at Michael, glaring as Michael backed away. Yet while his anger might have caused him a momentary jab of pain, he was no longer stuck in his desperate sadness.

Essentially, in his sadness the man was feeling sorry for himself and transmitting the message, Pity me. But those feelings only made the man feel more hopeless and depressed. Michael's intervention broke the man's destructive chain of thinking—the anger Michael induced gave the man a strong infusion of energy, and he directed his anger outward instead of at himself. So Michael's act drew the man out of his sense of hopeless depression, for anger is at a higher level of energy than depression is.

Similarly, there are therapy approaches that use this technique. For instance, in a Synanon group, the members use a form of attack therapy to confront someone with his problems. So if a person talks about being depressed, the group members may attack him or her, which can stimulate anger and self-examination. By contrast, if the group were only supportive and sympathetic, this might push the person back into embracing the problem, since it is producing all this sympathy and support.

Of course, this kind of verbal attack therapy might not be a good idea for someone who has low self-esteem. It might only further undermine the person's self-esteem. But attack therapy can respond to the true need of someone who is deeply sad about a particular event or in a state of chronic depression. Making him or her angry gets the juices going, and then maybe he or she can start working to overcome that problem.

In short, when responding to what people really need, rather than what they want, at times you may cause them some pain or put some obstacles in the way of what they want, to get them to move into a better, more healing place.

THE IMPORTANCE OF INTENTION IN COMPASSION

There is a critical difference between a harsh but compassionate action based on a benevolent intention to give the person what he really needs and a negative, egotistical action that is really cruel and hurtful. If you act out of compassion, you may act harshly, perhaps withholding shows of love or affection from someone, but your intention is to help the person in the long run, so there is a good outcome. That is quite different from acting selfishly, like withholding love to manipulate someone, or trying to buy love with offers of help. In the latter case, you are just playing games with someone, since you are only pretending to be compassionate and helpful, which can be really cruel and destructive. So for true compassion, you must have a good intent. By contrast, if you act seemingly for someone's good, but your intention is bad, that is not compassion.

A perfect example is a neighbor I once had. She was a very

critical, self-righteous person who felt she knew what was best for everyone. She would constantly tell people how to act and she would frequently tear people apart with harsh criticism of their behavior or appearance, pointing out what she thought wrong, claiming her judgment and advice was for their own good. For instance, she would tell her husband sometimes in front of her children, that he had done some task incorrectly, that he did not have any sense of style and that he needed her to go shopping with him because he would not make proper choices. Also, she sometimes made fun of her daughter in front of the girl's friends, by describing how she had committed some little mistake, which only made her daughter very upset. She felt her mother was ridiculing her in front of the other girls, but her mother would just laugh and tell her, "Oh, laugh at yourself; have a sense of humor." The woman claimed that her behavior was designed to be helpful, because she hoped her husband and daughter would learn from it. But in reality, it was done more in the spirit of putting down her husband and daughter and they experienced it as a put-down. Thus, her behavior definitely was not compassionate, and her husband and daughter did not experience it as such. Instead, they responded with anger and hurt, feeling upset, and were not motivated to change. And of course, they were right in sensing that she was not motivated by compassion, for as was later revealed when she consulted a psychiatrist for depression, she acted judgmentally and critically toward others because she felt inferior, and so by demeaning people, she felt more powerful and better about herself.

So that is an example of a person who is pretending to be compassionate by doing something that is harsh and painful (such as telling you your faults) and claiming it is done for your own good. But the action really is not compassionate, because it is not intended benevolently. Instead, the person is power-tripping or getting some other selfish benefit. And this is quite different from constructively pointing out problems to someone at an appropriate time or using an action to disrupt a person's destructive behavior or thought patterns, so you can help that person move through a difficult situation, as Michael did for the man whose house was on fire. For instance, the woman who was criticizing her daughter publicly might have done her daughter a service by quietly taking her aside to point out her errors and describe how she could improve. But when she announced the girl's flaws in front of company, the comments were just embarrassing to her daughter and did not help her improve in any way. Instead, her daughter just felt bad.

The same kind of process can occur when people seem very helpful and friendly on the surface, but in fact, they have very critical attitudes toward others, which they do not express. Some people are even brought up to be this way. They are taught to have a very warm, friendly exterior, but under the surface they may be repressing their real hostile feelings, which can become even more intense through this repression. In fact, some of these people may be sweet on the outside, but harbor vicious feelings within. And this kind of behavior can be quite dangerous, because their real intentions are negative, but they come across as very positive, benevolent, compassionate people.

Thus, just as it is important to be truly compassionate by having the right intention to help others, even though you may initially cause them some pain, it is important to be sensitive to others' motives when they offer to help in a way that seems critical. If their intentions seem good, then value the help they offer, even if it seems harsh. But if you question their intentions, then turn away —and again, look at your heart or inner voice to help you tell the difference.

Finally, consider both the value and the dangers of using diplomacy in showing compassion. Generally, if you are fueled by compassion, it is helpful to be diplomatic in expressing your negative feelings or criticisms, so people can better take in this message and respond to it positively, without anger, hostility or resistance. Thus, by diplomacy, with a compassionate, benevolent intention, you can point out problems to others so they can move on successfully.

At the same time, you need to be able to see through someone else's diplomatic approach, to determine if this diplomacy is inspired by a benevolent intent or conceals an egotistical action that is really cruel and hurtful. To do so, you need to look to your inner voice to pick up that person's true motive. In other words, you have to try to listen to his or her real intent on the inner level, rather than just on the surface. Then, once you have made the distinction, if you feel he or she truly wants to help, listen to the advice. But if you feel the apparent kindness masks a darker intention, then reject it and turn away.

HAVING HONOR

The sixth key principle of personal power and mastery is honor. This principle states that you should keep the promises you make to yourself and others, especially to those you are most closely associated with—members of your family, your friends, and your close associates.

THE HIERARCHY OF HONOR

There are essentially four levels of honor, with the highest levels requiring the highest degrees of commitment. The first and highest is to yourself and your sense of direction and purpose in life. To properly fulfill this commitment, you must be true to your identity and beliefs.

The second honor is to those you are close to, like your family, close friends, and associates. In turn, you may have subdivisions and levels within each category. For example, you may feel your highest honor at the second level is due to your spouse, then to your children, and then to your parents.

The third level of honor is due to those who need to be served and are worthy of benevolence and compassion, like the old woman to whom you offer your help at a bus station. In exercising this type of honor, you are essentially acting in keeping the principle of true service, described earlier. Accordingly, when you help, you should make your commitment to provide what the person really needs and offer your assistance willingly, without an ulterior motive for personal gain, for then you are no longer acting with honor. You are not motivated by real integrity and compassion.

The fourth honor is due to all others, and this honor is based on the ideal of operating in a spirit of a fair and equal exchange. This means that you should look for relationships based on mutual benefit and sharing. You should see these relationships as more or less equal and seek an exchange in which all parties gain, for this mutuality will help keep the relationship in balance, so it will go along smoothly.

Such a relationship based on an exchange is quite different from the ideal relationship based on giving service. In a service situation, you are giving 100 percent of yourself, and your gain should come only or primarily in the giving. But most of our interactions with others are based on an exchange or interchange of benefits and services to one another. And in this case, you should normally act with integrity or honor to someone as long as there is a relatively equal or fifty-fifty exchange.

THE ADVANTAGES OF BEING HONORABLE

There are several good reasons why it is advantageous to be honorable to others. First, it is good public relations, so to speak, because acting with honor helps to keep your relationships smooth. People see that they can trust and rely on you, and so, if they are motivated by goodwill, which most people prefer to be, they will act toward you in kind.

Second, on a broader societal level, it is important that people generally relate to each other in a spirit of trust, because trust is the basis of relationships; it is the glue that holds relationships together to create an orderly society. For people need to operate in terms of their mutual expectations of each other. They must have understanding, so one party can anticipate what the other party is going to do and act accordingly. Moreover, trust depends on each party taking the responsibility to keep promises and follow through on agreements.

By contrast, if people do not trust each other, chaos results. People get confused, do not know how to act, and communications break down. Also, if a promise is not kept, events can go badly, and others can feel upset as well as actually being harmed by their reliance on someone who fails to perform.

Failings of trust and honor do not have to involve large matters. They can involve any breach of promise, and the result is generally that events will not go as well as usual. This honor that keeps the world running smoothly depends on people acting fairly, in a spirit of good faith and trust, taking responsibility to keep their promises.

SMOOTHING OVER A DIFFICULT SITUATION

Another advantage of acting from honor is it can smooth over a potentially difficult situation; acting from honor can help to reassure someone who has been upset. For example, when a group of us were leaving a press party which had been held in a performance space next door to a bookstore, the store owner was upset because one of the presenters, Maria, had used some of his rattles and drums, and he thought some of them were missing, and an antique Hopi rattle looked like it was scratched. As we walked out, he complained, even after Maria showed him where she had returned the rattles and drums. He was still upset about the Hopi rattle, though it did not look so severely damaged, and Maria had only used it for a minute. He complained that the rattle had cost him forty-five dollars and now he could not sell it. At once Maria offered, "I'm sorry. I only shook the rattle a few times, but I'll pay for it. I have very little money, but I feel like I want to pay you."

As soon as she said this, the man's attitude changed. He had been feeling upset and taken advantage of when he thought his rattles and drums were missing and he saw his scratched rattle. But once Maria made this offer, he realized she wanted to be honorable and fair about the situation. So he told her, "No, no, that's all right. You don't have to pay me anything. What happened is just one of those things. And I can just put a little white paint on the rattle to touch it up." It was as if Maria's offer led him to realize he had been overreacting, and instead, he decided to be reasonable and act from a sense of honor too. So the situation ended with mutual good feelings. And it worked out well because Maria had opened up to him in an honorable way, and since he was an honorable person, he responded in kind. By contrast, if Maria had gone off and tried to ignore what had occurred, she could have left matters in a very negative state, and if the store owner were angry enough, he might even have wanted to take legal action. But by acting honorably, she healed the situation, and not only did she gain his goodwill, but also he did not ask her to pay for any unintentional damage she might have caused.

DISTINGUISHING BETWEEN GOOD AND BAD INTENTIONS

The ideal, as in the illustration above, should be to act honorably when you are dealing with a person of goodwill whom you can trust, or if you are involved in an even exchange. In such a case, when a person is coming from a goodwill place, where he or she is acting in a spirit of good faith, you can safely respond with goodwill, because you both have the same attitude of honor; so a reciprocal good faith exchange exists. Then you can deal fairly and equitably with each other.

On the other hand, if people are coming from a bad will place, so that they are acting in bad faith and are not being honorable, that is the time to take necessary steps to protect yourself, because if you try to act honorably toward someone who is dishonorable and acting in bad faith, he or she may try to take advantage of you.

A classic example of this is the con artist who relies on the other's trust to gain from the encounter. He can take advantage of the victim, because if a person is acting deviously or dishonestly, the other is no longer involved in a fair and equal exchange based on mutual trust. Thus, if you sense that a person is lying to you or concealing important information, you may need to respond in kind by being less than candid or even actively deceptive yourself, to protect yourself if you must or choose to continue dealing with this person. Or perhaps you might consider whether you have to relate to this person at all, since the ideal for the optimal relationship is mutual trust and honor. So if you can, it is better to pull away from someone if you cannot act with honor.

However, at times you may have to deal with someone coming from a bad will place (i.e., acting in bad faith), and then it is necessary to do whatever is appropriate, including being ruthless, to protect yourself. After all, if the person you are dealing with has no honor or integrity, there is no reason to show honor to him or her, and you will only get hurt if you show vulnerability to a person of ill will. In other words, you must be ready to deal with others based on what they give you, and if they are coming from a place of bad will, and you cannot avoid the situation or change them, you must be ready to respond accordingly.

For example, in a potentially dangerous situation, like a street encounter, you must do what is necessary to protect yourself. Or if you are involved in a debtor-creditor relationship, and you feel the debtor is trying to trick you, you may have to be equally manipulative ultimately to get the money that is due. Still another situation might be one in which someone asks your opinion in a challenging way and seems ready to pick a fight if you respond with an honest answer. Again, it might be better to avoid giving the honorable response, if you sense it might lead to a conflict you want to avoid, because the other person is not acting from a place of honor.

To determine the proper approach, once again tune in to your inner voice or self, to try to pick up the person's intent. In some cases, you will be able to sense this right away. But other times, if the person is very well guarded and slick, or your own sensitivity is lessened, it may take you some time to pick up accurate information.

Thus it is often good to proceed with a readiness to respond with honor, tempered by an equal readiness to exercise due caution. In so doing, you operate from the ideal of acting honorably, in which you both come from a place of goodwill and are ready to act as equals. But if the other person is not being straightforward or is otherwise threatening to harm you if you open yourself up, thereby taking advantage of your sense of honor, there is no longer an ethical requirement to behave honorably toward him or her.

Let's say you are in a dispute. If the person is willing to work it out, then the ideal is to try to be fair and seek a win-win solution, which may mean you both have to compromise a little. By contrast, if the person seems to be avoiding the issue, it may be necessary to get tough and take legal measures, which will result in more of a gain for you and a loss for the other person in the long run. For example, one man in a workshop, Tony, was involved in a minor accident; another man pulled out of a parking space and hit his car. There was no question that the man was responsible, and Tony learned that it would cost $150 to fix the fender. Tony went to the man, who owned a successful business and could easily pay for the repair, and the man at first said he would take care of the expense. But each time Tony came to pick up his money, the man was away from the office, out of town, still at home sleeping, or otherwise occupied. As a result, Tony felt certain the man was just trying to find excuses for avoiding him, so that he eventually took the matter to small claims court, won, and when the man still evaded paying, Tony finally managed to collect with the help of the sheriff. At the same time, the man ultimately paid about double the cost of the repair, because of legal expenses. For Tony, the process had been a real nuisance, but he approached it with determination, and in the end he felt vindicated. As he observed, "I felt it was only just that he should pay. And so I went after him. I felt it was the honorable thing to do."

Yet, in other cases, you may be able to change a person acting from bad will, by behaving as if the person is acting from goodwill, even if you sense he or she is not, because that person wants to preserve his or her appearance of integrity and honor. For example, I did some work for a person who I felt was trying to cheat me by falsely claiming to have forgotten his wallet and promising to bring the money over later, but then he continually made excuses for not coming. I had worked for him before and I knew his friends, so I kept acting as if I trusted him and accepted his excuses because I felt that if I gave him the chance to save face, eventually he would come through and pay me. In fact, in our last conversation, it was obvious that he wanted me to think well of him, even if he had been deceptive in the beginning, because he said, "Thank you so much for trusting me." It was as if my appearance of trust helped him to keep up an appearance of being honorable and ethical, so he could maintain his self-esteem. As a result, though he later ran into financial and personal problems, I heard from his friends that he would be calling me soon, to finally arrange to pay. Thus, in this case, since the man wanted to appear honorable and was willing to act to redeem his honor, it was worthwhile to give him the chance to do so, by appearing to trust him as if he were acting out of goodwill all along.

CHOOSING WHEN TO RESPOND WITH HONOR

Thus, it can sometimes be tricky to tell whether someone is acting from good or bad will and to know how to respond based on what you sense or know. For you have to choose whether to initiate a relationship or respond from good or bad will yourself, to match the actions of the other person.

Perhaps one way to think of this process of choosing is to imagine that you are putting on different heads. Your ideal head is your goodwill head, which acts out of honor and seeks to behave in an honorable way. If you feel the other person is motivated by goodwill or can be shifted into acting in this way, you can put on this goodwill head.

At other times, you may need to put on your bad will head, like a helmet, as a source of protection. Normally, you may go out without this armor, hoping to act in goodwill to others who will act in kind. But you know this bad will head is always there, behind the scenes, so you can put it on when you need it. And at times you may, because even though you may want to act honorably with everybody, at times you cannot, and must arm yourself or take devious paths. Otherwise, you are like an unprotected warrior in battle and someone charging at you from a place of bad will can easily lop off your unprotected goodwill head.

So that is why you need to combine acting out of goodwill and honor with acting out of caution and possibly putting on your bad will head. Then you can act with honor when desirable, but in other dangerous, negative, or uncertain situations, you can shield yourself.

HOW TO DEAL WITH PEOPLE MOTIVATED BY BAD WILL

If you do feel that someone is acting from bad will, while you are acting from goodwill, you have several options.

One is to try to clarify the situation by bringing the reason for the bad will out into the open. For instance, maybe the person has some pent-up anger which is causing him or her to act destructively, and maybe you can gently point this out and help him or her release the anger.

Another option might be not to deal at all with a person who is acting out of bad will, if possible. Just end the relationship and walk away.

In other cases, a more quick-witted or manipulative approach might be the answer. This might be particularly apropos, for instance, when you are confronted with a difficult situation that you can not avoid. Perhaps the person is an important client, a co-worker, or a relative. Or possibly you are suddenly involved in a face-to-face confrontation on the street. In such cases, you may need to talk yourself out of the situation or cleverly maneuver it.

In short, what to do depends on the situation. So walk with honor when you can, but be prepared to protect yourself if necessary by leaving, or choosing, though reluctantly, to respond with bad will.

DEALING WITH NEGATIVE OR BAD WILL PEOPLE AS YOU BECOME MORE SENSITIVE

You may notice as you develop your personal mastery that you become more sensitive to the attitudes and underlying intentions of others. That is because you become both more intuitive about others and more uncomfortable with negative or bad will people.

Accordingly, you may find it especially difficult to deal with people who are complaining, critical, or judgmental, or who are just not honorable people and who are eager to take advantage of people who are. Since you have been trying to become more honorable and positive, you are more sensitive to others' dishonorable motives, and hence it is more difficult, even painful, to be around such people or to respond to them on their level.

For example, when I was younger, my parents were ordinarily critical and judgmental, and I felt this was the honest and natural way to be. Conversely, when other people were not acting like this, I felt they were being dishonest in not saying how they really felt. But then, when I started studying many spiritual groups for a doctoral dissertation, I began to change, and I found that I no longer wanted to be around critical and negative people because I could feel their destructive energy, as if I were being bombarded by tiny negative energy particles that sapped my own energy and made me feel discouraged and depressed.

Likewise, when you are around people who are acting from bad will, you can feel personally attacked by them, even if they do not directly say or do anything to make you feel threatened. In fact, it may be increasingly difficult to deal with them as you work on evolving yourself because the same sensitivity that makes you more perceptive of and in tune with the forces of the world around you, will make you more sensitive and vulnerable to others' negative energy.

Thus it is important to be aware of the kind of people you encounter, so that you are prepared to deal with negative people. Then, if you feel you cannot change them because they are set in their ways, you can quickly choose one of the options discussed earlier (leaving the situation, or if you cannot, protecting yourself) when you deal with such a person.

DECIDING WHEN IT IS HONORABLE
NOT TO BE FULLY HONEST AND OPEN

Although the hallmark of being honorable is acting with commitment, honesty, and openness, except in dealing with a person of bad will, at times it may be appropriate not to be honest or open with a person of goodwill, because that will better help you assist him or her. This situation is most likely when you are dealing with someone who has a lack of knowledge or is operating under a delusion. In such a case, you have to ask yourself, Should I provide this knowledge or try to counter this delusion? Or should I act based on what this person knows or believes? Also consider the question, Will it profit me in the long run to be honorable and tell the truth to this person, or is it perhaps better to let the other person believe the delusion? However you answer these questions, you should consider what will benefit the person most, and take into consideration your own potential gains and difficulties in revealing the truth or not, so you come out with a win-win situation.

For example, if someone has fantasies about his or her greatness or importance and is looking to have those feelings reinforced with compliments and support, sometimes it may be better just to give the person the recognition he or she seeks, rather than pointing out his or her problem. In doing so, if the person is not quite ready to deal with the truth, you can at least help bolster his or her self-esteem. For it is not always the best course to be brutally honest, unless, of course, you feel the person vitally needs this information now or has shown he or she wants to know, however painful the truth may be.

A common example of when it may be better to withhold knowledge or perhaps modify the truth is in the case of healing, because to a great extent healing is influenced by a person's belief. A person may be feeling terrible, and a doctor may not be sure of whether the person will get well, or may even think the person will die. But even in such a situation, a doctor will often encourage the patient to feel he or she will get better, for then, feeling this way, the person is more likely to heal.

On the other hand, there may be times when it is important to bring a person back down to reality because his or her delusions are dangerous. For example, one man in a workshop described visiting his ninety-seven-year-old aunt in the hospital after she fell and broke her hip. From her hospital bed, she started telling him how she had been at her sister's the night before, when she fell. But the man knew this was not true because, as he explained, "Her sister died last year and the house had been sold." Perhaps he might have gone along with the woman's delusion by simply nodding. But he felt that she was trying to retreat into the past and needed to be brought back to present-day reality. And so he told her what was real and what was not:

> I didn't see how I could go along with her fantasy. So I told her that she was probably dreaming and that dreams can be very vivid and that she was simply remembering when she was there or dreaming about being there. But there was no way she could have physically been there.
>
> I thought it was necessary to help her keep her reality correct. So I had

to bring her down to reality. I felt she would only get more and more confused mentally otherwise.

In many everyday situations, by contrast, it may be fine to support someone's perceptions, even if you do not agree with them, simply because the situation is not that important, and this maintenance of delusions can help to keep everyday social interactions flowing smoothly. On the other hand, if someone is really seeking advice from you, rather than just social support, it is better to say what you really think.

For example, if you are at a party and somebody is wearing an outfit you do not like, it may not make a lot of sense to tell that person you think he or she looks awful. Even if the person asks you, "How do I look?" whether you should tell the truth depends on the situation. If he or she is asking in the course of a casual conversation, you might do well to say something innocuous like "Well, that's an interesting outfit." But if the person is really asking for advice on a purchase, then tell the truth.

By the same token, if someone has just spent a great deal of money for an item, and you think he or she has made a terrible mistake, it may be better to keep the relationship running smoothly by saying nothing, since the purchase has already been made. By contrast, if the person is now considering an action which you know or believe to be wrong, and particularly if he or she wants your opinion, then by all means, say what you honestly think. In this case, negative comments would probably only make the person feel bad about an action that has already been done, and perhaps he or she even will be angry at you for causing these feelings. So the remarks would serve no useful purpose.

In short, deciding whether or not to be honest can be a bit like a cost-benefit analysis, in that you are figuring out if telling the truth is worth the price, given the circumstances. And to decide, you have to ask yourself what the gains are for the person or for you if you tell the truth, as opposed to keeping what you know or believe to yourself. The problem can be a tricky one to resolve because ideally you want to follow the principles of true honor, which require openly and honestly saying what you think. But at times, it is to your benefit and to the benefit of the other person to say nothing or tell a "white lie," based on good intent.

What should you do and when? Again, ask your inner voice to

decide. Just be aware that this issue can sometimes come up, so when it does, consult your inner voice.

Exercise 4: **APPLYING THE PRINCIPLE OF HONOR IN RELATING TO OTHERS**

The following exercise is designed to help you in applying the principle of honor in relating to others in different situations.

As usual, begin by getting relaxed. Just focus on your breathing for a moment and calm down. Focus on your breath going in and out. In and out. And as you get relaxed, be aware that a part of you is going to stay alert and aware.

Now imagine that you are going to be having many encounters with different types of people. And when you do, you will know how to make the appropriate choices of what to do, and know that you will act in a spirit of honor when you can.

In your first encounter, see yourself coming from a place of honor, and see that the person you are going to relate to is also coming from that kind of place.

So see yourself in this situation with this person coming from a place of honor and goodwill. Maybe you're having a conversation, and this person asks you a question which you answer. Maybe this person wants you to do something. Maybe it's somebody you work for, somebody that you are in a business relationship with, or a person you're very close to.

Sometimes you feel you can say just about anything you want to this person. You can be totally truthful. And you feel this person is being totally truthful to you too.

So you feel very good about this relationship because you can relate in this way. You can be totally honest with each other. You feel the person can be totally honest with you.

Notice that you may have certain expectations of this person, and this person may have certain expectations of you. But you feel this person will try to meet your expectations, just as you will try to meet his or hers.

You also know that if there are any problems in having or meeting those expectations, you can share your feelings honestly and openly. And if you feel that perhaps you are not doing enough of this now, you feel you can do more of this in the future.

So just take a few moments to share with this person. As you do, you feel you can be totally open and the person can be totally open with you.

As you share, you might feel yourself in a warm bubble of white light. And this is how this relationship of total honor should feel—total communication, total honesty, total warmth. It's a totally protective kind of relationship. And you feel really good about it.

Now let that relationship go and move on to another relationship. And this is a relationship in which you are not sure of this person's intent. It may be somebody you know, or maybe somebody you don't.

But in either case, you're not sure you *really* know this person. You feel a kind of separation, a lack of clarity.

Maybe you want to try to resolve that. And you know you have a few options. You can try and talk about it. You might be able to leave the situation. Or maybe you need to do something else to protect yourself, if you're not sure you can trust this person and you feel he or she is coming from a place of ill will. So just see yourself resolving this uncertainty in some way.

Now move on to one last situation. And this situation involves an encounter with a person you feel that you definitely do not trust. It may be with a hostile person, a person who is angry. It may be an encounter on the street, maybe in a bar, maybe with someone at work who's not a very nice person. Or it may involve some other situation with someone you feel you can't trust.

So you are not in a situation in which you feel you can act with honor. Instead, you need to protect yourself in this encounter. So just imagine yourself putting up some defenses. You are aware that there is only so much you can do in dealing with this person.

Yet, although this may be a difficult situation, you feel that whatever you do, you'll come out feeling very powerful, because you've been able to sense where this person is coming from. You've been able to respond properly.

It's as if you've got two heads—one is the head that you'd like to wear, which is your head of honor. This is the head you put on when you feel you can deal openly and freely with someone.

But you've also got this other head. And this is the one you need to put on sometimes when you are dealing with someone you can't trust. You might see this special head being like a mask or like a helmet or part of a warrior's outfit. And sometimes you may need to put this on to protect yourself.

So when you are in a difficult situation or with someone you don't trust, you can put on this mask or helmet and feel completely protected.

Finally, separate yourself from all of these situations you have just experienced, and imagine yourself looking at them. You are seeing them on a screen in front of you, and you realize that you have the power to choose.

When you are with somebody you feel is very honorable, with whom you can act with honor, you might see yourself in a warm bubble of white light, where you can relate to that person and be totally open, feel totally protected.

Then there's this second situation in which you are not sure. So you want to tune in to the person and get a sense of where he or she is coming from. Then if the person is coming from a place of honor, you can act that way too, or if not, you can put on your protective helmet.

And finally, there's the third situation with the person who's not coming from a place of honor at all, so you need to protect yourself.

Now just be aware that you are standing outside all of these situations, looking at them, and you can sense where people are coming from. So in whatever situation you face, you can choose what action to take, what head to put on, so you can do what you need to do to relate to the person appropriately.

So now, with that image, that awareness that you have the ability to choose, start to come back. And count from five down to one. Five, four, feeling more awake. Three, two, more and more awake. One. Come back into the room.

6

•

Being Aware

The seventh major principle of gaining personal power and mastery is awareness. One type of awareness is paying attention to your inner voice, intuition, higher self, or whatever you want to call it. It is equally important to take note of what is happening in the environment, and then to reconcile these two sources of information, if there is any conflict. For example, your inner voice may give you cues to check out something in your outer environment, so you will look more carefully and gain some information you need.

Developing a finely tuned awareness to your surroundings can be critical not only to your success, but to your very survival. Police officers, for example, are forced to develop this kind of alertness by sensing potential danger ahead, so they can react accordingly. Likewise, anyone who is involved in a very dangerous profession or activity, like skiing, has to be very aware in order to avoid accidents. A skier, for instance, has to be very much attuned to the flow of the slope and other people's whereabouts before moving ahead, and must remain aware of these things while monitoring his or her speed.

At times it may seem as if there is too much to notice when events are happening swiftly—like when the police officer has to make a quick decision while pursuing a suspect or when a skier is whizzing rapidly down a swerving slope. But the information is processed automatically when you are very attuned and aware. In this state of superawareness all systems are operating at top speed and at top accuracy, so the information pours in quickly and you can react almost immediately and correctly without having to think how to respond.

BECOMING MORE SENSITIVE TO OTHERS

You can also use this awareness to be more sensitive to other people's feelings. Then you have a better idea of how to act and react.

As an example, if there is a build-up of tension at work (among others or toward you), you may be able to pick this up, although the signs of difficulty may not be immediately obvious, as certain rules of etiquette force these feelings to remain beneath the surface.

Similarly, you can pick up cues from other people when you meet them. A person's body language is a valuable source of information about his or her true nature or motivations in a situation (e.g., usually truthful or devious). For instance, a person starting a multilevel marketing company unexpectedly called to hire me as a consultant. Then he came over, we spoke for about two hours, and I had a sense that he was a very honest person. As a result, I believed him when he announced that he did not have his checkbook or charge card with him and did not have enough cash (about $160) to pay me, since he had been about to fly back to Los Angeles and had been referred to me at the last minute. And I believed him when he said he would mail me a check and told me his name, address and phone number for the bill. I even believed him when he said he did not have any business cards to give me, so I did not ask for identification because I felt that would be an insult, though I did ask him to sign a copy of the bill as an acknowledgment.

Under the circumstances, the man I had just met could have given me a fake name, address, or phone number, and then walked out the door, and I would not have been able to do anything. But I felt I could trust him, even though these other possibilities flashed through my mind as I agreed to let him send me a check and did not ask for verification. But after he left, I called the number and found it was correct. And I received the check within a few days.

Similarly, I have used this close awareness combined with intuition to make quick decisions about housemates, employees, and business associates, and almost always, my sense of the person has been exactly right. It is hard to pinpoint the exact reason for the intuition because the information comes back to you as an overall impression or gestalt which pulls together all the contributing pieces of data. It is like sending out a radar and then getting back a signal that all is clear, or that there is danger in the field, so pull back.

Generally, when you do get this intuitive sense of someone, you can trust it. Yet at the same time, you might check it afterward, just to reconfirm the accuracy of your perceptions. As you find they are correct, you will gain more confidence in tuning in to other people and acting in response to the information you receive.

WORKING WITH PREMONITIONS

Premonitions are another source of information to heed. How do you know when they are accurate? You should look for a certain tone or quality in the premonition suggesting whether or not it is true, and again that goes back to developing your inner knowing and learning what signals to look for, so you will know when to trust. Then, if you feel the premonition is likely to be true, you can prepare to deal with it accordingly.

Sensing and Interpreting Premonitions If you do get a premonition and are not sure whether to trust it, you might look at it more closely to check it out internally. For instance, start by acknowledging to yourself, I'm feeling this discomfort or uncertainty about something. Let me look at what is happening. Then you can briefly meditate on your premonition and ask yourself, What is this telling me?

In some cases, you may be getting this premonition because the situation is making you nervous, perhaps because it is a new experience and you are afraid. So you are asking yourself, Can I do it or not? And your nervousness is translating into a generalized fear about the situation. But then, once you start doing it, the feeling will go away. But in other cases, your feelings of concern may not be due to performance anxiety, but to the situation itself.

Thus it is important to look at the source of your premonition through this self-examination. So when you get a strong feeling that something is going to happen, perhaps take some time to look at exactly what that might be and what might be the reasons for your feelings, to assess their validity so you can decide how to deal with them. Once when I was throwing a press party with a group of people, I had some internal warnings that the party would not go well. Were these premonitions real? Or was I just anxious because this was a new, uncertain, and important event? When I looked more closely at my concerns, I realized there were a series of signs of potential problems, so I was right to feel alarmed and to take action to avert trouble. For example, the location seemed to be set, but still there was a misunderstanding about the arrangements. And then, as I reviewed other recent events, I picked up a sense of general disorganization, so I realized I would need to proceed with caution in working with the people who had set up this party.

Thus, as this story illustrates, it can sometimes be useful to examine your premonition in order to reconfirm it or determine if this is just a stray concern that has no real significance.

At other times, you may not have the leisure to do this, because you have to decide quickly whether or not to act on your premonition. In this case, perhaps evaluate the strength of your perception and ask yourself if you are projecting an internal worry, or if something in the environment might be triggering your concern.

For example, if you have a strong sense of danger while on the street, this could be a very quick, accurate assessment of conditions, although you may not consciously be picking up the individual perceptions that are causing this intense uneasiness. But if you look around, you might see them. Say, to the left there may be a dark alley, while farther down the street, you may see suspicious-looking people. You did not see these things consciously, but your peripheral vision was picking up signs of danger, and your inner voice interpreted this information as a warning. So such a premonition may be a real warning—not the work of your imagination.

Thus, whenever possible, try to determine whether the premonition is due to some real external cue or is perhaps coming from some internal source, such as a memory of a past experience or some unrelated fears or concerns. For example, maybe the place causing you to fear some looming danger just reminds you of some place similar where you had a scary experience as a kid. Then again, a premonition may be a combination of both external and internal cues, due to fears or concerns triggered by the environment itself, although those fears or concerns may not be justified. So, often you may get mixed messages in these premonitions, which is why you should get to the source of a particular signal, so you know whether and how to act on it.

However, when in doubt, if the signal is strong and suggests immediate danger, you should probably act quickly, because your premonition is like a survival instinct. Sometimes, however, people ignore these sensations, particularly when they are in a familiar environment or following their normal routine, because they feel that doing what they usually do should be safe. But then this failure to listen can result in a disaster. For instance, someone may be home and may get the feeling, Let's leave right now. The feeling may seem to come out of nowhere, but in fact it has been triggered by a fire which is just starting in a back room. The person may not be aware of this fire on a conscious level, but his or her subconscious is picking up the danger and sending a signal to leave now.

Unfortunately, it is often easy to ignore such a signal of danger, since you may not even be consciously aware of the feeling for perhaps fifteen to thirty seconds, although at other times this conscious awareness may result as soon as you pay attention to these signals sent out by your subconscious. In any event, when your subconscious speaks in the form of a premonition, it can be critical to act right away, because waiting may increase the danger. Yet, in other cases, there may be no danger.

The problem is, it is often hard to tell when premonitions are valid, because your intuition is not perfect. You can develop and improve your intuitive ability, so you are better at determining when to listen. But nevertheless, your intuition is not like your logic, where one and one makes two, and you know that certain relationships always occur. With your intuition, sometimes you are right, but sometimes you are not.

So the key to using your intuition successfully is to get feedback on how correct you are when you use it. Then, gradually, you will find yourself becoming more accurate, and as your success rate improves, you will gain more confidence in your intuition, though it will never be perfect.

You can use this feedback you get to improve, by noticing the differences in the feelings you get when your information is correct and when it is wrong. Then see how you feel when you get premonitions in the future. If this feeling more closely matches the feeling you have had when you were correct, you are more likely to be correct now. Or if your feeling more closely matches the feeling associated with incorrect information, then the premonition may be less likely to be correct.

In addition, when you do get wrong information, perhaps look more closely at the information and the circumstances under which you are picking it up. It may be that an inaccurate tuning process or an inaccurate feedback and interpretation of that feedback cycle is occurring. For instance, you may be projecting what you would like a situation or person to be, rather than picking up what is really out there. If that is the case, you can work on eliminating the projection or at least putting it out of the way, so you can assess the information or premonitions more accurately.

Dealing with Premonitions You Feel Are Valid If you do have a strong premonition which you believe is valid, there are a number of steps you can take to handle it.

First, if you sense a future difficulty or potential disaster, you can avoid it, correct it, or at least prepare for it. For example, if you have scheduled an event, and you have a strong feeling that those helping you are going to let you down, you could cancel the event if you can, bring other people into the program, or arrive early and take on tasks you think your original helpers may not perform. By responding to your premonition with careful planning or repair strategies, you can sometimes keep matters on track.

Second, you can visualize the feared situation in your mind in order to avoid that situation or change the outcome. Suppose you feel you are going to have a confrontation with somebody you do not want to confront, like a co-worker with whom you have previously had words. You might visualize that situation being resolved and the two of you feeling good about each other again. Or perhaps imagine that the person is not going to show up at a certain event, like an office party, or you are going to be able to avoid him or her at the party. As a result, you may be able to have some psychic influence on this other person, or when you do meet him or her again, the visualization may influence your feelings and reactions so that he or she responds more peaceably in turn and the bad situation is smoothed over.

Third, if you have a premonition about an event which is set and cannot be changed, you can make the best of it. For example, before my first press party for my book *Shaman Warrior,* I began to have strong doubts about the turnout, in part because the planned publicity and promotion were not working, though the party sponsor and I were actively spreading the word through private networking. Nevertheless, I imagined a very small turnout. So to prevent that I spent two days before the party going from event to event around the city, and the night before I handed out about two hundred fliers at a party. As a result, the impending disaster did not occur, since the last-minute blitz produced about fifty people (the majority of the total attendance of eighty), so I was able to avert the occurrence of what could have been a true premonition.

Finally, if you cannot do anything to forestall disasters, use the foreseen event as a learning experience. You can do this even before the actual event, if you see in the course of preparation that your premonition of difficulties does have some valid basis. Or you can do this after the event, as you assess what went wrong and why. In either case, you should review what you expect to occur or what has occurred and ask yourself, How can I best deal with such a situation in the future? or How can I learn from what happened? From these questions you may discover how to make matters go more smoothly in the future. Furthermore, you may see that you made certain connections with others that will prove valuable for the future as a result of the first event, so that may be another source of gain.

THE PROBLEM OF NOT BEING AWARE

In contrast to the many benefits of being aware, a lack of awareness can result in many problems.

To begin with, many mishaps may occur simply because you do not pay attention, although you get cues from your environment or an alarm rings in your mind. So in this case, the problem occurs because you simply are not observant of your surroundings or feelings. An example might be the person who is walking down a dark street at night, caught up in reveries, so he or she does not see the robber lurking in the shadows and does not notice his or her subconscious feelings of nervousness.

There can also be problems if you pay attention, but then tell yourself to ignore the signals of concern you are receiving, so that you do not respond to your awareness cues. One man at a workshop described how this happened when he returned home from shopping with his purchase, a mechanical device for a project he was making. He began to throw away the bag and the receipt, when he suddenly heard a little mental alarm telling him not to do so. But he did it anyway, and a few days later, he regretted it, when he found that the machine did not work as it should, but now he could not return it. As he described the experience:

> . . . I was throwing the bag and the receipt away, when ding-ding-ding-ding, some alarm goes off, and it says, Don't do that.
>
> But then I switched over into my logical part, which said, Oh, there's no reason you need to keep this. You have your check as your receipt. And so I threw it out.
>
> However, later that week, the item I bought got ruined when someone else used it . . . and if I had saved the receipt, I could have taken it back, because the receipt said that the machine could be used to do certain things, but then it didn't do this. . . . So I'm not going to let my logic get in the way the next time my alarm goes off. I'm going to listen to that alarm.

This failure to listen can in turn produce other problems, besides the immediate result due to failing to pay attention. Most important, if you do not listen to your inner alarm, if you tell yourself repeatedly when you hear it, Forget it, or I don't believe you, then you are effectively denying and devaluing a part of yourself. And if you do this often enough, you will turn off that part of you, and you will not hear any more messages, until you do something to turn on this part of you again, such as doing some guided meditations or taking some shaman journeys to look within and get reacquainted with and reactivate this part of yourself that has become dormant.

RECOGNIZING CIRCUMSTANCES THAT CAN MAKE YOU UNAWARE

At times, people fail to pay attention because they are too busy. They are rushing around, feel under pressure, and so do not take the time to look, or they push away any warning signals because they do not want to be bothered.

Then too, there may be special circumstances which make people unaware, because they want to believe that something is so, or they do not want to look too closely and discover that something is wrong. As the popular expression states, Ignorance is bliss, and sometimes people prefer not to know something, because this knowledge might disturb their current state of contentment.

A prime example of this is romantic love. When people are in love, they often tune out any qualities or behaviors that aren't consistent with the desired images of the person they love. For example, a woman may want to believe that her husband is a strong, successful person who loves her deeply, and she may seek to put out of her awareness any signs of potential trouble, like indications that her husband is not doing well at work, or is having an affair.

Similarly, people entering a business deal together may want to believe the best of their new partner and so may overlook signs that this person is someone who cannot be trusted or may not be as competent or experienced as he or she claims.

Problems of this sort can also occur in judging casual acquaintances. The person may seem outwardly normal, and you want to believe the person is as sane and ordinary as he or she looks. As a result, it may be easy to overlook or dismiss signs of trouble, such as a slight tension in the person's walk, which might be a sign of inner tension. For example, in reports of crazed people who suddenly attacked others, a common theme is how normal the person appeared. Yet when people look back, they start to recall signs that the person was not quite so normal, though they ignored those signs at the time.

Thus, stay alert when you start getting warning signals from your intuition or inner voice and don't ignore them. Often these cues are not immediately noticeable. Or you may not want to acknowledge that anything is wrong. But if your inner alarm is sounding, take a closer look. Certainly, it might be a false alarm, but very often your alarm will be on target, because it is picking up subtle cues from a person or situation, before you can notice them with your conscious mind.

So check out these warnings. For when your inner alarm is picking up some real danger, responding promptly can save you money, help you decide about relationships or business deals, or even save your life. On the other hand, when you do not listen, this is like going into a boat without a life preserver or radio. You may think you have no need to bring them because the day is fine and the sea is calm. And perhaps the day may stay that way. But if it does not, you will not hear the storm warnings, so you won't have time to get back to shore. And if you are thrown into the sea, you will not have your life preserver, so you might drown.

NOTING SIGNS OF SUCCESS OR TROUBLE

Finally, you may notice that if you are proceeding along a path that feels right for you, events seem to fall into place very smoothly, whereas when you have uncertainties, obstacles and signals may continually crop up that make the going even more difficult. Thus, if you find that things are going smoothly, you might take this as an indicator that you are doing what is right, whereas if you start to encounter many problems, this might be a sign to reevaluate your actions and associates more closely and maybe move on to something else.

The following account by one workshop participant illustrates the sense of confirmation that can occur when everything seems to go smoothly. She commented:

I went on a business trip back East and I operated very intuitively in terms of who I decided to call and how I decided to make presentations to people. . . .

And I couldn't believe how smoothly things fell into place. In one case I called this company official out of the blue, because I had his name on a letterhead sent to me as a promotional piece by someone else. Then, when I called, he invited me over to see him, and he actually turned out to be the wrong person in that firm to see about my particular project.

But then he referred me to someone else in the same company who does handle that line, and that person gave me the name of somebody else in another company. And when I called him he gave me the name of a third person.

Then when I called him, on the spur of the moment, he invited me out to drinks and dinner, and we really seemed to hit it off, and I'm confident a major business deal will come out of this.

And it all happened, I believe, because I was operating fully on a sense of intuition. So somehow things seemed to fall into place, as if I was following along with the flow of things, and things couldn't go wrong.

By contrast, when there are underlying problems and difficulties, you may pick up signs of trouble. These may occur in the form of all sorts of snafus, like messages not being delivered or someone sending you wrong information. Or these signs could be very subtle in how people relate to you. You might notice that people do not meet your eyes or they seem hesitant. Or sometimes you might feel a certain stiffness in their movements or a reserve in the way they present themselves to you.

When you do pick up signs of problems, it is often beneficial to bring the issues to the surface, unless you feel this revelation might stir up the difficulty even more (such as with an easily angered, sensitive person who has difficulty facing the truth directly). But generally this airing tends to have a releasing effect, because otherwise, the problem may continue to grind away underneath and tensions and hostility may continue to build. To begin this opening up process, perhaps tell someone who seems bothered, "I feel there may be something bothering you; maybe we should talk about it." Thus, tensions do not continue to percolate under the surface; you get them out in the open so you can resolve them. Otherwise, the tensions may build to the point where they literally explode.

Such an incident occurred when I was teaching in the South, where people tend to be much more reserved than in many other parts of the country. As a result, at times people would have hostile feelings that they did not express until the situation would suddenly explode. In one case, a professor nurtured his hatred toward another professor in the department for years because he was jealous of the other's success; in turn, the other professor was prejudiced against the first, who came from the Middle East, but he did not want to show this prejudice. This feud went on under the surface of ordinary pleasant relations until one day at a faculty meeting, a remark triggered one of them to begin yelling at the other, who yelled back, and they nearly came to blows before others in the department stood up and embarrassed them both into calming down.

Looking back, I could see the signs of hostility in the way the men related to each other—small physical cues, like a quick glance or a slight body motion. But at the time, everyone ignored them, although the signs were there to be seen by anyone paying attention.

In short, it is important to stay aware and pay attention to the signs you see along the way. Then, if they suggest success or problems ahead, you can act accordingly, to maximize your chances for success and reduce or eliminate any problems along the way.

RECONFIRMING YOUR PERCEPTIONS

Finally, what do you do when your perception of everyday events is at odds with your inner sense about those events? Suppose you meet someone and the outer signs suggest this is a kind, successful person, yet some inner feeling of distrust nags at you. So your perception and your inner sense are in conflict. Often your inner sense may be right, but this is when you really need to determine whether you should trust your inner sense or your perceptions.

A typical example was my experience with a travel promoter I worked with for about four months some years ago. He came across as a slick, sophisticated, warmhearted person, with a vision of organizing romantic trips for singles to luxurious getaways. He also spoke of setting up branch operations for a travel firm back East, which he claimed was worth $38 million and had twenty-two branches. He talked of company jets and lavish expense accounts. And he even set up an office in the San Francisco Bay Area, where he convinced many travelers to sign up for glamorous trips. The only problem was, there was no $38-million company with twenty-two branches, no jets, and no expense accounts. There was only a small start-up loan from a silent partner, and the promoter's dreams. And in time there were dozens of bad checks, broken promises, and cancelled trips, until the promoter fled after a gala fiasco which cost thousands. He eventually landed in jail because he had conned so many people out of a total of fifty thousand dollars.

Yet in the beginning, one woman did see through the scam with her inner sense, and for a while she monitored her perceptions closely to see if her inner feelings were accurate. For as she told me:

> When he interviewed me for a job, things just didn't seem right. It was just a vague feeling, and I wanted to be sure. So I started asking questions, and when I didn't get the full answers I wanted, I decided to pull back.

At the time, she had no hard facts against the man—just a feeling —and when he seemed to evade her questions at the interview, she chose to go with her feelings of distrust and so bailed out. Later, of course, she turned out to be completely right.

Thus, when you do get conflicting impressions from your feelings and your external perceptions, check out this inconsistency. Are the inaccuracies internal? External? Is there some way to reconcile the two? What source of information should you trust?

It can be hard to know, but as you examine your perceptions from different sources more and more, you will find you get better at sorting out what is true. No one is really sure how this process works, but somehow you will start making better choices automatically, so gradually you will become more successful in knowing when to trust that inner voice and when to go with your logical perceptions.

The process operates like a survival instinct, which suddenly gives you the signal to act, though there is no clear reason why you should do so. But then, after you do act, you find the quick response to your inner feelings has saved your life. Many people have averted very serious danger this way. They may be engaged in some activity and suddenly get a message to stop. Or somebody may be walking along the street, not consciously aware that part of a building has started to fall, but he or she suddenly senses, I've got to step out of the way, and does so, thus saving his or her life, as the section of the building hits the ground. Such examples frequently turn up in the newspapers. The person reports he or she had a sudden feeling of danger, just reacted automatically, and survived.

That is why you must check out those inner feelings and use them to guide you in paying attention and being aware. These feelings are not always right, but they often may be, and you will find that as you pay attention and check on them, you will not only get more of this inner feedback, but it will more often be right, and you will become more accurate in determining when to trust it and when not to do so.

7

•

Forming

a Purpose

The eighth major principle for gaining power and mastery is having a purpose or series of purposes. Further, these purposes should be clear, known to you, and they should be directed to beneficial ends.

TYPES OF PURPOSES

There are three basic types of purposes: personal, mutual, and community or social. Though each type is distinct, they overlap at points, and you can best achieve your own purposes if your personal purpose is aligned with these mutual and social purposes.

YOUR PERSONAL PURPOSE

Your personal purpose is essentially your spiritual path or your chosen path in everyday life. This is the purpose that tries to answer the questions, Where am I going? or Who am I?

For some people, this sense of purpose can develop very early in life; others come to it much later. But in either case, having this purpose is important because it gives you a sense of overall direction, so you know where you are going and you can assess your progress toward that goal along the way.

Today it can sometimes be very difficult to discover or choose this sense of purpose, or even keep a commitment to this purpose, because we are living in a very complex society with so many opportunities and choices. Also, people come from many different walks of life, so they may be affected by multiple influences. All these options can be confusing. Since there are so many choices, we have to decide who we are, and people often do this again and again, as social conditions, opportunities, and options change.

By contrast, in simpler societies or fairly stable cultures, like the America of several generations ago, it may be easier for people to develop a sense of purpose early in life and keep that clear direction. A key reason is that there are fewer choices and many major life decisions are already planned for people. For instance, in the past, women knew they were supposed to get married and raise families, while men traditionally followed in their fathers' business or line of work. So in some ways this reduction of choice may be much easier, though limiting, whereas today, trying to choose among the myriad of options can often be quite difficult.

MUTUAL PURPOSES

You have mutual purpose when you work with other people or when you seek to interact with the world in some way. For example, a group decides on a certain activity, and then everybody joins in achieving that limited purpose. You also have a mutual purpose when you are performing a shamanic or magical ritual and are seeking the help of nature in achieving your goals. In turn, your efforts will be most effective when you work with the energies and forces of nature in achieving this mutual goal, rather than trying to impose your will on an unwilling nature by giving commands or seeing yourself as superior to or outside of nature. It's like you are seeking to work *with* others and that contributes to your success. The process operates very similarly to working with other people. When you share mutual goals or cooperate with others, everyone is more willing to work together to achieve that goal. That would not be so if you tried to impose your goal on others who did not share it. Likewise, working with and in cooperation with nature operates in the same way.

A good example of this might be doing a group ritual to reinforce your commitment to working on some goal. But as you are performing this everything seems to go wrong—the wind suddenly whips up and interferes with what you are doing; it starts to rain; people seem oddly tired and distant. Perhaps this is an indication that it may be better not to do this ritual now, and perhaps reassess this mutual goal. It's like nature is, in its own way, sending you a signal that the time for action or the goal of that action or even the people you are working with aren't right. And then you can look to your inner voice again to help you decide what to do.

SOCIAL PURPOSE

Finally, the social purpose is the overall purpose of the world as it evolves to a more advanced state. It is this sense of purpose that has propelled society to achieve ever greater technological advances and to increase the store of world knowledge.

This dynamic has brought us to where we are today. As one society reaches its evolutionary plateau, other societies continue advancing, because there is a sense of purpose pushing humankind along. I think we can begin to see this in the world today: the U.S. seems to have plateaued, because we have drifted away from a sense of purpose. As a result, we are experiencing a confusion of values and are raising many questions about ethics. If we answer them well and move on with a new sense of purpose and clear goals, then we can regain our strength. But if not, other countries with "strong" societal purposes will soon lead the way for the next generations, for that is the natural process of social evolution. We can already see this now, since other societies with strong social purposes, like Japan, are pushing ahead of us economically.

In turn, this larger social purpose influences each individual, for a country's firm direction helps direct and motivate its citizens too. But in a country with no direction, people can feel confused and unsure of their own intentions and goals. And again we can see this in a comparison of the U.S. and Japan. Many people here seem to be floundering; we are experiencing a real moral crisis, as illustrated by the repeated revelations of the transgressions of our political and religious leaders. But the Japanese seem to be very goal directed; they seem to have a sense of unity and direction toward common goals that keeps their society working more harmoniously than ours does.

Developing a Unity of Personal, Mutual, and Social Purposes In summary then, there are three types of purposes, which operate to order action and choice on the individual, group, and societal level —personal, mutual, and social purpose, respectively. In turn, to the extent that these three purposes are working in harmony, we can feel grounded, committed, and balanced in working toward our goals.

THE VALUE OF A PURPOSE

From time to time, I have heard people say, like one woman at a workshop, "I'm tired of looking for a purpose, a real purpose, or a valuable purpose." She concluded, "Maybe I won't look for one, and . . . I don't think you have to have a purpose overall."

Yet, even as she said these words, she seemed uncertain and confused because, though she was denying it, she was still groping for a sense of who she is and what she really wants to do.

So while it might be fine to engage in some purposeless activity at times and just relax from having or working toward a purpose, people generally need one to provide overall structure, guidance, and focus for their lives. They need that sense of a larger direction to lead and motivate them.

Equally important, having a sense of purpose is reassuring, because as long as you feel this commitment, you have an overall sense of direction which makes you feel that you are acting correctly. With this sense of reassurance, you will have less fear or anxiety, even when things go wrong, because you will feel that if you keep going, you will be able to overcome any problems.

STAYING ATTUNED TO THE LARGER SOCIAL PURPOSE

You can add to your own sense of purpose by being aware of and attuned to overall social trends, because, as you feel more aligned with societal goals, you will feel more reassured about your own purpose. Moreover, you will get added support for your purpose from others, who will sense you are in harmony with these larger social goals and perhaps with their own. In turn, this convergence between personal and social or mutual goals can at times translate into economic gains, such as when you are satisfying a demand for some new service or product.

For example, you may be aware that we are now in the beginnings of a major social shift. We seem to be pulling back from a period of rampant individual greed and swinging toward conservation—back to ethics, morality, and the basic principles of order in society, like education, the family, and the value of the community. It is like a general cleansing because we have realized the dangers of individualism and self-interest getting out of control. This can be seen in the images of insider traders going to jail and scandal-ridden preachers being ousted from pulpits. There seems to be a call for a new soul-searching and a new consensus.

We are not returning to the antiestablishment theme of the sixties or the personal "me generation" of the seventies. Rather, the swing away from the success-greed ethos of the eighties seems to represent a synthesis between what has gone before and this new emphasis on the larger community.

You can see signs of this shift everywhere. For instance, community help groups have been growing in popularity, with more and more people volunteering, as is the case with one of the groups I belong to, Community Boards, which seeks to resolve conflicts among neighbors. By the same token, I think we are going to see even more and more philanthropists finding ways to give back to the community, and more signs of personal altruism rather than people placing their emphasis on trying to accumulate more wealth.

You can even see this shift in the toy industry, which reflects themes in the larger society. In the last few years, toys were getting more expensive and more high tech, and many toys, like realistic toy guns, emphasized a macho, individualistic ethic. But now there is a real swing back to the basics, to a concern with safety and basic play value, much like the renewed concern of the larger society with traditional ethical, social, and family roots. For example, there has been a growing interest in educational toys, as well as in social interaction games for adults that encourage communication.

Thus, the national purpose may shift as times change, and in turn, people need to respond by aligning their own purposes with this larger social purpose. Then doing so creates a mutual synergy. Accordingly, when you choose a purpose that is in tune with the times, you can operate more smoothly in life generally, for these larger social forces will support you, just as you support them.

Similarly, when you start working with magic and ritual to achieve personal or group goals, it helps if your purpose is aligned with those larger cycles and purposes. For then you will be better able to focus your own energy and obtain the goals you seek, for you will be supported by the overall flow of trends in the universe, in the same direction as your own. It is always more difficult to do something that cuts across the flow of events, attitudes, and trends of the times.

LARGER AND SMALLER PURPOSES

It is also important to distinguish between larger and usually more distant purposes and the smaller short-term purposes of everyday life. Many people, for example, have a larger guiding purpose that organizes their whole lives—say a feeling like I want to be creative and contribute to society—and a series of smaller purposes like I'm going to get a promotion this year, or I want to get married this year and start a family, or I'd like to make $150 in sales tomorrow. Likewise, you can break down your larger purposes into a series of smaller short-term steps or processes.

This distinction between larger and smaller purposes becomes important in planning magical acts or rituals to help you achieve what you want. Whether it is large or small, you have to be clear about your purpose, and you have to direct your energy toward achieving it. Furthermore, you must be fully focused on and committed to that goal. But the key difference is that you generally have to put more energy and commitment into achieving your larger purposes. Conversely, to fulfill a smaller purpose, you will have to do much less.

For instance, to achieve a small purpose by tomorrow, like completing a project for a deadline, you may only need to say a few words of affirmation and commitment to yourself, to smooth the process along and reassure yourself that it will be done well. By contrast, with a larger project or objective, like obtaining a promotion and raise so you can move to a larger residence, you may need a series of rituals in which you clarify your wish, decide on what acts you must take to achieve that desire, and see yourself succeed.

USING YOUR INTUITION TO SENSE YOUR PURPOSE

If you are not completely clear about your smaller or larger purpose, you can use your intuition to examine what you really want.

You do this by looking to your inner knowing. In the process, ask yourself questions like, What do I really like or dislike? since your likes are a key to your purpose. For your purpose should be something that you really respond to, something that turns you on.

As you look within and ask questions, you will get the answers which indicate whether or not you have the right purpose, at least for the present time. If your purpose is correct, you will get a strong feeling of rightness, a sense that you are doing what you want and are supposed to do. You will feel a sense of harmony and balance because you truly feel what you are doing is right.

CHOOSING A TENTATIVE PURPOSE

At times when you look within to determine your purpose, you may get a clear image of a particular goal. But at other times, you may feel your immediate purpose is simply to rest and enjoy yourself now, because you feel you are between larger or more definite purposes.

If you do get such a feeling of uncertainty or transition, this is perfectly fine, because you may not want to make a firm commitment to a particular purpose. Rather, you may prefer to let go of the idea of a definite purpose, because you need the time to experiment.

So in this case, you may want to try out a series of tentative purposes. But eventually you will be able to decide on one, as you get feedback from your experiences and discover which purpose suits you best. A person choosing a career may have this type of experience. Thinking of being a doctor, he or she may volunteer at a medical clinic. A person considering being a writer may explore working at a local paper. Another person investigating a career as a social worker may assist at a local agency. Then, with the information gained about himself or herself from these experiences, he or she can better decide what to do.

It is also fine to rest for a while with nothing specific in mind. If you are in the middle of a major transition and are unsure of a direction, a breather may be good, especially if you feel too pressured to decide. Perhaps take a brief trip, or tell yourself that for a week or two you are not going to decide. Taking this breather will relax you, so you can make your decision more easily, when you are better able to look at your true desires, free of excess strain.

HAVING YOUR OWN PURPOSE

Any purpose you choose should also be your own purpose, not somebody else's idea of your purpose. If you are trying to live somebody else's purpose, like your parents', you are not being really true to yourself. For then you are living somebody else's vision of your life, which is generally not going to work. So there's no point in working toward somebody else's goal. Just as people have many different purposes, so should you choose your own.

Furthermore, in choosing a purpose, recognize that not choosing a purpose is a purpose too, for some people prefer to be more relaxed and easygoing about working toward a purpose; they prefer to focus on day-to-day enjoyment, and this desire to enjoy the here and now is also a purpose. For a purpose is not necessarily achievement. Rather, finding your overall purpose involves choosing your essential outlook or value system by which to order your life. So you do not need to have a specific purpose that you feel compelled to achieve and thus struggle to achieve it. That struggle is fine if you have chosen that purpose and you know you have to work hard to attain it. But if you have chosen a less goal-oriented purpose for yourself, that is fine too. The key is just to know clearly what you want, so you can do what is necessary to achieve it, if you want it badly enough, or you can relax more, if that is what you really want.

Likewise, if at times you want to work toward a purpose, and at other times you do not, that is fine too. For part of a purpose may be not having a purpose at times, if you feel that is what you want.

In other words, it is important to have your own overall purpose in mind, because that gives you a larger sense of direction. But this purpose does not have to be directed toward a particular achievement—it can also be focused on having a certain state of being or a central core of values. Moreover, you can let go of your purpose at times, if you feel uncertain about its feasibility, if you are considering a new direction, or if you consider working toward a purpose too oppressive at the moment—as if you are taking a vacation from purpose. But, in the long run, it is generally best to have this overall sense of purpose, for it helps to keep you centered, directed, and self-aware.

In turn, suit your actions to the purpose you have chosen, and be ready to shift when that purpose no longer seems right or when you have chosen another one. For example, if you have selected a certain purpose that you have to work hard to achieve, and you feel sure it is what you want, make yourself persist. On the other hand, if you keep trying and never seem to succeed, you may have the wrong purpose or you may not think it worthwhile to keep struggling to attain it. If so, perhaps choose a more appropriate purpose, given what you want and are able to do to attain your goal.

BALANCING YOUR REAL PURPOSE WITH YOUR OBLIGATIONS

Although you have decided on your "real" purpose and have committed yourself to achieving it, you still may have to balance it with some real-life practical concerns, like How do I make a living while I strive to do what I really want? Artists, actors, writers, and people in any creative field often have this problem, as do entrepreneurs who are hoping to fulfill their dream.

What to do when you cannot immediately realize your goal depends on the circumstances and your priorities. For example, although you have this larger goal, it may make sense to do something else for a while to support yourself, while still keeping this goal, so you have both a source of income and a sense of identity and larger purpose.

A good example is the would-be actor or actress, working as a waiter or waitress. He or she knows the restaurant job is necessary for a while, though his or her real purpose, motivation, and sense of identity in life come from acting. Acting is the larger purpose, but he or she does not throw over the other source of income until the time is right.

Similarly, an entrepreneur who does not have much capital may start a business in his or her spare time. With sufficient funds, it might make sense to take a year off and devote oneself full-time to the business. But without the resources, the would-be entrepreneur may find it more sensible to start working on the larger goal during his or her leisure time.

Thus you have to keep a balance between your real purpose and day-to-day survival. For instance, while writing my own books and designing and marketing games, I have also ghostwritten a few books and articles for others. I would have preferred not to do these, but I continued until recently because the money was supporting my own writing and work on games. And I did it until I felt secure enough with my own work to stop ghostwriting.

In short, do what is necessary to keep going, while you keep your true purpose in mind.

DISTINGUISHING BETWEEN GOOD AND BAD PURPOSES

When you choose a purpose, it is also important to select a good one, one that is socially useful or beneficial to others as well as to yourself, because otherwise, in the long run, the negative effects will come back to you.

Such is what happened when many people began choosing the goal of making money for its own sake. Now, after the scandals, exposés, and disruptions to the U.S. economy caused by the pursuit of pure greed, people are finding that just making money is not a very satisfying goal. Furthermore, it can even be dangerous because it encourages the exploitation of others, and eventually, not just those exploited but society as a whole loses, for the victims become burdens on the system—such as becoming homeless, welfare recipients, or criminals. Thus there is a growing recognition that we need to return to larger community values and the traditional ethics of hard work and productivity, trampled over by the emphasis on pure greed. And so there is a new concern with ethics today, to restore the moral order of society.

Thus, on both a personal and social level, certain goals may not be desirable because they have undesirable side effects, just as may a drug. The drug may achieve the intended effect (curing the disease), but may cause other damages. By contrast, when people have a socially valuable goal, they will earn money in the course of pursuing that goal, because they are providing a true service and fulfilling a need.

ACTING HONORABLY TO ACHIEVE YOUR PURPOSE

Besides choosing a good purpose, keep in mind the principle of acting honorably to achieve your purpose. This means you should not step on other people in the course of pursuing your goal, be-

cause such ruthlessness creates negative feelings which can ultimately return to you and defeat your purpose. For example,
people who are affected by your negative actions may hurt you in
revenge. So in the long run, you can actually defeat your whole
purpose, if you exploit others to achieve it.

Thus it is important to act with integrity, because, if you do not,
your lack of integrity eventually catches up with you. A most
graphic example is the vengeance vendettas one typically sees in
organized crime. For even criminals have their own sense of ethics
and justice, so that if people do not act "honorably," they may
find a contract has been placed on their lives.

This same process of justice and revenge happens on other levels
too. Perhaps bureaucrats may be a bit more subtle, so they may
not physically stab somebody who is dishonorable, but they may
vigorously stab somebody verbally behind his or her back, and so
undermine him or her that way.

Thus there is a rough justice which happens when you act, and
this is a key reason for acting honorably. If you step on somebody
along the way you may get to your goal initially, but you can easily
be pulled down, and this happens again and again.

THE NEED FOR FLEXIBILITY

You must also combine your sense of purpose and direction with
flexibility and adaptability. In so doing, you are ready to adapt
when society or conditions change. You need a purpose to have
an overall structure, but you must be ready to modify it to flow
with the times. Whether your goal is for the long-term or tomorrow, you need to balance your purpose with flexibility.

Suppose you have one purpose related to your plans for your
present career. But then that career suddenly disappears, due to a
change in society. In this case, you have to change your purpose,
too, or you will be left behind. This happened to me soon after I
got my doctorate in sociology in 1976. A few years later, Reagan
was elected, and suddenly there was very little interest in sociolog-
ical and anthropological studies; now people were more interested
in financial success and business, not in expanding social pro-
grams, which had been a major thrust in the late 1960s and the
1970s. However, many of those who received doctorates in this
field at the same time I did refused to change. Instead, they spent
much of their time complaining about the direction society was

taking, and they felt frustrated because people did not understand their vision of society. But the result was they got left behind; they got stuck in dead-end jobs or could not find work.

By contrast, I felt that I had to change with the times, and so I shifted into private industry. As a result, I successfully taught and wrote books about sales, marketing, and business. And now I am ready to change again to work on projects involving resolving conflict and a concern with social issues, because as society shifts back toward a concern with community, away from business and financial gain, I want to adapt to these new times.

Likewise, day to day you need to be ready to change, though you need structure to keep you organized too. For example, you can keep a daily diary or calendar to provide direction, so you know what you are doing day by day, week by week, and so on. But then, with the changes each day brings, you can modify your schedule based on your priorities.

For instance, I keep a date book with me constantly, in which I have plotted out my daily life for the next four months. But each day, if more important things come up, I adjust it. Say I may postpone a project for a week or two because a higher priority has arisen. Yet the long-range purpose is still there, because I still plan to complete the project on a revised schedule. So the ideal is to have that long-term goal, but then also allow yourself the flexibility to change or reschedule that goal.

Similarly, you can use this approach in organizing any project (i.e., writing a book, teaching a class) and just about any life goal. To do so, start with a basic outline and estimate the required time or resources. Then as you implement the plan, remain receptive to any promising new alternatives, possibilities, or ideas that may come up. For later on it may make sense to make some changes, such as expanding some parts of your project and shortening others, shifting the topics you cover, or changing your orientation and marketing angle. Once again, your purpose or direction provides the starting point, but then you are flexible enough to adapt to new circumstances.

DEALING WITH OBSTACLES AND DISRUPTIONS

You also need this flexibility so you are ready to respond to obstacles and disruptions that may arise. In some cases, it may be necessary to overcome the challenge. But in other cases, these setbacks may be signs that you should abandon the goal. So learn to pay attention to your intuition or premonitions at these times to help you decide on what to do.

Suppose you are working on a job and you suddenly encounter a shortened deadline or some barrier to completing the task. Depending on the situation, it may be most appropriate to persevere, looking for ways to overcome the difficulties; or perhaps it may be better to postpone the project until the barrier has been removed. In either case, stay calm as you determine what is necessary, and do not let the disruption throw you. Having a sense of an overall purpose can help you do so, because you know you will eventually achieve your objective, since you are clear in your goal. You can just look at the obstacle as one more step on the path. You know you will still reach your destination eventually, but now you realize that your original timetable may not be appropriate. Thus you can readily adjust accordingly, confident that when the time is right, you will get there.

To make this easy assessment and adjustment, it helps to maintain the feeling of control that comes from a strong sense of purpose. Then you can couple this sense of exercising control with a feeling of detachment, which will help you in objectively assessing what you need to do and then in doing it. For instance, if a potential problem surfaces you can draw on this sense of control and detachment to step calmly out of the way. Then, when you feel that problem has subsided, you can step back onto the path.

You might do this when you encounter a negative, difficult person who is standing in your way. Such a person may feel threatened by you and is therefore coming up with many reasons why your idea will not work. Perhaps one way to cope is to let this person vent frustration for a while. Then, when he or she has released the anger and fear, you can rationally explain why the project is feasible and go on with the task.

On the other hand, if you keep running into so many disruptions and barriers that you feel you have lost sight of your purpose, perhaps you should ask yourself, Am I on the right path? It can be important to have a clear sense of purpose and persevere against obstacles and disruptions. However, if everything seems to be going wrong, this may indicate that you have made the wrong choice. Therefore, this may be a good time to look at your own situation more closely and try to reassess your direction.

Suppose somebody accepts a promotion and soon afterward

faces many difficulties, such as conflicts with co-workers and family members. Maybe accepting the promotion was not the right move. Sometimes people may take promotions because they feel they should move ahead and promotions show they are successful. But in reality, they do not want to take on those commitments, though they feel a pressure to do so. The result is ambivalence or unconscious resentment, which leads to signs that they have made the wrong choice. For instance, they may have family problems because they are venting their work tensions on their spouses. Or they may encounter office conflicts because co-workers pick up that they really do not like their jobs or they feel uncomfortable with their duties. Thus, when things repeatedly go wrong, this is a signal to reassess your current situation or choice to do something, for perhaps you should turn back or otherwise change your direction.

In other words, be ready to respond to challenges and willing to work to overcome them, because you have to be prepared to work toward a desired goal. But while a certain amount of struggle may be fine and even expected, a *great deal* of struggle suggests that maybe what you are seeking so diligently is not appropriate or meant to happen.

Thus take some time to look at the situation and see what your inner self has to say. If you are really committed to a goal and feel it is right to see it through, by all means, keep working on it. But if not, feel ready to let it go and choose another purpose. For the key is to combine purpose with flexibility, and that can mean changing your purpose in midstream, if that seems appropriate. Conversely, if you encounter a steady stream of obstacles and disruptions, this could be a signal it is time to change your purpose. But look to yourself to decide, for only you will know.

VIEWING YOUR PURPOSE AS AN ADVENTURE

Working toward your purpose and dealing with adversity will be easier if you view your progress as a form of adventure. Doing so will give a certain curiosity or anticipation about new developments. You are almost like an author creating the story of your life, and you approach this story with a sense of wonder about what comes on the next page. A part of you may be functioning as the director of your life, helping to plan and arrange the future. At the same time, another part of you is turning the pages of the novel or watching the screen and has a certain excitement in not being sure about the next plot twist. For you can not be sure of everything, and this attitude helps you approach life with a spirit of adventure.

There is a major advantage to regarding your life as an adventure, for if problems arise, you can better cope by distancing yourself from them, because you realize that when you turn the page, the problem will be solved and you can go on to something else. So that approach can help you keep going, despite any obstacles you may encounter. As the old country and western song by Johnny Cash goes, "This too shall pass." And you know it will, because the page will turn, the act will end, the chapter will be over—and that is a good way to look at any difficulty.

Thus, while it may be good to do some planning to achieve your purpose, still approach whatever happens with anticipation and excitement. When you do, you are prepared for what you might expect, but ready to accept whatever else might come. So you have an ideal balance between an overall direction and a willingness to respond and change. This balance is important because planning and organizing can help us stay in control, to some extent. But there is always some serendipity, and it is important to be ready to welcome it when it comes, so it does not throw you. In short, you are prepared by having a sense of purpose, but at the same time you have this attitude of adventure and anticipation, so you can easily adjust.

Exercise 5: **USING YOUR INNER VISION AND MAGIC TO ENVISION AND ACHIEVE YOUR PURPOSE**

Your inner vision or knowing can help you decide what your purpose should be. Then you can use your directed thought processes and magical ritual to achieve your desired goal.

Start by looking within to clarify exactly what you want, if you are unsure. Once you have decided on a goal, the whole point of magical ritual is to mobilize the energy within yourself and to draw on the assistance of the energies and forces of nature to help you get what you want.

The following exercise is designed to help you clarify your purpose so you can focus on achieving it. You can work on either a smaller, more limited purpose, such as a goal you want to attain today or tomorrow, or you can work on a much larger, more expansive one, such as your personal five-year plan or an even more complex purpose involving others. You can decide in advance or during the exercise.

As usual, start by getting relaxed. Again you must center down and concentrate on your breathing. Notice it going in and out. In and out. Also be aware that as you get relaxed, you'll continue to be aware.

Now start by thinking of some purpose. It might be a larger purpose that you have. It might be a purpose that you have for tomorrow. It might be something over the next week, two weeks, a month, a year, or five years.

Now see that purpose come into your mind. Perhaps see it on a screen in front of you. And maybe you'll see it described in writing. Maybe you'll visualize it. Maybe you'll see symbols. Whatever it is, you have a very clear image, a very clear picture of it.

Just look at it. And if it's the right purpose for you, you'll find that it becomes clearer as you look at it. It comes into better focus. It seems to come closer to you, so you can look at it very closely. And if it's not the right purpose, you'll see it waver or get fuzzy, and in that case, just change the channel or put on another film.

Now see another purpose come up there on your screen. And if you want to, you can use this screen of your mind to look at many different purposes which you have.

You can choose among them. It's as if you have this storage cabinet, like you might have for records or videotapes, of all the different purposes you have. So whenever you want to look at a purpose, you can put it on the screen. You can focus on it. You can make it clear and you can decide whether or not you want to work on achieving that purpose.

As you look, you can see that purpose being realized. You can see the steps leading up to the fulfillment of that purpose. And, with some purposes, there will be many things you have to do to achieve them.

Now if you wish, take a look at some of the things you need to do. And maybe consider if that's the purpose you want. Or if you have selected a purpose which you feel certain about or which you feel is easy to achieve, just feel good about this now. So now take some time just to observe your feelings and to sense whether or not this is the right purpose for you.

You'll notice that when it is the right purpose, the image will become clearer and clearer on the screen. And if it's not the right purpose, the image will fade away.

So experiment now and try out different purposes on your screen. Just look at them. Look at what you have to do to achieve them. And decide if you want to do that, so you can decide if you want a particular purpose or not.

You can sort through many potential purposes now, and you may find that some of them are purposes for right now, and some of them for a little while from now, and some of them for a time that's very far away.

But the timetable doesn't matter. For you can choose. You can tune in any purposes you want. And if they are the right purposes, they'll be clearer, and if they're not, they will be unclear and you can just let them go. So take some time to look through your cabinet and try glancing at different purposes.

Now, as you're looking at all these different purposes, choose one of them. Choose something which you'd like to achieve, that you'd like to commit yourself to achieving. Take the time really to look at this. You want to choose something you really want to do. It might be something that's very easy to do, or maybe it's not. Just examine this purpose, and notice what it means to you. Be aware of how it makes you feel. Really take a close look at this purpose.

As you look at it, imagine that you are like a director going onstage and looking at the actors and the set. For as you are carefully examining your purpose, it's as if you are carefully reviewing a little play in your mind. So continue to look at it and see what's happening. Really get in touch with your purpose. And get a sense of the motivations of the characters up there.

Also notice where your purpose is going. If you achieve it, ask yourself, What are the results? What kind of rewards do I expect to have when I achieve that purpose? How does having experienced that purpose now make me feel? What do I like about it? What feels good about it? And notice too if there are any problems that come up as a result of having this purpose. If so, ask yourself what you can do to get rid of these problems.

Then imagine your purpose as an object you can take with you and look at later, when you want to. Perhaps it's a picture, such as the picture of the stage that you have just seen. Maybe it's a pillow, which you can keep in your room. Maybe it's a wall hanging. Maybe it's like the page of a book. Or maybe it's anything else you can just look at. For it's like a reminder. When you look at it, you feel good because you know that object represents your purpose. It is who you are, who you want to be.

When you are ready, you can take that image with you. And you know you can always turn on the screen again, so you can look at your purpose closely, and you can look at other purposes too. Also know that you can always take this image, this picture, this pillow, this wall hanging, this page, whatever form you see this purpose in, and it will always be with you. For you can keep it with you and always look at it in your mind. Or maybe later, you can make a physical manifestation of your purpose, so it's something that you can always take with you and examine, recommit yourself to, and feel good about. For it's your purpose and it's you.

So now, with that feeling, step away from the screen you have been looking at. Turn off the projector or the television or whatever you have been watching.

And now get ready to return. In a moment start counting backward from five to one, and as you do, become more and more awake, more and more conscious. So now, begin to come back into the room. Five, more and more awake. Four, three, even more awake. Two. One. And when you are ready you can open your eyes and come back into the room.

REASSESSING YOUR PURPOSE
WITH YOUR INNER VISION

A close look at your purpose, as provided by the exercise just described, can also help you decide if you should change or abandon a current purpose. In one workshop, several participants saw images that suggested they might not have the right purpose and might need to find a new one. One engineer commented:

> While I was looking at this image, it disappeared, and I thought maybe it wasn't the right purpose for me. . . . It was a big sign that said, "how to" up there, and I thought that could suggest me, since I'm an engineer. But then, hey, it was gone. And I thought maybe what I need to do is reevaluate things in my life, because maybe it's time for a change.

Another woman found she had trouble even imagining a purpose because, as she later realized, she did not want to have a purpose right then. She had been feeling burned out and felt a need to drift without a particular purpose in mind, which showed up in her imagery—or, perhaps more accurately, in her lack of imagery. She did not want to see anything because she was not ready to make a commitment to a purpose at that time. She explained:

> The exercise helped me see I had to be less ambitious in my goals, at least for now. . . . I found I didn't have a purpose when I looked. Then I tried to find one . . . but I realized I'm not really ready for it because there are some very real obstacles to it. . . .
>
> The basic problem is I have a job I don't like. . . . I hate being a secretary. . . . I'm doing it because I have to have a job. . . . And I know that I have to realize that I have to make the best of it. . . . But I keep thinking I really should get out, because I hate my boss and I hate all the things about the job. But on the other hand, there are some very real reasons why I need to keep this job. They're practical reasons. I need the money, because the rent is high. . . .
>
> So I know it's not the right time. . . . I keep thinking that I should be working on finding something else . . . but I'm not at a point in my life where I can do that. You know, it really takes a lot of courage . . . to quit, and I have to make a living.
>
> So I feel too ambivalent about thinking about another purpose now. I guess I'm afraid to really look at it. It's just too scary for me to think about the whole question of my purpose now.

Thus, as these examples show, not to get a clear image of your purpose may be a sign that it is time to change or an indication that you are not quite ready to deal with this issue. If it is time for a change, you can look more closely at what you might want. Or if you are not quite ready, then perhaps wait for a while before you look again, or ask yourself what might be standing in the way of your gaining a clear sense of direction.

TAKING TIME TO ASK YOURSELF QUESTIONS

If you do find you have a sense of uncertainty about your purpose, or about anything else, for that matter, it can help to set aside private time to ask yourself questions. One especially good technique is the solo, during which you go off by yourself for thirty minutes to an hour and open yourself up, remaining receptive to whatever comes to you. A natural setting is ideal for helping to open you up. Then when you are in this quiet, meditative, and receptive state, you can ask your inner voice or personal guides any questions you have and listen for the answers. For instance, you can ask what you should do now or what your purpose should be.

The whole idea of this approach is to enter an altered state and listen to your inner self. In other words, you ask yourself a question with your conscious mind and then you open yourself up so that your unconscious responds to you. For example, if you are trying to clarify your purpose, your inner voice might give you certain insights about the skills you have now or what you should do next, which will help you make decisions. Or if your inner voice tells you this may not be the right time to do something, this is a sign to wait. Later, when you feel ready, you can ask again, to explore further what you want and what you must do to achieve it.

REVIEWING YOUR PURPOSE PERIODICALLY

In conclusion, it helps to review your overall and more limited purposes in life from time to time, to check your direction and see if you still feel you are on track. Then, if there are indications that you should change, you can explore that issue further. Use the exercises described in this chapter to help you do this review—and if you wish, develop your own visualizations and images to help you more closely examine your purpose and determine the steps to your goals (for example, instead of seeing your purpose flash before you on a screen, take, in your imagination, a journey to the beach and see your purpose appear before you in the water). The point is to use the images and associations that work best for you, but call on them fairly regularly. It is as if you are reviewing your current situation and your destination, so that you can carefully check your progress. Then, if you like where you are going, fine. If not, you can make a change, calling on your inner voice to help you decide on the most appropriate path for you.

8
•

Exercising Persistence
and Patience

The last two major principles on the path to personal power and mastery are persistence and patience.

Persistence is the key to success in virtually anything, as well as in attaining goals through shamanic journeys, magical rituals, and working with other methods of entering altered states of consciousness. Persistence means you must work at whatever you are doing in order to become successful. You have to stick with it and keep working on the goal regularly.

Initially, your efforts may not seem effective. But if you persevere, eventually these efforts will pay off, or you will learn from these efforts how to correct your mistakes, so your situation will improve. It is as if you have made a certain commitment to a direction. Then, as you stay on the path, gradually things start to fall into place, and your success rate starts to rise, which helps you to know you have made the correct choice.

You might think of the process as having made a promise to yourself, and to fulfill this promise you do whatever is necessary to accomplish it. In turn, this promise to yourself should flow out of your inner choice of purpose. When you get that sense of rightness, you make that commitment, and you need persistence to see it through.

DISTINGUISHING BETWEEN PERSISTENCE AND OBSTINANCE

Persistence, however, is quite different from being stuck and spinning your wheels. It is not the same as beating your head against the wall because you do not have the sense to stop. You should stop in those situations where you have no realistic hope of achievement.

A case of being stuck is somebody feeling that he or she would like to be an actor or singer, when there is no realistic hope of becoming one. Nevertheless, he or she continues, because of unrealistic wishes, since he or she has no talent, or because his or her mother would like it, or for some other unconvincing reason This is an example of obstinance, not persistence, because the person is tilting at windmills by continuing to focus on a goal he or she cannot really attain. So he or she is persisting in a poorly chosen goal.

By contrast, true persistence means having that inner sense of rightness first and then sticking to your purpose. Under these conditions eventually you will achieve your goal.

Many people in creative fields have this experience. They may go through a real struggle for years and years, and it may seem as if they are getting nowhere. But they have that confidence that what they are doing is right for them and so they persevere. And finally, after much failure, they succeed spectacularly. Such was the case for Barbra Streisand, Burt Reynolds, and hundreds of now-famous celebrities. In fact, a book called *Rejection* details the early failures of many famous people who turned these rejections around by persistent struggling.

THE IMPORTANCE OF FOLLOWING THROUGH

Persistence is critical, because you need to follow through for most successes. Even if you have a terrific idea, if you are too busy with other things or do not put enough energy into it, eventually you will give it up or you will fail, because you will not see it through. By contrast, persistence is a key to success.

About 10 percent of your success comes from the idea. But 90 percent of that success comes from following through and plodding away. For you need that follow-through to accomplish something. Otherwise, you just have the dream.

I have seen many cases of dreaming without following through, and the result is typically failure. A good example is when I have consulted with aspiring game inventors. I have given them suggestions on how to develop their raw ideas into workable, salable models, how to contact potential manufacturers once they have that model, or how to produce and distribute the finished product themselves.

But with the majority of people, the consultation is the last step. For after I explain how hard it will be to manufacture and distribute the product themselves or tell them how to prepare their model and make a presentation to a manufacturer, most people do not go any further. And so their ideas are aborted at this early stage because they do not follow through. Yet some of their ideas have great potential.

Thus, in every aspect of life, you need to follow through. Your ideas and talent can only get you so far. Then you need commitment and determination to make your endeavor a real success.

IMPROVING YOUR REPUTATION THROUGH PERSISTENCE

Persistence can help you break through barriers to success because when you persist, people start to take you seriously after a while and as a result, respond better to you and your idea. When you begin something, people may think, This may be an interesting idea, and Yet here's another person who wants to do that, but they do not give you or your idea much attention. But when you keep coming back, all of a sudden, people start to see you differently, as a person with a serious idea or plan to be reckoned with.

I had that experience when I first started designing games some years ago. At first, many professionals in the industry did not want to talk to me because they saw me as an amateur. But I kept calling them again and again to follow up. And after a few years, I came to know everyone, and now, returning to the field after many years out of the field, I find all the doors still open. Through persistence,

I got past the barriers that keep thousands of inventors out of the game industry.

The process works the same way in other fields. Your first year, only a few people will talk to you. But in the second year, another series of people will talk to you. And finally, all of the doors start opening, because people see that you are still there and you have not given up.

This is true in industry and in other pursuits. For example, when Jimmy Carter began his campaign, nobody took him seriously as a presidential candidate. But just by continuing to knock on doors, speak to groups, and otherwise persist, he started to gain credibility until finally, he won.

Of course, you need a certain charisma, talent, or ability to succeed. But beyond that, you need the persistence to follow through and gain the necessary credibility to support you in attaining your goal.

LEARNING FROM YOUR MISTAKES THROUGH PERSISTENCE

Having persistence also helps you to learn from the mistakes which may stand in the way of your success. In the beginning of any project, you may make a huge number of mistakes. But if you persist, not only can you learn from them, but you may even be able to go back to the people who saw you make these mistakes and win them over. This happens because they see you are still in there pushing and have acquired new knowledge, so they have a new respect for you.

For instance, I gained such knowledge after I had a huge disaster in the doll industry about four years ago. I had hired a doll designer on a free-lance basis, and gradually our work together evolved into a partnership. However, after a while, she began to think that she had enough talent to do without me, so when I introduced her to people, she would seek to form alliances with them so she could work with them directly without my being involved. I was not aware of this at the time; I only discovered it in retrospect.

At a gift show, I met the chief designer of a doll manufacturer, who liked many of my partner's dolls and agreed to license them. But a few months before the dolls were ready, I met a man who claimed to be a children's book publisher, although I later learned he had only hopes and no funding. However, he was convincing, and he claimed he wanted to publish a children's book I had written based on the dolls. Unfortunately, he gradually started changing our original concept (cute little devils), because he was afraid of public reaction to the devil imagery. So first he wanted to change the name of the dolls and then he suggested eliminating their red tails, then asked to change their whole appearance because he claimed his artist had come up with other designs. Meanwhile, the manufacturer agreed because the man stirred up excitement about the book. But in fact there was no book, because he did not have the money to pay the printer. However, the dolls still could have come out using the original design, if only I had called the manufacturer in time to explain what had happened, since they were about to go to press and were holding their catalog for a few days so they could include the new design of the dolls, based on this man's artwork, which never came.

But I did not call, because the doll designer had entered into an alliance with this man against me, and a few days before the catalog went to press, they came to me with a proposal—or actually, more of an ultimatum. They came over to my house together and essentially told me that they both had made so many changes that these were no longer the same dolls, and I had only contributed the concept. So if I did not go along with them, I would essentially be out of the project which I had originated.

Yet I agreed because at the time, I believed there would be a book and thought I might lose everything if I tried to intervene. I believed they would bring out the newly redesigned dolls, he would publish his book based on them, and I would be out of any agreement because these were no longer the original dolls.

But within a few days, their whole plan unraveled because the man could not pay his printer. So there was no book, no new artwork for the manufacturers, and because the manufacturer was not called in time to explain what had happened so the original doll designs could be used, there were no dolls in the catalog. The manufacturer was very angry about all the delay and confusion which had led to this sad state of affairs.

Yet after the project was effectively dead, and after the manufacturer had formed a negative view of me and my company, still I persisted. I waited for the negative feelings to subside, and then I started writing an occasional friendly letter to show that I had learned from the experience and was not about to quit. I described working with new designers, learning more about writing children's stories, and writing up a formal contract with the original designer and others, so that such confusion would never happen again. And the strategy worked. Finally, the president and the chief designer for the manufacturer responded. I met with them in New York, and they expressed renewed interest in these original and other dolls.

So the key is persistence. Even if you have made a huge faux pas with someone, if you come back with a new level of knowledge, if you acknowledge the mistakes of the past, you may find that suddenly the door reopens. And the reason is that he or she has a new respect for you because of your persistence and ability to learn from your bad experience. As a result, you can put the past behind you and proceed on a new and higher level because of what you have learned. In turn, it is your persistence that has given you this new knowledge and this new respect.

Exercise 6: **REAFFIRMING YOUR COMMITMENT TO PERSISTENCE**
At times, however, it can be difficult to persist. It takes hard work and commitment, and it may feel easier or more comfortable to do something else, but you need persistence ultimately to win. Accordingly, the following exercise is designed to help you persist, by reaffirming your commitment to your persistence to achieve a particular goal.

Start again by getting relaxed. Just focus on your breathing. Just notice it going in and out, in and out. You're feeling more and more relaxed.

Meanwhile, as you get relaxed, you're going to stay alert and aware.

Now think of some task or project that you have in mind, something that you want to do. But maybe you haven't had time to do it. Maybe you've been very busy. But this task is something you'd like to get done.

And now imagine recommitting yourself to it. See yourself doing it, planning it. You are taking whatever steps are necessary to make it happen. And as you see yourself doing it or thinking of doing it, you feel a strong sense of commitment.

You might even see yourself holding a stake or other strong object and putting it in the ground to symbolize that this task is something you're going to do, something that you want to do. You're going to make it happen.

Now, as you look, you may see in front of you a large map representing the commitment you are making to follow a path to your goal. Notice that there are various pathways on this map. These pathways represent the various ways you can go about doing this task. You can choose any pathway, but you are determined to follow that path.

Now, if you want, look ahead along the path, and near the end, you see a flag. The flag marks the end of the project, the end of your commitment. And like a runner in a race, you're determined to get to that flag. You've made getting to the end of the path, to the flag, a goal. You've made this your commitment, and you've planted your flag ahead of you on the path. For you have made this flag the object that you are going to commit yourself to, and you know you are going to get to it.

Along the way, you may notice some obstacles. Perhaps there are some stones. Maybe there is some water you have to climb over or go through. Maybe you see some cliffs ahead that present a challenge. And you know it might be hard getting where you want to go. You might have to struggle. But you feel that sense of commitment, and you know you are going to go through whatever obstacles are there. And you know you can do it.

Furthermore, you know the resources you need to achieve your goal will be there. Say you have to go across the water, you know a boat will be there. If you have to go across a cliff, you know you'll be able to jump over or perhaps there may be a plane to take you over. So whatever the situation, you will get through because you have that commitment and determination. And as long as you have that you'll be able to find the way through.

So see yourself going along the path and moving through whatever obstacles may come up, to whatever goal or object you have ahead of you. You see the obstacles along the way just disappearing as you go through. And you feel a sense of strength, commitment, and determination as you go.

Also notice how that commitment to determination gives you a strong sense of power that serves to propel you along the path. So as you keep going, feel that power. It's like a suit of armor surrounding you. It helps you get through. And you keep going. And you're willing to face whatever comes.

So now just see yourself getting there and getting closer and closer to your goal. As you move ahead, you feel a strong sense of satisfaction because you are persistent, because you have kept going. Whatever the obstacles were, you kept going through them. You persisted in overcoming the barriers you encountered along the way.

And now experience yourself being there, enjoying the fruits of your satisfaction for having persisted. Experience the rewards of whatever goal you set.

And now, when you're ready, you can turn back along the path to the beginning. Or if you prefer, just let the image go.

And now count backward from five to one, and as you do, see that image fading and start coming back into the room. Five, four, you're becoming more and more awake. Three, coming closer and closer to reality. Two. One. Then, when you feel ready, open your eyes and come back into the room.

RECOMMITTING YOURSELF TO YOUR GOAL

You may find as you do different exercises that some of your goals reoccur, though perhaps you look at your goal a little differently each time. This is fine; it acts like a recommitment, a reaffirmation that you want to keep pursuing the goal. Then too, this process reminds you of your decision to persevere with this goal.

Furthermore, in practicing these exercises, you may like working with certain images or symbols. If so, just choose the ones you feel comfortable with and use them again. Say a certain exercise or set of images has worked well for one purpose; you might try using that exercise or those images to work with another goal.

Or if you are between goals or do not want to have any goals because you are feeling burned out and just want to relax (as one woman said, ''My main goal right now is not doing much. I just want to relax, let everything go''), then do just that. Acknowledge that you do not feel like working on any goals right now, although eventually you will, for we all need an overall purpose and goals. Then, when you are ready, you can clarify those goals and from time to time use these exercises to recommit yourself to them.

HAVING THE PATIENCE TO ACCEPT THINGS AS THEY ARE

Finally, after you have your purpose and sense of commitment to whatever you are doing, you also need patience to realize and accept that some things may take time.

Patience is closely related to persistence, in that both involve following through on a goal. However, when you have persistence, you are actively attempting to keep moving toward your goal. But patience is a more receptive mode, in which you are able to sit back, relax, and let matters unfold, for you are aware that the process may not happen as quickly as you would like, but you are willing to accept that and wait for the right time. For you know, as the old proverb states, that every activity has a time or season and every time or season has its ideal activities. So patience is understanding that events will happen when it is appropriate for them to happen, and accepting and working within that framework.

Thus, patience goes hand in hand with waiting, though it is a calm and comfortable sort of waiting, because you are not impatient or expectant, and you are not anxious as you anticipate what will happen. Also, you are not feeling annoyed that your goal is not being attained sooner. Rather, you are accepting matters as they are, at the same time that you might be working to fulfill your overall purpose or more short-time goals.

For example, when I was at the New York toy fair, showing my games and the games of other inventors, my purpose was clearly to show them to as many manufacturers as possible and to sell some manufacturers on these ideas. To that end, I was making phone calls, seeing as many as ten people a day, and dragging around two large suitcases full of models. So I was actively trying to fulfill this purpose by persistently contacting people. But at the same time, I approached the task with patience, so I had a sense of also taking it easy, even as I was persisting in achieving my purpose. As a result, if I was not able to reach somebody even after numerous calls, I just accepted this and did not become tense. Instead, I just acknowledged that I had to call again; he or she was not ready to talk with me yet, but might be tomorrow. So I was able to maintain this feeling of being relaxed and comfortable, regardless of the outcome. And the result is I managed to see almost everybody and I did so without feeling tense or pressured.

Thus, patience and persistence form a nice counterbalance. They allow you to successfully balance any efforts to push ahead through persistence with an attitude of acceptance that springs from patience. In fact, the process is like having a good blend of Type A and Type B personality traits. The Type A personality is the go-getter: the person who is aggressive, action oriented, and sometimes very tense. By contrast, the Type B person has a more easygoing style and is not easily stressed. The ideal is to have both types of qualities in balance, just as you should seek to have a balanced measure of persistence and patience.

THE BENEFITS OF PATIENCE

Besides making you more relaxed and less stressed about any endeavor, having patience provides a number of benefits because of the other abilities that patience gives you.

First, being patient allows you to pull back and look at a situation more objectively, to decide how best to handle it. This is because patience helps to defuse any emotion that may be clouding your vision. Instead, you can review your current situation or make decisions about your purpose in a more detached way. In other words, with patience, you become aware of what is happening in your life now; you sense how it is flowing, think about your direction, and accept current developments as they are. This is a very balanced and harmonious approach to life.

Second, being patient lets you take time to get the information you need to make decisions. For example, ask yourself, What is the most profitable or productive thing for me to do for myself right now? Then you can wait for your inner knowing to respond and for events to indicate an appropriate course. In turn, when you wait, your patience gives you the ability to accept what comes, without growing anxious.

Third, being patient makes you able to accept that you need time to grow and learn. Patience means acknowledging that not everything is going to resolve itself as soon as you might like, particularly if you are in a period of transition, such as when you are changing jobs, locations, or relationships. So you need to be willing to live with uncertainty as the situation evolves, and when you have this willingness, this period can be a chance to learn and grow.

Fourth, being patient can help you better accept yourself and be satisfied with your identity and your progress. For having patience includes accepting whatever comes when you do your best. As a result, when you look on what you are doing with this attitude of patient acceptance, you can feel satisfied with what you are doing, as long as you feel your goal is appropriate and as long as you persist and continue giving your all. For you know that you are doing all you can ask of yourself, and therefore you can feel pleased with your efforts and accepting of the outcome.

For example, when good athletes enter a sports event, they seek to do their very best. Winning is important, of course, but if they do not win, they are not devastated. Rather, they accept this defeat, learn from it, perhaps work harder, and the next time, when they once more give their best to the competition, the time may be right for them to win.

Thus, should you encounter any disappointments or barriers, patience can help you through the difficulties because it lets you accept the way things happen, recognize that maybe you need to do a bit more to achieve your goal and go on without the regret that would trap you in the past.

In turn, this attitude goes well with persistence, for your patience encourages you by telling you that all will work out in good time. So while your persistence will help you push forward, your patience will help you to be receptive and accept what happens and the conditions you encounter. Then this approach will in turn help give you the positive optimistic outlook to keep going. Thus, in spite of any adversity this combination of patience with persistence can inspire you to keep on going, for you feel confident that you will ultimately succeed.

Perhaps one way to envision the balance between patience and persistence is through the image of a full glass of water. In order to have more water come in, you have to release the water that is there. Doing so is like persistence—it is the active process of pouring out. But then your patience is like the glass sitting there being refilled. And then, once the glass is full, the water is ready to be released again through your persistence.

Likewise, in doing a magical ritual, persistence is like your focus and concentration in sending the energy out and exercising your will. To perform an effective ritual, you generally need to repeat the images, symbols, magical words, and other gestures that are designed to express your purpose—and in that repetition, there is persistence. But then, after you exert that focus of will and energy, your patience comes into play, waiting for the energy to respond and the desired act to occur. Also, your patience comes in realizing that you may have to do this act of willing at least a couple of times for it to be effective. And finally, your patience comes in realizing that you must not only wait for, but be accepting of the response.

THE RELATIONSHIP OF PATIENCE TO
THE OTHER PRINCIPLES

Having patience is thus the last of the ten major principles of the path and it is related to all of the others, just as they are all related to each other, in the following way. The key is to have *patience* and *persistence* in working on your *purpose*. For this purpose, you should choose the right action and be *aware* of what you want to do and how to do it. You should also have the necessary *self-control* and *courage* to see this purpose through. Also, you should work with others in a spirit of *service, compassion,* and *honor,* for in so doing, when you finally achieve your goal, you will do so in a balanced and harmonious way.

•

PART TWO

Power
Words
and
Objects

9
•

Gaining Power
with Power Words

Power words, as the phrase implies, are used to give you a sense of power. You just say or think the word and you feel its power, and others may sense your power or the power of the word as well.

While you can use a power word to give yourself a momentary charge of energy on the spur of the moment—like when you feel threatened by someone on the street or are about to start a challenging project—a major purpose for these words is using them in a magical ritual, which is designed to achieve a goal.

Power words help you get into a ritual state by emphasizing the gravity of the occasion. They also help you converse with your inner self or with any spiritual beings or entities that you evoke in the course of the ritual, as will be discussed. You can then use this communication to gain helpful information and draw on the power that comes from this alternate time and space.

CHOOSING YOUR POWER WORDS

When you work with power words, you can use any magical or power language. There are certain established languages that have a long tradition, and often it is simpler to use the words that are already there, with the meanings and symbols attached to them. For example, a group called the New Reformed Order of the Golden Dawn, which started in the late 1800s, has developed a whole series of magical rituals and magical words, which can easily be drawn on. Likewise, you can use the Enochian Keys, a symbolic system for getting in touch with this magical reality, developed by the well-known ceremonial magician, Aleister Crowley.

However, it is also possible to develop your own magical language, as long as it has meaning for you. Or you could work with the language developed by someone in a magical group to which you belong, as long as you feel comfortable with that language and that group.

Essentially, whether you create your own language or use one developed by someone else, the source of the language is much the same. Typically, it comes from someone who has been working with magic or altered states of reality for a while. When in an altered state, he or she gets in touch with his or her inner self, personal ally, or spiritual being, and has the sense that this entity is speaking magical words to him or her. Then he or she writes down these words and uses them in ritual him or herself, or shares them with his or her students.

Usually, these words come from the organizers or founders of a magical group or tradition, who have seen or heard these words in a trance state, and often feel these words have been specially given to them. However, sometimes other group members might get their own language communications while in trance, and share these with fellow members. Or you might find your own words in a trance state.

But, whatever the source, the process of gaining power from these words is the same. Gradually, you start working with these words in ritual or meditation, and they build up a certain power and meaning as a result of their associations and continued use.

THE DIFFERENCE BETWEEN USING POWER WORDS AND SPEAKING IN TONGUES

The use of power words is quite different from speaking in tongues, though both involve languages derived from an altered consciousness state. The key difference when people speak in tongues is that they are not using a specific codified language. Rather, they spontaneously begin speaking a stream of words, which may even sound like a form of gibberish, with no particular meaningful content. It is as if they are relaying whatever comes into their minds, which they may not be able to translate meaningfully. The content is more emotional than verbal, as if they are drawing on their feelings welling up from the subconscious while spouting these words, which some people may believe are coming to them from God.

By contrast, magical or power words, phrases, or statements have a certain meaning, and one tries to control the use of the words. Also, individual magical words may have specific references. A particular word may, for example, refer to a certain kind of energy or light, or it may be designed to evoke a certain entity at a certain time; the word is not used only to give a certain feeling.

Thus, there is an emphasis on using magical words which have a specific meaning, to gain power or exercise control, which is quite different from the more emotional, spontaneous and expressive quality of speaking in tongues.

DEVELOPING AND USING YOUR OWN POWER LANGUAGE

You can obtain your own repertoire of power words through trance, through friends or associates who start using those words, or by drawing on established magical or spiritual traditions. Any of these sources is fine, and it is important to be flexible so you can select those words that feel most comfortable for you, whether already established or newly coined and transformed into words with magical meaning by you. For different people have different systems, reflecting different backgrounds in magic and spiritual traditions and different personal styles.

Sometimes these power words may come from a foreign language. For example, the ODF group, described in my book *Shaman Warrior*, sometimes used the Fermese language, developed by its founder, Michael, in its rituals. Certain words had special meanings, and this very foreignness helped to contribute to the feeling that people were entering this altered ritual space. For instance, a member would say something like "Aloway, aminay," to ask a spirit or energy form in nature to come forward, as the group members stood in their ritual circle.

However, you do not have to use foreign words. You can use English words, if you prefer, as long as the words have a power reference or magical meaning for you. Or you can use made-up words, or even sounds. For example, while some of the members of ODF preferred to work in Fermese, many others preferred the familiarity of English words. I find the use of English more meaningful myself, since I write in English all the time.

So the particular words you choose do not matter. The key is choosing the words that feel comfortable or resonate for you, and as you keep using them in magical or ritual contexts, they will develop a certain power of their own. This occurs because by using them you invest them with power, much as you might energize and charge an object to become a power object, which will be discussed in Chapters 10 and 11. Later, when you use these words you have charged with power in a ritual context, you draw on your previous work and associations with these words to increase your power.

The use of certain words may also have physiological effect. This theory has been espoused by students of Eastern traditions, who suggest that words like *om* and *on* cause different vibrations when they are chanted, so they have different physiological effects. Thus, chanting "om" will make you feel differently from chanting "on," because of the different resonances of those sounds.

In short, there may be a scientific basis for the different experiences you have using different words. However, you do not need this scientific understanding to experience the effect. So just use the words that feel comfortable for you, whether they are made-up words from another source, or originated by you, and whether they are English words, foreign words, or words from any previously developed magical language. You can invest any language with your power, whether or not it already has power or meaning from other sources. Once you do, you can use the magical power of that language to help you focus your power and attain your goals, in rituals and in everyday life.

THE USES OF POWER WORDS AND
MAGICAL LANGUAGE

There are a number of reasons to use power words or a magical language to help you in rituals and everyday life. These include the following:

First, a special language can help you *express certain principles or ideas telegraphically,* and this focus can give these ideas more immediacy and power. For example, instead of saying a whole sentence, like, OK, now I'm going to draw a magical circle, you use a single word or phrase. Saying this power word or phrase as you draw the circle helps reinforce that you are drawing the circle and that it has certain magical meanings. Since the word or phrase is also much shorter than a formal statement of the idea, its use makes the experience more intense, because it is less likely to distract you from your altered or ritual state of consciousness.

Second, using special words or language can make it easier for you to *communicate with your inner self or any allies or spirits* you want to contact, because you may view these entities as unable to communicate in ordinary language. You may feel this since both you and these entities are in an altered or higher state of consciousness, and therefore you need this higher form of language in order to communicate. You may also feel that this language provides you with a more intense or clearer channel, so you can communicate more intimately and directly.

Third, you may find that your inner self or the beings you contact in this other dimension talk to you in another language or in a code which you need to interpret later, so if you become familiar with this language, you can *interpret the meanings of any unfamiliar words or sounds.* Some people involved in channeling do this, for example. They report that their voices are talking to them in another language, which they translate later. If you feel you are getting messages in a tongue you do not understand, you can preserve them for later translation if you write down the words; or tape the message, if you say it aloud. Then review what you have written or listen to the tape, looking for any patterns which have meaning for you. For example, a recurring phrase or series of sounds might prove meaningful if you focus on these, asking yourself what these mean, and then notice what thoughts or images are triggered. Later, you can interpret these ideas that come to you. It may be that these patterns are speaking to you in some way, as if through a series of levels of meaning, if only you pay attention and investigate, moving up from the very deepest levels of consciousness where these symbols or signals may originate to the more accessible thoughts and images which have clearer meanings for you.

Fourth, special words can make it easier to *get into another state*, because they help set the tone or mood, just as putting on a robe may help you feel more involved in a ritual. The costume may not be necessary for the ritual itself, but putting it on is like telling yourself, I'm stepping into this magical world now. The process operates much like a costume party, where the costumes help everyone feel in the spirit of things. Likewise, power words add to this magical feeling. One group that uses such techniques is a group called the Society for Creative Anachronism, whose members can step into another world and who are devoted to recreating the world of the Middle Ages. Members attend meetings in medieval costumes and sometimes speak traditional Middle English. Together the dress and the speech help members to experience an altered state in which they share in a past worldview. Similarly, there are certain symbols, modes of dress, and other characteristics associated with entry into the magical world. The use of power words and language is just one more factor contributing to that altered state.

Fifth, special words can *add to the impact of the ritual* by making it feel more out of the ordinary, and therefore more significant, much in the same way that wearing a costume or setting up a ritual environment do. Special words help to separate the ritual from the mundane, for they are different from the everyday words used for ordinary purposes.

Sixth, if everyone in a group uses the same power words and symbols, these words can *strengthen the feeling of being part of a powerful group*. Moreover, group members can use this magical language to communicate with each other quickly and privately. For example, when Michael and other members of the ODF were out in the field and saw members of another group, they would speak Fermese for privacy. So Fermese became a code system to keep their magical secrets. Of course, if you are working on your own, this use is not relevant. But in a group, you may at times want to use a special language for this purpose.

Seventh, power words or a magical language can sometimes

acquire a special forcefulness or power, so that they can be used when you need extra power. For example, they might be effective in a banishing ritual, if you feel negative energy or spirits lingering, whereas ordinary words might not dispel these negative forces. In turn, the power words will acquire a much greater intensity because of the magical charge associated with them, so you will find them more effective when you use them next.

For example, Michael had a friend who once felt he was surrounded by unfriendly spirits and negative energy. So Michael used some Fermese words of banishment to get rid of those beings and forces and afterward he felt the spirits suddenly stop bothering the man. Michael believed that the spirits or energy responded so quickly because he used powerful words. If he had used ordinary language, the spirit might have thought he was trying to persuade it gently, and so might have been less inclined to leave.

In turn, power words can gain much of their extra power through use in previous rituals, by yourself or others who have shared in the use of a word with a magical historical tradition. Their use operates to charge them with power, much like using a car charges up the battery. In other words, with use, these words gain power; they gain more of a charge of energy, so they have more power to give when you use them in a ritual.

Furthermore, in some cases, people use special alphabets or words as a way to *send information secretly* or to *invest another object with their magical power.* This occurs when you carve a magical name on an object. You can write on the same object in ordinary English, but you may find the magical words or names in English or other languages more powerful, because of their more esoteric, secret, and private quality. The everyday English words may just seem very ordinary and mundane, but the magical words or letters make the object feel more special and powerful. In addition, if these words have been invested with power through ritual use, you may feel these very words transfer some of their power to the object too, making it more magical and special.

Finally, magical or power words can serve as a memory trigger, to help you recall and then step into an alternate reality or ritual state you have experienced before. This trigger can develop, because as you use the words, they acquire certain associations with the emotional state you are experiencing. As a result, when you use them again, you trigger that emotional state and return to that place again. As one man observed:

The words can help to anchor you physically. So when you use them, you may remember something that happened to you when you used those words before. For example, a word can trigger you to be happy or sad. Then, when you hear or use that word again, it helps you to get back to the same place. . . . So if you're used to using a particular word when you're in a certain state, if you want to get there again, you can use the word. . . .

Magical words can also help transport you into an altered state because they clear away distractions and focus you on the ritual or state you are seeking.

GAINING ACCESS TO MAGICAL OR POWER WORDS

Depending on your methods, it can be easy or difficult to acquire power words. If you are developing your own or taking them from your reading, you can easily come up with words. On the other hand, if you are part of a magical group, you may experience some delay in learning these words, because the group may want you to achieve a certain level of magical or personal mastery before granting access to the words it considers power words. For example, Michael did not introduce ODF members to the Fermese language until he felt they had advanced to a certain magical level.

Thus, you may find limitations on your access to power words when you work within a group that has a hierarchical system of teachings. But otherwise feel free to choose the words you want.

Exercise 7: **FINDING AND USING YOUR OWN POWER WORDS**
The following exercise is designed to help you discover and choose your personal power words:

Start off by just getting relaxed and concentrating on your breathing. Let it go in and out. In and out. Feel yourself settling down and getting centered. And as you get relaxed, know that you'll pay attention and stay alert.

Now imagine that you are in a quiet place. You're preparing to do some kind of ritual meditation. Just stand in that place or sit down. You feel very, very centered while you are there.

If you want, you can make a circle of protection around yourself. And call on the assistance of anyone you want. You can call on a spiritual guide or spiritual beings, call on guardians, whomever you want, as a source of protection and assistance.

Now, as you are standing or sitting there, start off by just listening. Soon you may hear the vibration of a sound like *om* or *on* or *an* coming through to you. So just listen to that sound and feel it vibrating through you. Let yourself just resonate to that sound.

Now you feel ready to receive your power words and you stand up or straighten up to listen. Perhaps you may hear some English words, but then, as you're standing or sitting there, you may hear some other words coming to you. These are powerful words, magical words, words that you can use to help create the space that you're in, to add to the ritual, to help you get what you want.

So just listen and let the words come to you. They may be in English, they may be foreign words; maybe they're just sounds or syllables. And as they come, you get an image or sound or feeling with each of these words.

Now, select a couple of these words to focus on, maybe one at a time, and, as you focus, pay attention to the image, the sound, the associations, the symbol, whatever is connected with that word or sound.

As you focus on that image, sound, or emotion, you can hear that word or sound reverberating. And as it does, it is charged with power, and you know you can call on that word in the future and draw on that power. And later on, you can call on that word again and again, and you can continue to charge it with that particular symbol or emotion or image.

Now you may hear another word or sound, and you can do the same thing with that. For you may notice that this word or sound also has different sounds or images or emotions attached to it. So just notice the associations that come to you when you hear that word or sound.

Now, just listen to that word or sound reverberate through you and feel that emotion, see that image, notice the symbols or thoughts associated with that word or sound, and know that later you can always call on that word or that sound again, and it will bring forth associations that you had just now.

Now do this one more time. Take one more word or sound; as you're standing or sitting there meditating, notice the emotions, the images, or the symbols and thoughts that come to mind as you hear that word or sound.

You might even imagine yourself in a capsule, totally surrounded by that sound or that word repeating over and over again. As it does, you feel suffused with power, as you experience those associations you have with it, as you feel the feelings, and observe those images, those thoughts, and those symbols. So now just experience the intensity of that power, as that word or sound reverberates through you.

You might even see that capsule of power expand, and as it does, the sound might grow louder, the word might grow stronger. For you feel yourself and everything around you charged with power—power from outside you, your own power. So just feel that power associated with that sound or word.

Finally, finish charging that word or sound and imagine that bubble or circle, if you've had one around you, disintegrating, disappearing. So you're standing there doing a ritual or sitting there meditating, wherever you are.

Now imagine something you'd like to have, some object or goal. It could be near, within the next few days, or it could be something that's a little further off, but it's something you want.

Now, see yourself asking for it and doing a ritual to make it happen. And as you do this, you are calling on those words, those three words or sounds that you've experienced. And you're using them in a ritual or a meditation. You're calling on that power and those images, on those feelings and those thoughts and symbols, and you're directing them toward the goal that you want.

Experience doing that now. See the power of those words, feel the energy of those words helping you get exactly what you want. It might help if you repeat those words or sounds again and again, or just listen to them as they loudly resound around you. Perhaps you can use them to call on any assistants or spiritual guides. Or you can use them to draw on your own power and increase it. Just concentrate for a minute on that.

And as you concentrate, you can see that energy, the power in those words or sounds infusing your goal, making it more likely to occur. You can see that goal being achieved. You can see those words making it a reality. You can experience that power charging your goals, making you feel charged. So now you are feeling very definite, very certain, and the energy of those words or sounds is feeding into that feeling of certainty and purpose, so you feel that certainty and purpose even more strongly.

Now gradually come back. Start to release that image. Start to release the sounds and words. See yourself standing or sitting back in that circle where you are meditating. And then start counting backward from five to one. As you do, start coming back into the room again. Five, starting to wake up now. Four, more and more awake. Three, two, more and more awake. One, and you are back in the room. And when you are ready, just open your eyes.

During this exercise, you may think of familiar words or sounds. You may also hear made-up words you create yourself. Or you may find yourself drawing on traditional power words or names. In one workshop, for example, a man called on Shiva, the Hindu goddess and used the ancient Egyptian word *hu,* which is associated with beginnings and creativity. It does not matter where your words and symbols come from, as long as they feel comfortable or resonate for you.

10

•

Using Power Objects to Gain Influence and Power: The Staff, Sword, and Magical Knife

Just about any object can become a power object if you invest it with power. However, there are certain objects which are especially designed to focus and extend power—the staff, sword, and magical knife, sometimes referred to as an *athame*. These long objects play a primarily active role in rituals. This chapter will focus on the use of these objects; chapter 11 on other types of power objects.

Essentially, these objects work because the power flows out of you and is projected into these objects. This energy is focused and directed through the object and then flows out from it in a more concentrated form so you can work with this focused energy to have a direct influence on other things or people. Also, this energy focus can help to make you more aware, alert, and attentive, so that you are more perceptive about what you need to know or do in achieving your goals.

THE ROOTS OF POWER OBJECTS

The use of power objects goes back to the beginning of time, when our distant ancestors first used sticks and other weapons against animals and at times, against each other. They not only fought with these objects but, anthropologists believe, they charged them with power, so these objects would be more effective in killing the animal or dispatching an enemy.

In time, many myths and legends developed about the power of some of these objects. The Arthurian legend, for example, describes a sword, Excalibur, that is lodged in a rock. According to the legend, anyone who could pull the sword out of the rock would become invincible against enemies. So this was a sword with both practical and magical properties. It was used like an ordinary sword in battle, but it magically gave its user—King Arthur—a supreme power over others.

Other tales are told about magic staffs, wands, and knives. But in all of these myths, the theme is the same: these objects have both practical and magical applications. And essentially, this is the way magic or power objects are used today—they are both practical and magical at the same time.

Moreover, they operate on both levels as an extension of yourself; when you work with a power object, you become one with this object. It becomes an extension of your own powers and abilities, both practical and spiritual. For essentially, the power object acts as a channel for your own power, to focus and magnify it, on both the practical and spiritual level.

THE TYPES OF POWER IN OBJECTS

The power in an object can be either receptive or active. Certain objects are generally used in a more receptive mode, like talismans, five-pointed stars known as pentagrams or pentacles, which are the small flat objects, such as plates, on which pentagrams are drawn. Alternatively, to pick up information or offer protection, other objects are used in a more active way, such as staffs, wands, and knives, to direct and control power. But any power object can be used in either way, just as anything can become a power object if you invest it with power, even a lowly pebble. However, in this chapter, I will be focusing on the use of the longer objects, such as swords, staffs, and knives, which are usually active, though they can be receptive too.

An active power object might be used to control the spiritual, magical, or natural energies around you. The active object can also help you cut through into other realities or dimensions of experience. You can achieve these ends without a power object, but the power object can extend or amplify the power within you—and it can give you more confidence in your own abilities, which will help you express more power too.

Similarly, you can gain power from an object if someone else has charged it with his or her own power. Then you can draw on that power to supplement your own. However, it is important to recognize that a power object has no real power of its own. Rather, it gets its power through the person who charges it or uses it to direct his or her own power through it.

Generally, you invest the object anew with your power each time. Thus, when you are not using it, your object is essentially at rest in a neutral state. But you can also charge your object to store up power so that it acts like a battery, and if someone else has charged an object to act like a battery, you can draw on that power as well.

THE IMPORTANCE OF FOCUSING YOUR ENERGY

A key to success in working with power objects is focusing your energy and any energy you feel is already in the object. Focusing makes the difference between an undirected, undisciplined, ineffective object and a directed, disciplined object which becomes a powerful extension of your energy.

Although the average person will not be able to distinguish them, an experienced user of power objects can tell an undisciplined object from a disciplined one. If you hold up an undisciplined object, you might envision the energy around it as a fuzzy cloud of diffused, unfocused, and scattered energy. By contrast, a disciplined object has a more directed, focused charge of energy, so that it is like a single high-powered light beam of energy streaming through it. Such focused and channeled energy is necessary to achieve a magical effect.

Once you concentrate the energy in this way, it starts flowing through the object, and experienced practitioners can actually see it projecting out, normally up to about six inches. However, as you work with the object and concentrate especially hard on projecting your energy through it, the beam might extend to six feet, or even farther, so you can sense changes in the energy field and pick up information as far as about a mile away, such as whether someone is coming along the road or over a hill.

Perhaps you can imagine this energy beam as a laser with a beam of very concentrated light energy surging through the object and cutting through the space ahead. In turn, you can use this intense energy much like radar, to sense what is ahead of you. Many times I saw Michael do this when I went out in the field with him. He would move his staff around and then point it to sense the kind of energy ahead. Then he would tell whether he picked up concentrations of energy or felt people coming down the path.

Also, you can use this projection of energy as an extension of your own will. Say you are doing a ritual to focus on achieving a goal; you can visualize the energy going through your power object, directed at helping you achieve your objective. For instance, if you want a certain job, you might imagine your desire or will to make that job yours, traveling like a beam of light through your staff and energizing you in the interview, so you are clear and convincing and get the job. Similarly, if you were directing your will in a field outdoors, perhaps to shift a concentration of energy in nature from one place to another, you would concentrate on projecting this beam of your own energy and then directing it to shift the energy in front of you. You might want to work with pure energy forms in the field to practice focusing and directing your energy, so you can later apply the technique to a real-life situation, such as getting a job.

You can also use this focused energy in everyday, nonritual situations to pick up information, protect yourself, or take some action, and you will be more powerful because of the concentrated energy. For example, you might walk down a street with a staff that looks like an ordinary walking stick. But if you have charged it with your energy, it may indeed have this concentrated power, so you can use it to sense what is ahead of you, which could be very useful in dangerous parts of town, because this will help you sense the presence of outside negative energy patterns. Then, as with power objects in general, your staff might have a very practical use, perhaps as a shield or weapon if you are attacked, and you will be able to use it this way with even more effectiveness and power, because you have already focused your energy in it.

A DEMONSTRATION OF WORKING WITH
POWER OBJECTS

The following demonstration, based on one I have used in one of my workshops, will give you a sense of how a power object can focus energy.

To get started, lower the lights if you can to create a setting more conducive to sensing energy. Next, one person should extend a staff or other long power object, and simply hold it quietly and steadily with an unfocused state of mind for about a minute. Then, still holding the object in the same way, this person should concentrate on focusing his or her energy so that he or she projects it through the object like an energy beam, while the others observe closely to see if they notice anything different about the object or the way he or she is holding it, compared to the way it looked when the person was not trying to focus any energy through it.

If you are doing the demonstration, avoid suggesting to the others what they may see. Just say something like, "Now I'm going to focus on concentrating my energy. See if you notice any change in the way I am holding the object."

Then start moving the staff or other object and ask, "As I move this around, do you notice anything?" Wait for responses. If no one volunteers an observation, you can comment that in these demonstrations, people sometimes notice a beam of energy moving and shifting. Then ask if anyone might have noticed that.

Then you can explain a bit further about possible observations in these demonstrations. However, try to get people to say as much as possible before you describe what others may see, to avoid shaping the observers' responses. It is sometimes difficult to avoid doing this, because first-time observers may not know how to look for subtle shifts of energy. So they may need some help in directing their attention, but this guidance may not only help them look closely; it may also shape what they see. Thus, suggest as little as possible, though some suggestion may be necessary.

In the demonstration, people often see an aura of energy emerge around the staff, and when the person starts moving the staff around and focuses energy through it, they may see a light beam of energy projecting a few inches from the tip. You can explain this, if people have not already noticed it.

Then, for a demonstration of the effects of this energy, ask people to hold out their hands as you move the staff in front of them and concentrate on projecting your energy through it. As you move it by, you can ask, "Do you notice any difference when I hold it in front of your hands?"

Again, wait for people to respond without prompting first. Afterward, you can reveal what people commonly experience, namely, that their hands may feel warmer when the staff is pointed at their hands from a few inches away. Presumably, they feel the warmth because of the energy being projected from the person directing it through the tip of the staff.

AN EXPERIMENT IN SENSING THE POWER

After you have done the basic demonstration, you can have people hold out their hands and close their eyes while you move the staff around, and ask them to sense whether or not the staff is in front of them. The person holding the staff should focus on sending his energy through it. Before starting this experiment, make sure that when people have their eyes open, they can actually feel the difference between having the staff in front of them and not having it there. (Typically, their hands will feel warmer when the staff is in front of them.)

In general, people do seem able to tell the difference. However, the experiment seems to work best when you move the staff slowly, because it may take some time for the energy to build up and for the person to respond when the energy is first directed at him or her, and for the energy to disperse or for the person to stop feeling the projection of energy when the staff is moved away.

This occurred a number of times when I used this demonstration at workshops. When one person moved the staff quickly, with a definite break, rather than slowly and gently, there seemed to be no connection, or even an inverse correlation, between people's feelings and the presence of the staff. The experience of projecting and sensing energy is a very subtle one, in which energy builds up or dissipates only gradually. As a person grows sensitive to this energy, he or she may feel a strength, warmth, pressure, or perhaps a tingling, suggesting this energy is present in a more concentrated, directed form. But then, when the source of energy is removed, this more intense sensation seems to gradually fade.

Thus, you must move the staff slowly, so the person sensing the energy has time to adjust. Otherwise, there may not seem to be much connection between the position of the staff and the subject's response.

Exercise 8: **EXPERIENCING THE ENERGY OF A POWER OBJECT**
The following exercise is designed to help you experience the feeling of projecting energy through a power object. Then, when you are actually working with power objects, you can use this visualization to help you draw on and project your own power.

Once again, start by focusing on your breathing going in and out. In and out. You are feeling very centered, very grounded, very relaxed. At the same time, you're going to stay very alert and awake.

Now imagine that you are standing or seated in some kind of ritual or meditative space, and you are holding a power object. It might be a staff; it might be a wand. You feel it in your hands; you feel its strength. Imagine your own power and energy flowing into it.

Now, hold this object out in front of you. Notice the power and energy streaming through it. You might notice that there is an aura around it. At first it is kind of fuzzy. But now, as you focus your energy on this object and send it through this object, you notice this energy starting to come together and become more intense. It's closing in around the object.

And now you experience all this energy rising up from inside you. It's swirling around, invigorating you, empowering you. And perhaps you see yourself drawing on this energy from different sources. Perhaps some of the energy is coming up from the earth and swirling up through you. And maybe some of the energy is coming in from the air and swirling down through you.

Now you might imagine these streams of energy meeting in the center of your body. And you see them forming this white ball of energy, and now you see this energy coming down your arm and out through your hand that is holding this object. And you can see the energy pouring out from you into this object that you are holding. It's coming out from the object like a white beam of light, like a laser beam.

Now, as you hold this object, move it around. Notice how the energy moves. You might notice that the beam is extending farther and farther as you put more and more energy into your object.

And now just move the object and the energy around, so you can get a sense of what's out there. It's almost as if you are getting an energy picture of the world around you.

You might feel certain pressures here and there. It's as if you're picking up certain denser areas of energy and feeling the resistance. Then, as you move the object around, you might feel other areas where the energy can go through easily, and in some areas, you may feel even more lightness, almost as if there's a channel which the energy can go through.

Keep moving your object around. And now you might notice the environment you are in. You could be out in the country. You might be in the city. In a house. Outdoors. Wherever you want to be.

So now just move your staff or other power object around. And just try to feel the energy that's there. It's almost like drawing a picture of energy as you move it. So move your object in front of you, up and down, all around, trying to pick up this energy picture around you.

As you do, you might notice concentrations of energy. You will feel the pressure is stronger or firmer here as your energy beam comes against these areas. Elsewhere you might notice areas where the energy is looser. Here your energy beam goes right through. You might notice mixed areas, where you feel a variety of pressures. So just move your object around and pick up the patterns of energy that are around you.

You also might notice, as you move your power object, that you are picking up objects, so that if you close your eyes as you move your object, you are getting an energy portrait of the physical objects in the room or area where you are. Perhaps there might be a certain heaviness if there is a desk or tree. Or there might be a bit more lightness in the energy if you are just sensing a pillow or a bush. So just scan around, getting a radar or energy picture of the world around you.

And now see if you can change any of that energy. You can project your own energy out through this beam that you are sending out. So now see if you can shift around any of the energy ahead of you. Perhaps move it over to your left or to the right. Or if an object is there, see if you can push it over to one side with your energy. So experiment for a while with moving the objects and energies that are in front of you.

As you do, notice how your beam of energy pushes certain energy forms very easily, while others may be harder to move. But just keep concentrating, and the stronger the energy you exert, the more you can move the energy that is in front of you.

And as you do this, know that you can use this energy in ritual work to achieve the objectives you want, to have power and control in guiding the energies in the fields around you when you do a ritual.

Perhaps as you experience this feeling of control and power, you might get a sense of something you want, some goal you have. As you do, continue to feel this power and control as you work with the energy and move it around, and this gives you a sense of power you can use to attain your goal. For just as you have the power to move that energy with your power object, so you can move the energy that's needed to achieve your goal.

So now, as you experience that power, that feeling of control as you move the energy around, see yourself achieving that goal you want, and you feel very powerful as you do.

And now, as you do this, you might get a sense of the energy surrounding you in the form of a big bubble of powerful energy. And you can draw on this energy at any time, direct it through you, and it will provide you with even more power to go through your power object, so you have even more power to control and direct the energy streaming through this, and you can likewise direct all of this energy into your goals. So now, for a while, just continue to visualize and experience all that power and see yourself achieving your goal.

Then, when you are ready, start to let go of that power. Let go of the goals. Draw back the energy that you have been projecting out of your power object and start pulling it back into you. Gradually, all of that energy is pulled back in.

As this happens, you can lower your power object. Put it down in front of you or just hold it by your side. Then you can start moving out of this ritual, this magical space that you have been in.

Now, start counting backward, from five to one, and as you do, continue to let the energy go, wake up, and come back into the room. Five, letting it go, becoming more and more awake. Four, even more awake. Three, two, almost back in the room. One. Now you are back and can open your eyes.

EMPOWERING YOUR POWER OBJECT AND KEEPING IT CHARGED

Since your power object essentially gets its power from those who use it, these visualization and power projection techniques are designed to help you charge it with power. And not only do you need to charge it, but also to keep it charged, to keep it working properly, because your power object is much like a car. You need to keep your battery charged and gas in the car if it is to run, and you also have to tune it up from time to time. So in much the same way, you have to keep your power objects charged up and work with them from time to time to keep them functioning well.

Charging Your Object Initially When you first get an object, a good way to charge it is by seeing the energy streaming through it, and if you are doing any exercises to practice seeing in an unfocused way to look into altered realities (see Chapter 1), you can combine charging your objects with the exercises. Your object will be even more powerful if you can do this initial charging for a week or so.

More specifically, you can charge your object in this way. Start by extending the object while you look at something else in this unfocused, seeing way. As you do so, imagine the energy coming out from you, pouring into your arm and into the object. You might use the visualization described in exercise 8 in which the energy comes up through the earth and down from the air, and spirals around to form a white ball of glowing energy inside you. Then you can see this energy entering and permeating your object.

After you have charged your object, you can direct it to achieve a specific intention. For example, you can project your will to have an immediate influence on the energy around you or you can project your energy into a goal you want to achieve.

You can also make your object more aggressive or more receptive than you are. If you feel that you need more power than you have personally, you can direct more energetic, aggressive, and active power into your object, so that when you feel like being more assertive, you can use your object to help you. On the other hand, if you feel that you need to be more receptive, you can charge your object accordingly.

In addition, you can make your object adaptable, so it can change its function depending upon your purpose. Thus at times it can be more aggressive than you are normally, and at other times it can be more receptive.

Deciding Whether to Let Others Use Your Object People working with power objects frequently ask whether they can let others touch their objects or how the energy of others affects their objects. People have different responses to the question.

Some people want to keep their objects private and may even keep them in a special place so that they have this magical quality of being different, separate, and apart. However, this is not necessary for keeping your objects charged and powerful, and many people do not mind if other people touch their objects.

The choice is up to you, and when you charge your object, you can build into your charge the idea that other people can touch or work with your object, or that they cannot. Also, you can build in protections to keep the object charged with your own energy, no matter who uses it. For example, you can charge your object with enough of your own energy to override other people's energy. You can also protect yourself against somebody's negative energy with an advance charge, so that it is protected against a person with such energy touching it. This way, your object will recycle this negative energy into positive energy. Alternatively, if you pick up your object after other people have touched it, you can simply do a quick mental cleansing ritual in which you shake off the other people's energy. So, because of all these options, it does not really matter whether somebody else touches your object, for you can either charge it in advance to reject or convert others' energy, or you can just cleanse it afterward.

You can do this because your power object is really like a working tool that you are using to achieve certain goals. It is not like an object of worship which has to be kept sacred and apart in order to maintain that special character, unless you feel more comfortable regarding your object in this way.

Recharging Your Object If you have not used your power object for a while, it is helpful to recharge it from time to time, because your power object is like a battery where you can store power. When you work with your power object regularly, it continues to build up energy. But if you let it go for a while, it will run down, much like a battery. So you will need to do a bit more to charge it up again. However, you can recharge it at any time.

You can recharge your object by visualizing your energy pouring into it successively over time, so the charge builds up or is renewed each time you charge it or use it, and as a result, your object becomes more powerful. You can do this charging process at special times, or you might do it any time when you have the object with you for any purpose. For example, if you are just walking along the street, you can do a quick visualization and charge your object.

Another way to charge it, which works best when you first get an object, is to dream with the object. Lay it beside you when you go to sleep and use your seeing and conscious projection abilities to help you program a dream. Take some time before you go to sleep to get in a quiet, meditative state. Then, holding your object, focus your attention on having a dream about it, just as you might focus your attention on dreaming about an event, person, or question. At the same time, use your seeing to visualize yourself pumping energy into your object, as well as to focus on what you would like to dream about. For example, you might want to dream about using your object in a ritual to attain some goal. Or you might just visualize your object being empowered and charged in the course of your dreaming.

If you do use this dream-charging technique, notice any changes in your dreams. See if you have any more dreams than usual, or notice any qualitative differences. These changes may occur because you are focusing on your object before you go to sleep in a dreamlike hypnogogic state, so that you are in a sense dreaming your object into your dreams, and the object may show up in various forms. Thus, if you have been focusing on dreaming about your staff, you might look for objects that are stafflike in your dreams. Or sometimes your dream may transform your object, so that it may not appear in its usual physical form, but may be present in associations with it, such as experiencing a feeling of power or accomplishing a task you have been working on with your object.

This dream process can be an extremely powerful way to charge your object, because the dream power comes from a deep unconscious level. However, it is best not to use this technique for longer than two weeks, because the object will generally reach the peak of its charge in that time, and you may become drained if you keep trying to charge it beyond that time. Also, if you keep charging your object after it is fully charged, it may become overcharged and begin to discharge excess energy until it loses its power.

Developing a Name and Persona for Your Object After charging your object, you can also give it a name so it becomes like a living spirit, or you can personify it by assigning it certain personality qualities. By pumping in your energy like this, you will give your object a life force or spirit of its own. In fact, some people may help to create personas for their object by getting an object like a staff, with heads of animals on it. Or they may carve certain images on their object, to give it a personality.

You may also notice that after charging, your object may sometimes take on a life of its own, although you did not intend this. For instance, your object may pick up information that supplements or contradicts your own perceptions or knowledge. Suppose you meet someone new and you get a sense of his or her qualities. If you focus on that person with your object, it may tell you something different, and sometimes your object may be more accurate, because you have invested it with so much energy and power. Likewise, if you are out in the field experimenting, say trying to locate a crystal hidden in a series of inverted cups, your object may know better than you where the crystal is.

Thus, after working with your object for a while, you may feel that it has developed its own sense of awareness or perception. It seems to have become an alter ego for you, now that you have charged it with all this energy, so it can start picking up information on its own, and as it gets better at this, you can trust its perceptions more.

Using Your Object Regularly One way to recharge your object continually and to have it available whenever you want it, is to carry it and use it regularly. For instance, if you are using an ordinary-looking object, like a walking stick for a staff, you can keep it with you and no one will know why you are using it. Likewise, you can charge an executive toy with energy and use it to pick up information in the course of your daily routine, and no one will know what you are doing. So you can readily use a power object to pick up information without being obvious.

In turn, the more you exercise your power object, the more life you give it, and the more you practice with it, the better you will get in using it, and the more powerful it will become.

WAYS OF USING YOUR POWER OBJECT

You can use an active power object, like a staff or sword, for a variety of purposes. Most often, as already noted, you can use it to exercise more control and extend your will. Also, you can use it to receive information and ideas more intensely. While you might distinguish these two functions as active and receptive, in practice you will often use them simultaneously or consecutively. For instance, you may use an object to pick up information, and then based on that information, you will use it to seek to control or extend your will.

Picking up Information Your object might best be seen as a receiver that draws in information. Thus, pay attention to movements, vibrations, or even words or phrases that come to you while you are holding it. If you feel that you are receiving something and you want to perceive it carefully, let this energy or information come to you by drawing it into your object and then carefully notice what you perceive through your different senses. This approach can be particularly useful if you are meditating or asking for answers in a ritual. Thus you are using your object to draw the answers to you.

Using Your Object in a Ritual Another key use of power objects is in rituals, and when you use longer objects, like staffs or swords, they are primarily used in an active rather than perceptive mode. In this context they may have a variety of symbolic associations. For example, swords and wands may be associated with the air, because they move through it, or with fire, because they are active sources of power. Whatever your associations with these objects, they can symbolically interact with other objects in the ritual, such as the pentacle or flat plate, with a pentragram, which is usually associated with earth, the chalice, usually associated with water, or the incense burner (censer), usually associated with fire. These symbolic associations help to add texture to the ritual and to move you into an altered consciousness.

When you are in this state, these active tools are commonly used either to invoke spiritual entities or to banish them. You can call on entities to help or protect you, or get rid of entities you feel are disturbing you or are endangering your ritual work.

Using Power Objects to Banish and Invoke in Nonritual Settings You can also use your power objects to banish or invoke energy in everyday, nonritual situations, such as when you encounter some negative energy on a walk in the country or city. For example, while walking in the country, Michael and some friends noticed a concentration of energy ahead; it looked like a dark blur in the trees. They felt it was negative, so Michael held out his staff and directed some energy at it. As soon as he did, this black spot started to dissipate and cleared away.

You can apply this to everyday life, and even if you do not actually use your power object, you can visualize yourself using it to get rid of negative energy. Suppose you are working in an office, where you feel a lot of tension around you. You might imagine yourself sending out a beam of energy to dissipate the negative energy in the room. Or perhaps you might imagine that you are sending out a beam of white protective light to create a bubble or field of protective energy around yourself.

By using your power object or your image of your power object, you can thus change your feelings about your environment. But at the same time, your act of banishing or invoking energy has a real physical effect, since thoughts and images have real physical presences or energy forces. As a result, banishing something with energy is like hitting a physical being with a physical object. Essentially, you are focusing an energy charge with your thinking, seeing, feeling, or willing, which acts like a laser or bullet to break up any concentrations of negative energy in the form of everyday hostile feelings between people or appearances of negative spiritual beings in a ritual. In any case, those who are perceptive of energy can see it in various forms.

In fact, this process seems similar to a Catholic exorcism, in which negative energy is characterized as a demon. The priest trained in exorcism will in essence direct positive, healing energy at this being to force it to leave. Certain traditional ritual acts and words are also used, which send out a banishing energy force. Much the same thing happens, though perhaps less dramatically, when somebody does a banishing ritual or sends out positive energy to break up negative energy—on a path, in a room, on a street, or within a person or group of people.

Feeling the Reality of Energy from Power Objects This power used for banishing or evoking is effective not only because of its influence on other energies, but also because other people can actually feel your energy. They may not really understand it, but they can feel a pressure or an odd sense of discomfort, and so they may pull back or be drawn to you, depending on how you have been concentrating on directing the energy away from you or toward you.

For example, once Michael used such energy to cause a police officer to back off when he and some of his friends were driving rather fast and a police officer stopped them. They had magical equipment in the backseat, which they had charged with power, and when the officer began to search the car, he suddenly stiffened and recoiled when he saw this equipment. According to Michael, it was as if he were burned by the power of these objects. The officer suddenly looked very confused, quickly shut the door, and said, "You can go." He did not even write a ticket because he was so disoriented.

Thus, you can use others' sensitivity to the energy of your power objects to protect yourself by influencing others to withdraw from you. Say, if you extend your power object, a hostile person may not understand why, but he or she will get a feeling that leads him or her to draw back. If one of your regular power objects is not available, you can actually charge any available object with this power and produce almost the same effect, although one of your regular, already-charged objects might be more powerful. But any object can work if necessary.

For instance, Michael was walking in an isolated area when he suddenly noticed some people following him. He felt uncomfortable about them, although he did not know why, so he picked up a pebble from the road, charged it with energy to repel them, and replaced it. When they came near the pebble, they suddenly veered off the path into the woods, and then after walking about ten feet, they came back out of the woods. This diversion slowed them down and put much more space between them and Michael, so he felt safe. He felt he had defused a potentially bad situation with the pebble. Likewise, you can protect yourself with your power object or by turning any handy object into a power object to push people you feel uncomfortable about away—to discourage them from approaching because people feel the energy repelling them or attracting them, if you choose to direct it in this way.

Creating the Space to Work with Power In an uncomfortable or uncertain situation, it helps if you can create a sense of space around yourself; and again, your power object can give you this sense of separation. For example, in a tense office environment, you can use your power object or an image of it to create a protective circle around your own work area. Then you can separate yourself psychically from the negative people or circumstances you perceive there.

In other situations, it may be good to create an actual physical space between yourself and individuals, situations, or energy forms, as Michael did by charging the pebble. Likewise, you may want to do this if you feel people on the street may pose a danger and want to keep your distance. Also, in a ritual or when working with energy forms in a field, it can also be important to keep a sense of space around you so you feel removed from your immediate surroundings and the everyday world. Moreover, if you notice various energy forms and are not certain whether they are positive, keeping a sense of space will give you a chance to react. Then, if you feel unwanted energy approaching, you can project your own energy to repel or disperse it, just as you might in an uncertain street encounter. In the street or in fieldwork, about thirty feet of space is a safe distance.

Using Your Object to Extend Your Power All of these procedures that have been discussed work with or without an object, for your object essentially acts as a booster in your work with energy, by focusing your concentration. Also, the energy from an object you have charged can supplement your own energy in a ritual as if you are tapping the power of a generator. Or perhaps imagine that you have charged the object like a battery in a flashlight so that when you call on your object, you are turning on the flashlight, sending out this powerful beam of light energy, which affects both the natural and the spiritual world.

In turn, the extent of your object's power depends on how you have charged it with your own energy, and how you are using it. If you are just holding a staff and putting some energy into it, but not really working with it, only a small amount of energy will project from it. An example might be a simple demonstration of the object's power when the demonstrator is not trying to achieve a particular goal. In this case, the energy will generally look like a transparent beam about six inches long, if you have the ability to perceive it.

By contrast, in a ritual, banishing, or invocation, the beam may extend much farther. When I went out in the field with Michael and his group, sometimes people would report a long beam of energy, several feet long coming from Michael's staff.

In fact, sometimes when you are really working hard to send out your energy or be receptive, this beam can extend to a mile, according to Michael. This might occur if you are trying to sense whether someone is present on the other side of a hill or if you are trying to influence somebody from a distance, as when a man at one of our gatherings did a ritual to influence a difficult roommate to move. He visualized a long beam of energy projecting from his staff and going across town to pressure his roommate into leaving, and a few days later, his roommate did. Perhaps his roommate might have been planning to leave anyway, but the man felt the ritual had provided an extra push.

Other Everyday Ways of Working with Power and Power Objects Besides some of the examples already given, there are many other ways power objects and projections of power can influence everyday life. In fact, you can work with your power object to develop the ability to project energy and power generally. Then you can use these projections without the actual object, to help you experience and use more power.

An excellent example is using a projection of power to feel in charge as you walk through a room occupied by strangers, as at a cocktail party, at a job interview or when you go into any room where you feel uncertain about events. To feel more in control of your environment, you might imagine that you are sending out beams of energy from yourself to the four corners of the room. As these beams project outward, imagine them cleansing the room and attaching to the corners like four steel beams, giving you total stability and control as you walk along. Thus, with this image, you can see yourself taking charge of everything around you, and you can experience yourself penetrating any negative or resistant energy.

Another everyday use of power objects is to put a charge on your food to improve its taste. To do so, visualize yourself holding a power object, or actually hold one, and imagine powerful, vital energy pouring into the food, so it becomes ever more flavorful. At one of my workshops, a man reported doing this with crystals, most often before he and his wife had company, to give their guests a special treat. Others reported that when they charged the food, people at a gathering tended to be more active, energetic, and enthusiastic. One man suggested that this action helped put people in a more peaceful, harmonious state of mind. One woman thought charging the food might help set the stage for romance. As she commented, "If you want a romantic evening, you might charge the meal and the table before your date comes, and that might help to make it a more exciting and stimulating evening."

Another common use for power objects or imagery is to protect your house, car, or other possessions. To do so, when you leave your house, imagine surrounding it with protective energy, or beam this energy out through your power object into the house. Similarly, you might visualize a bubble of protective energy encasing your car when you park, or even as you are driving it, so you feel more protected too.

You can also project energy to charge yourself up for virtually any activity for which you need to be especially alert, such as preparing for an exam or starting a new project.

In short, there are many ways in which you can use power objects and power imagery in everyday life. You can project energy with your power object, such as a staff, in a ritual or in a street encounter, if you happen to have the object with you. But in other cases, you can simply visualize the projection. Also, by practicing with your power object, you can develop the ability to visualize and project energy and images of power generally and then apply this ability in a virtually unlimited variety of situations, whenever you need an extra charge of energy and power.

Cutting Gateways into Other Realities You can also use your power object to enter into other realities by going more deeply into an altered state of consciousness to pick up information and insights not ordinarily available to you. You can do this through trance or by cutting a gateway into another reality, so you imagine yourself stepping into this other world.

You can do this physically during a ritual, by using your power object to cut a gap in the energy field around you, then stepping through the gap and feeling yourself on the other side, or if you prefer, simply look through the gap. I will be discussing this further in Chapter 17, which covers rituals.

You can also visualize yourself cutting this gateway and then see yourself looking or stepping through, so that you see into another reality. When you are there, you may see spiritual beings, energy forms, or perhaps an alien landscape representing your images of your experience on this other side.

Exercise 9: **CREATING A GATEWAY INTO ANOTHER REALITY**

The following exercise is designed to give you this experience of creating a gateway into another reality. If you wish, you can hold a power object during this visualization to intensify the feeling of cutting through a gateway. Or you can simply visualize holding the object.

Start again by getting relaxed. Concentrate on your breathing, going in and out. In and out. And as you relax, you're going to pay attention and stay alert. At the same time, you're going to be able to go deeply inward and concentrate on other realms.

Now, as you're holding your power object, imagine that you're in some kind of ritual space and you're standing up, holding your power object.

Imagine that as you are holding your object, you are drawing a circle around you, a protective circle. It's a way of stepping out of the mundane, everyday world into a magical, spiritual reality. And this circle will help you look into other realms, other levels of existence.

Now, holding your object, continue drawing this circle, and as you draw it, you see a white protective circle of light surrounding you. And you feel very comfortable, very warm, very safe there. So just experience being very comfortable in this warm, protective bubble of white protective light.

Now, still holding your power object, sense the power flowing from you into it. You can feel the energy coming up into you from the earth and flowing around inside you. You can feel the energy coming down from the air and flowing around you too. And you can see these two streams of energy coming together in your center to form a white glowing ball of energy within you, and it's pouring its energy out into your power object.

Next, start moving forward in your circle, and you can see in front of you a kind of wall, or maybe it's like a screen in front of you, and it's right on the boundary of this white protective ball of energy around you.

As you look, notice the beginnings of an opening. Or you can draw this opening, if you want, with your power object. To do this, just move your knife or wand or sword or whatever power object you are using.

Now, as you continue to move your object up and down, you start enlarging this opening, and you feel perfectly comfortable and safe doing so, because all of this white protective energy forms a close bubble of protection around you. At the same time, you feel all this power coming into you and out of you, so you feel very protected, safe, and powerful.

Yet you're curious. You want to explore. So you continue to open up this hole, this opening in the wall or screen of energy in front of you. And as this opening gets larger, there's space enough for you to look through or move through it.

But the first step is just looking through it, so you feel safe and protected. So now just peer through this opening and see what's there on the other side.

You may see a flat white surface. Or maybe you see other colors too. You may see shapes of different sizes. There may be spheres or other geometrical forms. Or perhaps you see rocks or maybe some trees. For this place you see may look like our own world, or maybe it looks like someplace else. But however it looks, you have a feeling that this is somehow a very unique, strange, and different place.

So you're curious about it. You want to see more. And you feel you can go into it, feeling very protected and very safe, knowing you can come back at any time through the opening you have created.

When you feel ready, you can step into this gateway and walk through it, into the special place you have seen on the other side. Step across the opening now, holding your staff or your sword or other power object. Just walk into that space, and as you do, you feel very protected because the white light around you comes with you, and you continue to feel the power that comes with you. It's as if you have a chain of power behind you, and you are continuing to pull your power from it, from the earth and from the air. So as you walk along, you feel continually charged with power from this chain of power behind you.

Now move ahead with your power object, sensing your way. As you move on, you can feel the energy fields around you, and you can see and feel the shapes of energy that appear around you. Perhaps some assume the forms of animals; perhaps some take on a human shape; and perhaps some move and shift, like ever-changing shapes of energy.

Whatever you see, just look around, pay attention, and be aware. Notice the landscape. Are there trees? Plants? Anything growing? Look up in the sky. What color is it? Is there a sun? Any clouds? Any strange objects in the sky?

Now look on the ground again. Are there any animals around? Do they look familiar or unique? How about the objects you see? Are they perhaps strange or different? Larger or smaller than usual?

Now see if there are any people. Or perhaps you may observe humanlike spiritual forms. Maybe you see some light or energy forms, like pure intelligence. Or perhaps there are other kinds of beings you have never seen before.

Just keep looking around and see what you see. You don't have to interact or talk to anybody as you look. For no one can see you, because you are invisible, protected by the white light around you.

Now you may see a path. If so, you can follow it. Notice where you are now. Is there any water around? Any fire? Look up in the sky. Are there any birds there now? What sort of colors do you see? Notice if you smell anything. You might listen to any sounds you hear and notice if they are different or the same as the sounds you are familiar with.

Now, perhaps you might be getting a message. If so, you are either hearing it or picking it up with your power object. The message may be something you would like to know now, and you feel it offers you some great wisdom or insight. It's as if you suddenly understand something you have wanted to know. And whatever it is, you will remember it and you can bring it back with you.

Then, when you feel ready, you can turn around and start going back, bringing the message, if you have one, with you. You are heading back toward the opening. Soon you are there. And once you are, step back into your circle.

Now, turn around and close the opening, knowing that when you want to, you can always open it again. You can explore more on this other side, and you can go there for messages whenever you want. But now you're leaving that other world behind, so close the gateway.

Now, see yourself back within your protective white circle again, feeling the energy around you and feeling warm, protected, and very comfortable.

Then, when you feel ready, you can gradually let go of this image and gradually see the circle disappear. As it does, lower your staff or other power object and let go of all the energy you have drawn in. Just release it back into the earth, back into the air, and feel very centered back in your body again.

And now count backward from five to one, and as you do, you become more and more awake, more and more alert. Five, four, becoming more and more awake. Three, coming back into the room. Two, one. And when you are ready, you can open your eyes.

11

•

Other Objects
Used to Achieve
Influence and Power

The more aggressive power objects, like the staff, sword, and magical knife, described in the previous chapter, are only one small category of power objects. Virtually any object can become a power object if you charge it with power. This chapter looks at the range of other objects and how to use and charge them for your purpose.

CREATING AND USING TALISMANS

One of the most common types of power objects is the talisman, which can be created from virtually anything. It is essentially an object which you charge with power for a specific purpose. Most typically it is used for good luck, like a "lucky" charm, or to ward off a harmful force, spirit, event, or even a person.

You can use a found object for this purpose, or you can make one, generally out of wood or clay. The object might be just an abstract shape or form you like, an animal image you respond to, or you can create an image of a specific person or thing. A good example is the voodoo doll, which has a long history of destructive associations. But such an object can be used for good as well as ill, to heal as well as harm, depending on your intention and how you charge it. However, it is generally best for you to use these objects only for positive purposes, because using an object for bad ends (for example, sticking pins into a voodoo doll) sets up a negative charge which can come back and harm you. So it is best not to put out negative energy when you work with talismans or other magical objects.

While specially made objects may have a certain appeal because you can create or obtain one which looks like something magical, you can turn just about any object into a talisman if you charge it. For example, if you charge a common penny and then give it to someone, he or she might feel energy coming from it, or it might bring him or her luck, depending on how you charge it.

THE EFFECT OF POWER OBJECTS

A charged talisman or other power object may have an effect on someone for several reasons. One factor is the power of suggestion. The person knows he has a charged object, and this knowledge can affect the person's thoughts or feelings. For instance, when someone finds his or her image (such as a voodoo doll or photograph) stuck with pins, he or she thinks that someone is trying to cause bad luck or illness, and this belief alone might cause him or her to act and feel differently, thus bringing that misfortune on him or herself. The appearance of the object may thus trigger the conditions which lead to the effects intended by the practitioner.

However, the charged object may also get its power from real energy, according to many who work with magic and psychic phenomena. Practitioners generally believe that your thoughts assume a real physical form. Thus, when you project your energy and intentions into an object, a real charge of energy occurs, perhaps like an electromagnetic force field. Essentially, what happens is that when you clearly visualize your goal, you build up energy, and when you combine what you see or think with your will, you physically project the desired charge into the object. So your own force combined with intention charges the object. Thus, you are not just imagining or thinking about charging the object; the power and intensity of your vision and your thoughts take on a physical form, like electromagnetic energy.

To be sure, scientists do not yet understand this process, but people working with these energies report that anyone can actually see this energy. Of course, an experienced practitioner will be better able to see it, but a person who is shown how to look can quickly learn to see something, and even an untrained person may sometimes see something. For example, when you charge an object or go outdoors and send energy to some form in nature, many people can observe an aura forming around the object, which may grow larger as more of a charge is projected at it. Similarly, some people who are very sensitive to these energies can transmit their energy to heal by touch or projecting healing energy over a distance. Also, they may be able to read auras accurately or sense the presence of disease in a person's body, because they can see or feel energies indicating this that the average person might not.

Kirlian photography likewise supports the claim that visualization and energy projection have real physical effects. Thelma Moss of UCLA and other researchers have photographed the field of energy or aura surrounding people, and their photographs suggest that this energy field expands when it is used for projection. For instance, they have shown that the aura seems to expand around healers' fingers when they do a healing, and then little flashes of energy, like leaping flames, may project out toward the person they are trying to heal.

This evidence suggests that sending out energy has a physical effect; the process of projecting energy to charge an object is not limited to the mind. So when you charge a talisman or other power object, you are projecting real energy into it. Everybody may not have the ability to observe it, but many people can, and most can learn. Also, Kirlian photography provides additional validation of the reality of this energy.

FEELING A CONNECTION OF RESONANCE WITH A POWER OBJECT

Many power objects are typically neutral until they are charged, although you may feel a more intense connection or resonance with a certain object. If so, you will generally find this object easier to charge and more powerful for you. This feeling of connection serves as a channel, or bridge, so that you are better able to pour your energy into the object.

In some cases, a quality of the object itself gives it this special feeling of power. For instance, some people feel that crystals have a certain life energy or force within them so that they act like special receptors and certain people may respond more to their particular wavelength of energy.

On the other hand, you may respond more powerfully to some objects because your experiences, values, and personality trigger this connection or resonance. For example, when I began setting up a workshop at a San Francisco gallery devoted to shamanic art, I was immediately attracted to a red rattle etched with the black silhouette of a female shaman. I have long been attracted to those two colors, and the image itself looked like the cover design of my *Shaman Warrior* book. When I gave the workshop about six weeks later, the rattle was still there, and I felt a strong urge to have it. It had a special feeling of power for me, perhaps reinforced by the fact that it was still there, as if it were waiting for me. So whether or not there was special power inherent in the object, I felt it had a special power for me. Similarly, I felt a certain affinity for the staff I used in studying with the teacher described in *Shaman Warrior*.

It is hard to say whether the object itself or your own associations produce that feeling of connection. But whatever the source of this feeling of linkage, it is quite common when people select power objects. And this same feeling of connection frequently occurs when people choose objects of any kind.

For instance, people may feel a certain affinity for a piece of jewelry. In an art gallery, they may experience a certain resonance with one painting. Or they may respond with a strong emotional charge to a particular house. Or someone may decide on a particular project because he or she feels right about doing it at this time.

So for whatever reason, we have a certain emotional connection to particular things, including power objects. The object itself may be neutral, but you respond to it because it has special associations for you. In turn, feeling this special affinity will help to make this object even more powerful for you.

CREATING AND WORKING WITH
A SINGLE-USE POWER OBJECT

While many power objects will be ones that you choose to keep, use, and charge on a regular basis, you can also create a single-use power object, which you just charge for the moment. A good example is the pebble or coin you charge on the spur of the moment for a particular purpose, such as described in Chapter 10, when Michael charged a pebble to repel people who were following him.

Similarly, any object you happen to find can be charged for a particular purpose you have at the time. Then, once that purpose is done, since you have charged the object only for a brief use, that power diffuses, and thereafter the object becomes ordinary again.

Empowering Common Objects You can also charge these common objects to keep their power over a period of time, generally as long as you continue to see or work with that object. One man in a workshop described how, as a child, he had empowered a toy lion. He put a small amulet on a chain around its neck, and suddenly he felt the lion become a protector of his bedroom. And yet he was not sure he could trust that power. He explained:

> The charge stayed in the lion for months. I didn't think the power was harmful, and yet I had an uneasy sense, like I didn't know what would happen . . . and I was wondering if anything would. . . . But then, as I grew up, I thought less and less about that lion, and eventually it became just another ordinary stuffed animal like all the rest.

This process of charging everyday objects is much like the way children empower dolls and action figures with a certain vitality and personality. The dolls seem to take on a special independent power of thought and feeling. When I was three or four, I had a Suzy doll that was more than half my own height—perhaps 24 or 26 inches. I thought of her as a real person; it was as if I had charged her with my energy to make her an alter ego. In fact, she seemed so real that as I began growing taller than she, I became concerned because she did not grow.

A lot of children relate to some toys in this animate way. They give their toys names and personalities, then they talk to them, take care of them, or see them as real protectors or playmates. In doing so they charge these inanimate objects in a sense to make them come alive; to give them power.

Similarly, you can invest your energy in any object, to give it power and make it real to you. Then, just like children, you can communicate with this object and direct it to help you attain your ends. And later, when you are finished with this object and put it aside, it will eventually lose its charge.

TECHNIQUES FOR CHARGING OBJECTS

There are a variety of techniques for charging objects, whether for a single purpose or for regular use. Also, you can build in any intent you choose, regardless of the technique you use.

One approach is simply to breathe on the object. As you do, direct your energy toward the object with each breath.

Another method is to use chants or incantations. The words can be English words, traditional words of power from some religious or magical tradition, or any words that feel powerful to you. You can use these chants or incantations as part of a larger ritual, in which charging the object is just one of your goals. Or you can just focus on charging this object with your words. In either case, place the object in front of you and chant over it, or hum or sing to it. As you chant, hum, or sing, focus on sending your power into the object, and project your intent.

Still another approach is to visualize your energy pouring into the object, perhaps by imagining a very clear and direct beam of energy coming from you, carrying your intention to the object. You can use a staff or other long object as a focus to concentrate this energy. Or you can send it directly from different parts of your body, because even if you use an object to assist you, you are sending the energy directly out of yourself.

Charging the Object from Different Parts of Your Body While you can direct energy from any part of your body, your object may be more powerful or sensitive if you use the part of your body associated with your intention for the object.

For example, if you wish the object to pick up information or insights based on observation or perception, focus on sending energy directly from your eyes as you look straight ahead. If you want the object to make you more sensitive to emotions, feelings, or sensations gained through touch, send your energy through your heart or hands. Finally, if you have more aggressive purposes (to gain power or control), you can send the energy charge out of your stomach, solar plexus, or abdomen, which is the center of your will, according to the chakra energy system, derived from the Hindu system of kundalini.

PROJECTING YOUR INTENTION
WHEN YOU DIRECT YOUR CHARGE

Whatever system of energy projection you use—visualization, willing, touch—seek to project your intention into the object along the energy beam you set up. This projection of intention is critical, because your intention determines whether the object will become a receiver of information, a sensor of feelings, or a projection of your will.

Thus, start by clarifying your intention for the object, so you can use the appropriate projection. However, you do not need to limit this projection to a single intention, for you can send a combination of intentions, if you want the object to have a variety of uses.

Some Common Purposes for Charging Objects While you may want to charge an object for a specific purpose (like helping you feel more powerful in an interview or giving you more insight and a better memory for a test), you can also empower an object for a broader purpose. Some of the most common uses are to attract or invoke, or to repel or banish. When you charge an object to attract or invoke, you are essentially projecting into it a positive charge which draws people, objects, or energy forces toward it. By contrast, in repelling or banishing, you are directing a negative charge into it, which pushes away people, objects, or energy.

The key difference between attracting and invoking is that in the former you are drawing people or things from the everyday world to you. By contrast, invoking means calling up spirits or energy forms to appear or assist you. The difference between repelling and banishing is that repelling refers to influencing people and everyday objects to move away from you or get out of your way, while banishing influences spirits or energy forms to go away.

For example, you might invoke the assistance of spiritual beings or call on natural energy forms by visualizing these forms or forces coming toward you or your power object. Then you can draw on the strength or insights of these forces or beings. Conversely, you can charge your object to banish undesirable energy forces. The charged object will act like a generator to send out the banishing energy you have put into it.

Choosing Having One Purpose or Many You can decide on the number of different purposes with which to charge an object. Some people find it especially convenient to charge an object for many different purposes—so they may charge it both to attract and repel, or to invoke and banish. Other people like an object with a single purpose, because they feel it is particularly powerful, since it is focused on one activity.

So it is really a matter of personal preference. You can use one object for a variety of purposes or have separate objects for particular uses. Or perhaps do a little of both over time and find out what works best for you.

Keeping an Object Charged or Discharging the Energy After Use Another consideration in working with power objects is whether to leave the object charged after use or let the energy go. Again, this is a matter of choice. If you plan to keep the object and use it exclusively for magical or ritual purposes, it may make sense to keep it charged and perhaps store it in a special place. Conversely, if it is an everyday or natural object and you intend to leave it behind when you are finished, it makes sense to release the energy, so it will not linger to affect passersby. In fact, some magical practitioners who work outdoors or in public places feel it is common courtesy to release energy from such objects. As one workshop participant put it, "It's not nice to leave your old energy hanging around. You should clear it out, just like you clear out your dishes in a self-service restaurant."

Whatever you decide, you can include this among the intentions you project when you charge the object. For example, if you have decided to release the energy after you are done, concentrate on sending out the image of the energy dissipating and this will help you break the connection with the object after you are finished. When you are done you can then reinforce that message by seeing the energy disappear, although regardless of whether you do this, the energy will dissipate on its own. Eventually, any energy you put into an object will disperse, just as a neglected battery will wear down. However, if you focus on the energy discharging when you initially charge the object, or if you imagine this discharge when you are done working, the discharge will happen more quickly, and these objects will be less likely to harbor lingering bits of energy.

Alternatively, if you want your object to hold onto its energy charge, project this intention before using the object, and immediately after you use it, to reinforce this intention. Then that charge will remain for some time, although, because of the general process of energy dispersal, it too will gradually dissipate, unless you continue to work with that object or recharge it.

HOW A CHARGED OBJECT FEELS

When you charge an object yourself or are near a charged object, you may have certain feelings as you sense the energy. Many people have a real surge of feeling when they charge an object. They may experience this as a kind of tingling or vibrating sensation, or perhaps a feeling of vibrancy suggesting that more energy is now there. Frequently, people also report feeling warm around a charged object, as in the workshop demonstration described in Chapter 10, when people sensed the presence of the charged staff. This radiation of real heat might be expected, since the projection of energy creates a real physical impact on the energy in the area, as described earlier in this chapter. Thus, not only may you be able to see the effects of this energy charge, as noted in the above discussion of auras and Kirlian photography, but you may also be able to feel this energy charge.

PICKING UP FEELINGS FROM OBJECTS

As you become more sensitive to these energy charges in objects, you will become more likely to pick up feelings and images from the objects and surroundings you encounter in everyday life. In fact, you may pick up feelings and images from objects that were charged long ago and still preserve some of that charge. Although much of the energy may have dissipated over time, if the charge is strong enough, some traces may linger, and with increased sensitivity, you may be able to sense that.

For example, one man in a workshop, who had been exploring magical and spiritual practices for about ten years, reported feeling very sensitive in a wax museum where medieval objects of torture were displayed. As he walked by the glass cases, he felt a sense of doom and gloom, as if he were projected back into the Middle Ages, and he sensed the agony and tension experienced by those who had been tortured. After several minutes, he felt weak and shaky and rushed out, not wanting to be around these objects.

Conversely, if you enter a room filled with spiritual objects, like the temple of worship of an Eastern guru, you may feel a strong sense of awe and spirituality. Some people also report feeling a sense of positive warmth and loving energy in the objects and the environment, as if the place has been continually charged by the guru and the love of his worshippers.

Such environments with many charged objects can feel especially powerful because there is a synergistic effect, so that you feel suffused by the energy that is all around you. But with fewer objects or only one object to pick up energy from, you need to be more sensitive, though you can develop this ability with practice and training, just as you can learn to see and feel the charge around your own working objects.

Children may be especially sensitive to these feelings, even without any training, while adults generally need to train for this sensitivity. According to many people involved in psychic work, this is so because we are born with greater sensitivity to these positive and negative energy forms than we later have as adults. As children, we are more open to our feelings. But adults may lose this sensitivity, unless they work on keeping it, because in growing up we typically learn to turn off these feelings, because our parents tell us these feelings are strange. And so we become trained to shut them out.

I remember my own experience of feeling this great sensitivity when I read the children's book *Babar the Elephant* at the age of three. When I saw a picture of Babar getting sick and turning green, I felt sick also. In fact, I actually had my parents paste the pages together, because every time I saw that picture, it made me feel quite ill. But when I happened to see that picture again as an adult, I no longer felt that negative charge. Indeed, I felt nothing at all. It was just another picture.

Certainly, learning to turn off this intense sensitivity may help us adjust and keep us sane in the face of the tremendous negativity and tension in modern urban life. Otherwise, with the raw feelings of childhood, we might feel continually oppressed by this negative energy. However, it is possible to develop this sensitivity to objects and the environment and yet be able to shut off these feelings at will. Thus, you can have the best of both worlds: you can recapture that feeling, sensing nature of the child, but you can combine it with the control, balance, and air of objectivity and detachment needed by the adult.

Exercise 10:

CHARGING YOUR POWER OBJECT WITH YOUR INTENTION

You may find it helpful to use a visualization in charging your object. The following visualization is designed as a guide. You can hold your object while you do it or you can just visualize yourself charging a particular object without also holding it.

As usual, start by getting relaxed, and for a moment, just concentrate on your breathing. Notice it going in and out. In and out. And as you relax, you'll be alert and pay attention.

Now either use the object which you are holding or imagine you are holding an object and extend your arm so that you have the object in front of you.

Now, visualize the energy from the earth coming up through your feet and the energy from the air coming down. The two energies meet inside of you, and they swirl around, the energy from the earth coming up, and the energy from the air swirling around and coming down.

And these two energies meet inside of you to form a big white bubble of glowing, living energy. You can feel it within you, warm and glowing.

Now imagine this bubble of energy pouring out from you, and depending on how you want to charge your object, this energy can pour out from any place you want it to.

If you want this object to pick up information or have insight, visualize this energy rising up inside you and coming out through the center of your forehead. As it does, it pours into your object with this intention that this object is going to be very perceptive and receptive and it's going to increase your sight and insight. For as you exert your energy with that intention, your object is gaining this kind of power. So if you want your object to do this, just concentrate on this image of the energy pouring out of your forehead into your object, giving it the power of sight and vision.

And as this occurs, you can notice your object becoming charged with power. Maybe it vibrates. Maybe you notice the aura around it expanding. You're feeling it becoming very, very powerful.

Now, if you want to, charge your object with your will; if you want it to be an object that you can use for your control, create that intention. For if you want this object can be used to attract people, repel them, invoke, or banish; you can use it to assert control with active, assertive energy. So if you want to charge an object with any of these intentions, see the energy within you pouring out from your abdomen or stomach. It's coming out like a beam, a strong white beam, and charging your object.

As the energy pours out, be aware of your object. It may feel very strong and powerful now in your hands. Perhaps feel it vibrate. For as you concentrate on your object, you can experience that strength. Your object feels strong and firm. Now you can direct that strong and powerful energy. You can control it. And you can direct that powerful, controlling energy into other things that you want to direct and control. So just experience that directing, controlling energy pouring out from your abdomen and into your object.

And now, if you want your object to be a sensing, feeling object, visualize the same energy coming out from either your hands or your heart. So your sense of feeling pours into this object, so you can use it to pick up "feeling" energy. You might use it for healing or for picking up information about how somebody feels. You might also use this object to pick up healing energy yourself, so you feel better using this object.

Now, focus on sending that healing energy charge into your object. And as you do, you can see this beam of energy pouring out of your hands or out of your heart, and as it does, you feel very good and very warm. And your object too feels very sensitive, surrounded by this energy field that can pick up other feeling energy. Just concentrate on feeling and experiencing that energy for a while.

And now, if you want, pick one of those modes of energy, or maybe a combination of them, and as you hold your object, direct that power to a particular goal or objective you want to achieve. You might be using feeling energy, maybe seeing, receptive, perceptive energy, or you might be sending out controlling, directing energy. Just focus on using your object which is imbued with all this power, all this charge of energy to attain that particular objective.

As you do this, as you are using your object to this end, you find your object very, very effective. You've charged it with all of your energy for this purpose, and you feel this goal becoming more real, more vital for you, because you have charged it in this way.

So continue to hold that image. Feel the powerful charge of your object, and feel how all your energy going through it is sending out your intention, helping you realize your goal.

Then, when you feel a sense of completion for having achieved or given power to that goal or objective, you can start letting out your energy from your object. And if you want, the charge will stay there. Of if you want, you can withdraw the charge, and the object will become neutral again.

Now, whether you choose to retain the charge or withdraw it, pull back this beam of light energy you have sent out as perceiving, healing, or directive energy. Just pull it back into your body. And know that your object will be charged or not charged, as you choose.

So continue to feel that energy coming back, and as it does, it again forms a white ball. Then you feel this energy from the ball disperse again, and you feel yourself coming back into a neutral state, knowing that whenever you want, you can create and draw on this energy ball and use it again to charge your object.

You can charge this object again, or you can charge another object. And you can choose any purpose that you want for any object. And if you want, you can have any object with any number of purposes, for you can charge a single object with all three purposes. Or if you prefer, the object can be charged with one purpose, one type of energy.

So now just come back to a neutral state, and feel all the energy disperse and go. And if you're extending your object, you can drop your hands and let your object rest by your side.

Now, start counting backward from five to one, and as you do, feel more and more awake. Five, four, becoming more and more awake. Three, more and more awake. Two, one. Open your eyes and come back into the room.

Sometimes during this visualization, you may have some especially powerful experiences with energy that make this a very effective method of charging an object. One man in a workshop, for example, experienced his hands becoming a part of his object, so the object truly became an extension of himself. Another man felt he had tuned into the source of all energy creation and felt a powerful resonance sweep through him as a result. If you get such images or sensations during this visualization, that indicates you have tapped into a strong well of power and are giving your object an especially strong charge. In turn, the stronger the energy and intention which you send into your object, the more you empower yourself in achieving your objective.

12

•

Power Objects
for Special Uses

Besides the more general-purpose power objects described in Chapters 10 and 11, there are objects which have special uses and powers. These include salt, rattles, drums, feathers, smoke, dowsing rods, and crystals. This chapter will touch on these objects and their uses and discuss how to choose your object.

SALT

Generally salt is used for protection. For example, if you are doing a ritual or meditating, you might scatter salt around the area to give an enclosed sense of safety. Some people draw a circle of protection by projecting their own energy or using a power object to create the circle, but others like to use salt as a strong symbol of protection by creating a clear visible boundary which keeps unwanted things out and protects those within the boundary.

Some people also scatter salt around their houses for protection.

Or they may place it around a room or surround themselves with it during a special activity.

Salt's special association with protection lies in the nature of salt itself. Because it is derived from acid, salt has a certain cleansing, astringent quality, so it can be used for several medical practices, such as cleaning a wound. Then too, salt is white, a color associated with purity; you may even see this association in advertisements. Morton salt once had an advertisement featuring a little girl holding an umbrella in the rain, accompanied by the slogan "When It Rains, It Pours." Although the most direct meaning of the ad was how the salt would still pour in the rain, the ad might also suggest to some an association of salt with the cleansing and purifying quality of rain.

Thus, given these many associations with cleansing and purification, salt is often used in a ritual or meditative setting to protect by keeping what is within its circle cleansed and pure and keeping out any impurities.

RATTLES AND DRUMS

Rattles are generally used because their sound can help one enter a trance state. The repetition of the rattling pulls one's awareness away from the everyday world into another environment. In fact, the rattle does not even have to be charged with any special powers or have any symbolic qualities, because just its sound is conducive to an altered state. However, many people do charge their rattles and imbue them with particular symbols and powers.

For example, when the American Indians make rattles, they simultaneously charge the rattles with a certain intention—perhaps a healing quality. Then, when they use this rattle to attain an altered state, the energy will make it be especially effective for this purpose: healing or being healed. In turn, when the healer or sick person knows the rattle has been designed for this purpose, this awareness helps to focus and intensify the purpose of the trance.

Similarly, the repetition of the sound of a drum can itself take you into this altered reality, but at the same time you can charge the drum with a special energy or intention to enhance a particular ritual. For example, when American Indians make their drums, they may charge them with animal spirits, with certain associations, such as medicine animals, associated with healing, or with others that bring power.

Typically, the makers create rattles or drums with certain qualities or personalities by chanting while making them. The process is much the same as the projection of energy discussed before. They focus on sending their desired intention into the objects as they rattle, drum, or chant.

However, remember that drums or rattles can be neutral objects for their sounds alone have the power to create an altered consciousness state.

PENDULUMS AND DIVINATION

The pendulum is frequently used as a divining tool. Just about any small object at the end of a chain will do, but some people like crystals, which they feel have special perceptive powers.

The pendulum is moved back and forth, to give yes, no, or maybe answers, much like the Ouija board.

You do not have to charge pendulums to get this information, but frequently people will charge them to make them more accurate or receptive.

Essentially, the pendulum is a medium for getting information from your inner self, because it magnifies your inner reactions so you can bring them into awareness. This occurs because as you move the pendulum back and forth, your subtle body movements trigger it to move in certain directions. These body movements reflect your true feelings because you have preprogrammed yourself to know a certain movement has a certain meaning, such as a forward movement means yes; a sideways movement means no, and a circular movement means maybe.

If you just ask yourself a question, you may not be able to answer consciously because you are not sensitive enough to tune in to your inner knowledge. However, a signaling device like a pendulum can magnify your inner knowing or desires. For instance, you might get a slight internal vibration when you feel the answer is yes, but you cannot pick it up consciously. The pendulum will magnify this vibration; thus your body movement will show that your response is yes.

Generally, people use physical objects for pendulums. But you can also make your own body a pendulum, or even visualize your body as that pendulum. To do this, stand up, get in a meditative state, and tell yourself that your body movement is going to tell you the answer to your question, using the same directional movements to indicate yes, no, or maybe as in a pendulum. Then ask your question and let your body move, or see your body moving in your mind. Thus you can use your body as a pendulum to get access to information that you might not have consciously.

FEATHERS AND LEAVES

Feathers and leaves can also be used for a number of purposes. Frequently, they are used in cleansing rituals for such purposes as sweeping an area clean, or cleansing one's body.

For example, Central American Indian healers will tie together different kinds of leaves and shake them over somebody, to cleanse that person. Similarly, you can shake some leaves or even have a group of leaves in front of you to cleanse an area, yourself, or another person.

You might also use feathers to cleanse. And since feathers are associated with birds and flying, they can help you move into another reality. To do so, think of your inner self or consciousness flying from the mundane world into an altered time and space. Meanwhile, you might be holding, shaking, or surrounding yourself with the feathers, to help you move into this other world. Or to prepare for this flight, perhaps first use the feathers or leaves to clean the area; then you may feel more comfortable moving into this other world. Or you might just cleanse an area you feel is full of negativity.

For instance, at a workshop, one man described using feathers to give his house a general cleansing. Also, he reported using feathers when a woman friend stayed over, carrying negative feelings from work. In his view, this negativity made his home feel uncomfortable.

Usually I enjoyed spending time with her. But . . . occasionally she would get all wrapped up in work or in something else that was negative and bring that home with her. Then I would feel it when we were together in bed, and I didn't want to have anything to do with that. So I would stay on my own side to avoid this energy, and then, when she got up to go to the bathroom, I would take a feather and sweep her side of the bed with it, so I could get rid of that negative energy. Then, after that, I could be close to her again.

However, I did it when she was out of the room for a few minutes, because I didn't want her to know what I was doing. I wasn't sure she would understand. But it didn't matter that she didn't know. After I cleared out the area with the feather, it would feel free of that negativity and clean.

SMOKE

Smoke can also purify or transport you into an altered state. Sometimes smoke is used in conjunction with leaves or feathers which help to raise and direct the smoke.

You can purify by blowing or fanning smoke at someone. The smoke particles draw any negative energy out of him or her and take it away, just as the smoke rises and dissipates in the air. For instance, many Central American healers blow tobacco smoke at their patients. This smoke serves to cleanse and purify, and it scatters disease or evil spirits. You can also envelop someone in a quick cleansing bath of smoke.

DOWSING RODS

Dowsing rods are good for picking up information about a place. Traditionally, they are associated with locating water underground, but they can sense the location of other objects. For instance, I have gone with groups to locate buried pipes and metals.

Dowsing rods traditionally have been made from forked sticks of wood. The dowser watches for a twitch or a dip in the rod, signifying that the object has been located. Today, many dowsers make the rods with other materials, such as two wire hangers, a common low-cost approach. To create a working tool from these, the dowser straightens the rods, bends up one end as a handle, and cuts the other end off so that the rods are each two to three feet long. Then the dowser moves, extending these two rods, but holding them loosely, so the rods can move. When the rods cross, the dowser has found the object.

In essence, the dowsing rod functions like a Geiger counter. It helps you focus on the desired object and magnifies the particular vibration you pick up which is associated with that object. In turn, directing your energy and intention into the rod helps to tune you into the same vibration level as the object you are trying to find, whether water, pipes, or metal. Thus, when you approach that object, the rod responds to that vibration because your own consciousness has been attuned to that same vibration level. The rod twitches, dips, or crosses to indicate this match between your own vibration level and the vibration you are directing the rod to pick up.

However, you may not need the rod to do this, because it really just magnifies the perceptions your own body is picking up, as the pendulum does. That's why some people report being able to dowse for water or other objects without a rod, because they have gotten so sensitive to these different objects and their energies. On the other hand, most people do not claim to be so sensitive, so they feel the need for a dowsing rod.

USING POWER OBJECTS
ASSOCIATED WITH NATURAL ELEMENTS IN RITUAL

There are also certain special-purpose power objects associated with particular elements, which are used to draw on these elemental energies in rituals. As a result, the experience of these energies is intensified, so they can be directed more forcefully to achieving the ritual goal. Typically, this is done by combining these objects with the ordinary working tools, which are often used to focus energy, like the staff, wand, or magical knife, to create a more powerful charge through their combined energies.

The pentacle (or disk with the pentagram) is normally associated with the earth and stability. The chalice or cup is associated with water and fluidity and thus with the reception of energy. And the censer may be associated with either air or fire, depending on one's ritual tradition and individual associations. The censer is associated with fire because it is used to burn things, and with air because the smoke from the censer rises into the air. Similarly, the sword, wand, and knife may be associated with forceful, active fire, because of their power to direct and control, or with the freedom and free-moving qualities of air, because these objects move through the air during rituals.

In a ritual, these power objects remind you of their associations, which you can incorporate into the ritual to reinforce your intentions. For instance, if you are seeking stability, you may use the pentacle. If you want to bring a more fluid quality to your life, you may emphasize the cup or other objects, such as those associated with water, like seashells or watercress.

However, since people may have different purposes and different associations with objects, you should choose the energies or symbols that work best for you. Thus, in a particular ritual, you may only want to use one kind of object to emphasize this purpose. Or you might use objects representing the different elements to have a balance of energies in your ritual.

CRYSTALS

Crystals have recently gained a special prominence and popularity among power objects. While other objects may be essentially neutral when at rest (though they have many symbolic associations), crystals have an inherent ability to receive and intensify energy. They are able to resonate or vibrate in response to the energies they pick up, which is one reason crystals are used as receivers. Scientists have found that crystals can pick up and focus energy because of their chemical makeup.

Thus, while you can use crystals much like other objects, for protection and to get information, they can also help you see and receive more, because of their special properties.

Types of Crystals You can use crystals in a number of forms. Some people affix them to the tip of a staff, to help them send out stronger, more focused energy or receive stronger signals. Many people wear them as jewelry, particularly in necklaces.

Some people wear their crystals regularly as they might wear any attractive piece of jewelry, and many crystals are produced in attractive designs for this purpose. However, some people only wear their crystals when they are doing a ritual, meditating, or looking for special information. At other times, they conceal their crystals, because they want to give them a special quality.

Different types of crystals are designed for specific purposes, although any crystal might be adapted for different purposes. As noted, some of the more decorative, attractive crystals are designed to be worn as jewelry, whereas other crystals, particularly larger ones, are designed to be working crystals, since they are supposed to have more power.

How to Use Crystals The following techniques are designed to help you use crystals for their main purposes: focusing the energy you send out and receiving information more clearly, or creating an energy field of protection.

One way that crystals can help you receive information is by making you more receptive to your dreams. The crystal is used in much the same way as the staff (see Chapter 10). Put your crystal under your pillow, and before you drift off to sleep, remind yourself that your crystal is there to pick up information and that it will be incorporated in your dreams in some form. This technique will help you become more receptive.

In particular, you might use your crystal in conjunction with the techniques for programming your dreams to ask certain questions or to have lucid dreams (see Chapter 1). Since the crystal helps you become more aware and receptive, its use makes you more likely to get the information you seek or to have lucid dreams.

Other common uses are picking up information about others or making predictions. The crystal ball has traditionally been used for this purpose. As you look into the ball your vision may seem out of focus; everything may have a diffuse look, which induces a receptive, altered state. Then, as you gaze into the ball in this altered state, this unfocused vision or diffused appearance may help trigger your associations to the information you seek. Then too, the resonance of the crystal itself may help to draw you into this altered state, and its ability to act as a receiver may heighten your awareness.

In other words, the crystal may be effective for two reasons. First, it may be an especially receptive device because of its own mechanical or chemical makeup. And second, it may make you more receptive because of the way you look at the crystal ball, so that it diffuses your field of vision. As a result, it is easy to project your inner consciousness into this field of vision, so that you are better able to see a response to your question. In effect, the crystal operates like a mental screen onto which you project your inner vision. But at the same time, you may see much more vividly in the crystal because it is an especially receptive object.

The crystal may also help you feel more intensely because of its energy-focusing properties. At a workshop, one man reported that he placed crystals around the room to make himself feel better:

> I sometimes put crystals under my pillow at night or in the corners of the room, because I like the feeling. If I want to feel calmer, the crystal helps me feel calmer. Or at other times, when I want to be more alert, it helps me feel more energized.

The man also reported that these crystals seemed to alleviate disease symptoms, like headaches. This occurs, according to many people who work with crystals, because the crystal, as a receiver, draws in negative energy, transforms it into positive energy, and sends it back. Or the crystal may have this effect because the sufferer imagines the symptoms being absorbed by the crystal and transformed into a feeling of wellness. Whatever the reason, the crystal seems to create a more positive, soothing energy field by washing away the negative energy or making it positive. This soothing quality of crystals is a reason that people in high-stress or negative, disease-ridden environments like hospitals may surround themselves with them.

In addition, you can combine crystals with other images or activities associated with eliminating negativity and stress or with purification and cleansing, to reinforce their power. One such activity is taking a shower, which many people find both physically and psychologically cleansing. Thus you might have a crystal nearby when you shower.

However, you do not need to take a shower actually to do this psychological cleansing. Instead, just visualize yourself taking the shower, or you can move—or imagine yourself moving—just place your hands over your head and shoulders, to cleanse yourself with the healing energy of your hands, as if you are giving yourself an energy shower. Wearing a crystal might also intensify this experience of cleansing.

Finally, if you are using your crystal for cleansing (or to draw in negative energy), it helps to cleanse the crystal itself, to release any accumulated negativity. In time, this energy may simply disperse, but some people prefer to clear out the negative energy immediately after using the crystal.

CHOOSING POWER OBJECTS TO SUIT YOUR PURPOSE

By having a variety of power objects to work with, you can choose the most appropriate to your individual purpose. It's like having a whole table of objects you can use. Then you can decide in advance on your objective and the most suitable object, just as a surgeon chooses certain tools for an operation, or a mechanic has his own set of tools for a repair.

You might think of your power objects in much the same way— as a bag of tools from which you can pick for specific purposes. If you want, you can carry your tools with you in a bag. You can even use a common-looking case, like an attaché case, so your container for magical tools looks perfectly ordinary to others. Or if you have a particular purpose in mind, you might choose your objects accordingly and just take those with you.

USING YOURSELF AS A POWER OBJECT

While all of these power objects may be helpful because of your associations with them and their ability to absorb, focus, or disperse energy, you do not really need an object to perform any of these actions. Instead, you can use yourself as a power object and use your power of visualization, sensing or knowing, to fulfill the functions of an object.

However, like any tools, power objects facilitate your action. Thus, while you may be able to pry a top from a jar with your hands, you can open it more easily with a screwdriver. Power objects operate in much the same way, since they extend your own ability and give you one more tool you can use.

But you can create your own object through your powers of visualization, charge it mentally, and use it much as you would a real power object. Your work may be a little easier with the real object, but after some practice with visualization, you can create virtually the same effect. Similarly, you can imagine the energy pouring out of your forehead, hands, abdomen, or other parts of your body, without using an object.

For example, in a ritual, try drawing a protective pentagram in the air with your staff or knife. Or just focus on sending out energy to create that pentagram with your power of vision. However you do this, sensitive observers may see signs of this energy projection. For instance, some observers report seeing sparkles or energy trails where someone has drawn a pentagram or projected his or her energy for some purpose. Also, if someone has done a ritual and has not dispersed the energy, people sometimes report lingering signs of these energy forms. In fact, some people experience these energy forms as so real that they cleanse the area before doing ritual or meditation.

Some people also experience a change in temperature when someone is doing these visualizations—a drop in temperature, when some people work, a rise in temperature when others work, and generally these perceptions of individual practitioners are consistent. This may occur because certain people tend to produce more warmth around them when they are working with energy, while others tend to create a cooler atmosphere.

CHOOSING TO USE POWER OBJECTS OR VISUALIZATIONS

Whether it is better to use a real power object or just a visualization depends on the situation and your own ability to visualize. You can use a visualization in place of just about any object (i.e., instead of drawing a circle around a pentagram with your staff, you just imagine yourself doing this).

The real physical object is valuable because it focuses your attention and helps to set the mood and leads you into a magical state by reminding you and any other participants that you are about to do a ritual. Yet you can put yourself in the mood by going to the ritual setting (i.e., outdoors or a special room), and visualizing these power objects around you. Doing so may be easier with the real object, but mentally creating the symbols may at times be more convenient, especially in a setting where physical objects are not appropriate, like an office. To achieve a goal in such a setting, you can use visualization to perform a miniritual in your mind on the spot.

However, working with the actual power objects helps to prepare you for visualizing later. Conversely, if you have not worked with these physical objects, visualization may be harder. This process works much like witnessing an action on stage or in a film; subsequently, you can better reproduce that action yourself, because you have a model. Thus using the physical power objects gives you a model for your visualization.

Once you are able to visualize, you can use what you prefer for the occasion—a real power object or a visualization.

RECOGNIZING THAT THERE IS NO "RIGHT" WAY

You can choose whatever feels right for you at the time because there is no single right way, although members of magical and spiritual groups sometimes claim otherwise. They do so because they grow accustomed to certain power objects and magical practices. Moreover, groups may have very strong leaders with fixed ideas, who pass on these techniques to others, who in turn use them as models. Then each group's members come to feel that their leader's way is the only way.

However, the approach of a particular group represents just one model, and if you like it, go ahead and use it. But if you have other associations, equipment, or techniques you prefer, use those.

Certainly, it may be easier to follow a model that already exists, particularly since its users may have more experience than you have in working with these energies and altered states. But you can create your own models for magical and spiritual work, and you should use what is appropriate for you and what feels comfortable, based on your own symbols and needs.

To summarize, feel free to choose the objects and methods that work best for you. There is no single right way.

Exercise 11:

USING YOUR POWER OBJECT FOR A PARTICULAR PURPOSE
The following visualization is designed to help you focus on using your power objects for a specific purpose.

Start by getting relaxed as usual, and focus on your breathing going in and out. In and out. At the same time, you're going to stay awake and alert.

If you want to hold your power object, do so, but you can also visualize an object. And you can choose any object you want. Just pick an object now.

Now, pick an objective, something you want to do. It might be an everyday goal. It might have to do with work. It might have to do with relationships. Just get something in your mind that you'd like to accomplish at some time. It could be tomorrow. It could be over the next week. It could be further in the future, six months or a year off. Just get this purpose very clear in your mind.

Then imagine yourself standing in front of a table with all kinds of power objects on it. You may notice a crystal on it. You may see a knife, a staff, a wand. There may be a chalice. You may notice a drum or a rattle. Or you may see some talismans. You may even see stones that have a meaning to you or jewelry. And maybe you see salt or a pentacle. Maybe there's a censer too.

So just look at this table with these different objects. And think of the symbolic associations that you have with these objects and their different uses. For example, if your objective is protection, you can use the salt. If you wish to be more flexible, you can use some water. If you desire more power, you can use the fire.

Also note that some objects may bring you information and be receptive, while you might use other objects to direct your will or be assertive. Other objects might help you send out or receive healing energy.

Now take from the table whatever objects you think you need. You can work with them.

Now, select one of these objects and have your goal in mind. Then see yourself charging that object with your intention. See that objective you want and see the object in front of you. It's as if your objective and your object are one. So, in charging your object, you can achieve your objective. See yourself standing there with that object, charging it, and know that you can draw on the power of that object and direct it toward your goal.

Now you can see a beam of energy pouring out from your object toward your goal, and it's the kind of object or energy that you need to achieve that goal. And if you feel you need to use a combination of objects to achieve your goal, that's fine. Just take these other objects from the table and charge them with your intention too. And you will see a beam of energy pouring out from them as well.

Now, if you want to take these charged objects with you to help you achieve your objective, go ahead and do that. For example, if your goal has to do with your office, you might take your objects there. Maybe you can take a crystal with you, if you want to draw on it for insight. Or if you are going into a house and want to protect yourself, perhaps have some salt with you, as a sign of protection. Or if you're involved in a relationship and want it to be closer, you might have an object with you that suggests a closer relationship to you.

So whatever your goal is, whatever your objects are, just focus on the activity you want to happen and see your object helping you to make it happen. And your object can help you do this because it focuses your power and magnifies your own energy so you attain your goals.

Then, when you feel that you have sufficiently energized the situation, you can draw back from it, taking your objects with you. You can take those objects back to the table you took them from.

Now, you are standing in front of the table with the objects. And if you want to leave the objects charged, you can do that. Or if you want to have them discharged, see the energy dissipate. Do whatever feels most comfortable for you, leaving the objects charged or uncharged.

Now, see yourself walking away from that table and feeling very good about what occurred. And you feel very secure, very confident that what you want to happen will happen, because you've seen it happen, and you've used your objects to make it happen. And you know you can always go back to that table and use those objects again to make whatever you want happen.

So now, walking away from the table, holding any power objects you have with you, start to come back and let go of that energy.

And now, start counting backward from five to one. And as you do so, feel more and more awake, more completely back in the room. Five, four, feeling more and more awake. Three, two, almost entirely back in the room. One. When you are ready, you can open your eyes.

CHARGING THE OBJECTS IN A ROOM

While the process of charging is generally confined to smaller, more movable objects, like those discussed thus far, you can also charge the larger objects in a room, or even the room itself, to create a charged environment designed to achieve some purpose. You do this just as you would with smaller objects—send out your energy to these objects in the room and focus on imbuing them with a particular intention. Say you want to have a more fluid environment, use water imagery. Or if you want a room to feel more alive and vital, charge it with the image and associations of fire.

For example, one man at a workshop described charging his kitchen by beaming his energy into different objects, like the stove and refrigerator. The result, he felt, was that food tasted better, and there was a high level of energy in the room.

SHOULD OTHERS HANDLE YOUR OBJECTS?

A final consideration is whether or not to let others handle your power objects. People differ in their response to this question, and your own ideas may vary for different objects. You might keep your staff, wand, or knife private, as discussed earlier, and permit access to objects that are more general in purpose.

For example, some objects are out in the open, like refrigerators and stoves, and it is perfectly fine to leave them charged up and accessible to others. It is obvious that such objects are going to be touched by others, unless you happen to keep them in a special ritual room.

Generally, it is fine to let others handle your magical or power objects, as long as you take certain precautions to keep others from weakening your energy or polluting the object with negative feelings. These precautions include the following:

· You can override other people's energy by projecting enough of your own so that people who have negative or very weak energy will not suddenly flood your object with their energy and cause it to lose its charge.
· Also, you can override other people's energy by directing the object to cast out or dissipate anyone else's energy. Thus your own energy will remain powerful.
· Another protection is to neutralize the object so that after you finish working with it, any energy you had charged it with is gone. As a result, if anyone else works with it, there is no effect on your energy, and you can later return, eliminate any leftover or negative energy from the other person, and recharge the object.
· Still another possibility is to charge your object with the intention that only those with positive energy can use it. On the other hand, you can charge your object to transform negative energy into a positive charge, in case someone with negative energy tries to use the object.

In short, if you do these precharging activities, you can use your object regardless of who touches it. For you have protected your object in advance of having it recycle others' energy, dissipate it, or simply become neutral so it is not affected by this energy.

Thus, it is for you to decide whether others can handle your objects, and if so, what precautions, if any, you need to take. You may decide that some objects are fine for anybody to handle, while you may have certain special objects that you want to keep separate.

Also consider the person who may use your object in deciding what to do. For instance, you may allow certain people with whom you have a resonance or rapport to touch your objects, especially if you are sharing rituals or visualizations with them, and thus feel that you have much in common and so feel comfortable sharing with them. By contrast, you may have acquaintances or relatives who think magical activity is weird, or wrong, so you do not want to introduce these people to your objects.

Also, consider people's attitudes toward the objects themselves. For example, if people believe these objects are charged, they will treat them with a certain respect, so you might feel quite comfortable letting them handle, or even work with, your objects because they are receptive to the activities.

On the other hand, if people are not sensitive to these energies, you may still feel at ease when they handle your objects because they are not going to notice anything special about these objects. So you can feel safe when such people touch them because they are operating in a neutral state.

Conversely, the attitude of skeptics, who look down on this activity, can undermine your work with your object. These people can lead you to question your actions and thereby release or reverse the energy charge you have put into your object. Thus it is advisable to keep your object away from such people, or at least, do not tell them the use of a particular object. For as long as they do not know their attitude will not matter because they will pay no attention to your object. They will think it is just an everyday object and so, like those who are unaware, they can handle your object at will, because they do not know its true purpose.

Thus, under some circumstances, feel free to let some or all people handle your objects. But in other cases, you may want to keep some or all of your objects away from certain types of people.

13
•
Using Psychometry to Gain Insights about Others

Psychometry involves picking up information from an object by sensing the energy imprint left by others who have owned or touched it, or by other influences on the object. This process of picking up information is the reverse of building up a power object. In building up an object, you are putting your own energy into it and creating your own force field around it. Also, you are using the power object to protect your energy and direct your will.

By contrast, psychometry involves the more receptive use of power objects—you are trying to get a feeling of the energy that is already in or around the object rather than trying to impose your own energy on it. Then, from this energy, you are trying to pick up information about the object's history, its current and possibly previous owners, its origin, and other relevant information.

To some extent, your own perceptions and energy will influence and be incorporated into what you see or feel, because you can not totally remove yourself from the observation-reception process. As a result, when you start picking up information about an object, certain images may be triggered, and certain symbols may have particular meanings for you. This occurs because your images and symbols reflect your particular mode of perception.

Nevertheless, put aside as much of yourself as possible, so you can pick up as much as you can from the object without filtering the information through your own system of symbols and meanings. You cannot do this completely because your own framework of perception, symbols, and energy interacts with the forces you are picking up from the object. But eliminate yourself as much as you can.

With yourself as far removed as possible, you can pick up information and insights from the energy invested in the object by others or by events in its past. According to the basic premise of psychometry, you can do this because owners of an object invest a certain amount of their own energy into it, which translates into thoughts, feelings, and perceptions that can be picked up from that object. Accordingly, not only can you pick up information about the most recent owner and events befalling the object, but you can also pick up information from the energy invested into the object over the course of its history. The older traces of energy may fade and become less influential over time, but they will still be there.

Thus, in using psychometry, you seek to draw out the information and feelings you can receive from the energy that is there.

PICKING UP INFORMATION FROM AN OBJECT

To pick up information from an object, start by sensing or perceiving the energy there. Hold the object and let the power circulate through it. Then feel that power as it circulates through the object, and let that energy flow from the object into your mind. In turn, try to open yourself to this energy and pick up whatever information you can, in whatever form it comes to you.

When you do this, it is usually best to follow your initial impression, since it is spontaneous and intuitive and thus likely to be most accurate. Often when you get these impressions in the form of images, feelings, or words, you cannot tell why a particular impression is important to you. But the key to picking up information effectively is just to let these impressions come through. Later you can try to interpret them or get feedback from the owner of the object, to check the accuracy of your impressions.

It is important to separate this initial phase of receptivity to impressions from the second phase of interpreting impressions. If you try to attach the meanings immediately, you can interfere with this open, receptive process.

This two-step process works in the same way as brainstorming or any creative, intuitive process; there are two stages. In the first, you let your creativity flow. Then you analyze and evaluate your ideas. For example, in the first phase of writing, you just start getting the ideas down on paper. Then the internal editor comes out in the second phase to polish what you have written. Likewise, when I design a game, I start by coming up with lots of ideas and then, to refine them, I play with them, test them, and make my logical decisions. And in market testing, the marketers use the same two-step process. They get consumers' immediate impressions of advertising or product packages. Then they analyze their responses logically.

EXPERIENCING YOUR IMPRESSIONS IN DIFFERENT FORMS

You may experience your impressions in different forms, since people perceive and feel energy in different ways. Some people will experience a feeling like a tingling, that conveys an emotion or overall sense of the object or its owner. Other people may see images. Still others may hear sounds or words, or have thoughts triggered by their experiences of the object. And many times, people get a mixture of impressions.

These differences occur because there are basically three modes of perceptions and therefore, three different ways in which the object can communicate with you—through your feelings, your visual sense, or your aural sense or thoughts. Initially, just follow these feelings, images, or thoughts as your senses pick them up. Later you can work on further developing particular areas of your perception, so you can get information of a different type or have a more well-rounded impression that draws on all three forms of perception. (For example, if you typically just get feelings, you might want to work on receiving more visual or aural information.) But to get comfortable with the process, start with your natural tendencies.

THE SOURCE OF YOUR IMPRESSIONS

Your pictures, feelings, or thoughts derive both from your own meaning-response system and from the energy imprinted in the object. It is as if the energy impression triggers your receptors to respond in a certain way. The object is like a camera that takes photographs of the energy structures it encounters. As a result, when someone holds or owns the object, the object gets an impression of that person.

Thus, the more energy he or she puts into the object, the stronger the impression or image, just as the more light let into a camera, the greater the exposure. Once this impression or image is formed, it stays in that object, just as any imprint or photograph retains an image. However, as time elapses or the object is passed into other hands, that image can gradually fade. But some impression will still remain, so if you are sensitive enough, you can pick it up.

INTERPRETING YOUR IMPRESSIONS

Since these energy impressions may be coming from two sources —from you and from the object—it can sometimes be hard to distinguish the origins of an impression. Also, if an owner or user of the object is present, you might pick up information not only from the object itself, but also from that person's thoughts about the object, as well as your impressions of that person. Thus the object can be a focus for many different sources of information.

Thus, a key to accurate interpretation is discerning the source of the information. Is it the object itself, the owner's thoughts about the object, your own impressions of the owner's appearance or personality? It may be hard to tell exactly what you are picking up from where. However, with practice you will develop a greater discernment, so you can pinpoint the information coming from the object itself and tell how you are filtering it through your own meaning-response system. Then you can better interpret the experience.

This process of discernment is much like getting in touch with your inner knowing. At first, you may pick up a lot of extraneous chatter and images. But as you pay more attention to your inner knowing, you get better at knowing what you know. Similarly, you will gradually get better at sorting out the impressions coming from the object, from its owner, and from yourself.

As you work on interpreting the images, thoughts, and feelings you pick up through psychometry, recognize that you bring your own meaning-response system to this process. As a result, images and impressions will vary in meaning from person to person.

Thus some of the images that you pick up may be very literal or they may be symbolic, pointing to some other, deeper meaning. Their significance depends on your own way of registering impressions, so look within your own meaning-response system to understand a particular image. Suppose you look at an object and see an image of a drum, while another person thinks of a fish. The two images are totally different, but they may have the same inner meanings. You may be thinking of the fluidity of the drum's sound; meanwhile, the other person may associate the fish with its fluid movement through water. Thus, although the two images are totally different, the meaning behind them is very similar. So you need to examine what your impressions mean to you. There is no set formula for discovering meanings.

This is the case because people in modern societies come from such diverse backgrounds and have such a broad range of experiences. By contrast, in more traditional cultures, people often have fixed associations with certain objects and images. But this system of shared meanings works in traditional cultures because people have grown up with the same meaning system. Thus a jaguar may have the same meaning for all the families within a Central American Indian tribe. However, in modern society, our varied backgrounds lead us to develop idiosyncratic responses.

Accordingly, you need to ask yourself what a particular image or impression means to you. As you do, certain images or impressions will come to have specific and constant meanings for you. In other words, whenever you see a particular symbol or image, it will have the same meaning for you.

At first, you may experience some confusion since different images may suggest the same meaning, or a particular image may have different meanings. However, with practice, you will find a clearer association of images and meanings. So gradually you will be better able to interpret the impressions you receive, for you will better know what they mean.

Developing this ability can take time, but be patient. Refining the meanings you associate with different impressions is like acquiring any skill. With more practice, clearer meanings will emerge, so you will become more focused in your interpretations.

CLARIFYING YOUR IMPRESSIONS

Besides looking at the meanings of your impressions, you will also get more accurate information if you work on clarifying your perceptions. Initially, the images, thoughts, or feelings you perceive may tend to be vague or blurry. You get just an overall impression. But you can make your perceptions more concrete by asking your inner self for additional details. Rather than just randomly letting images and impressions come to you, ask yourself specific questions about your first images and impressions. Then you will get more detailed information. And if you want still more, ask even more questions to clarify and refine your perceptions further. For instance, suppose as you hold up an object, you get a fleeting image of a house in a meadow. You might ask where this is, who lives in the house, what the house signifies. Also, you might look more closely at the house to see its color, style, and workmanship, and then perhaps go inside your imagination to look at the rooms and explore the meanings of these rooms to you.

PARALLELS WITH OTHER MEANS OF
RECEIVING INFORMATION

Psychometry is similar in many ways to other aids to getting intuitive information about a person, like tarot cards, because it operates like a sensor to tune you in to the energies of others. As such, it is simply one more tool for sensing the energies in an object, to help you understand the object's owner.

At the same time, using an object which is important to someone else can help you develop a feeling of connection to that person, since you are linked through the object. With this single object, you can tune in on many different levels, to understand the multifaceted nature of a human being.

Using an object can also confirm or supplement the information you receive from other intuitive methods. Furthermore, if the information from the object contradicts that from another intuitive approach, you might examine your methods or the accuracy of the information to see why they don't match; maybe something is wrong in one or both of these areas. For example, if a person's object tells you one thing and your intuitive sense of the person's appearance disagrees, perhaps this person is deceptive—is not what he or she first appears to be. Or maybe your intuitive sense was wrong when you used one of these techniques. Look to your inner knowing to decide which is true.

STOPPING YOUR LOGICAL MIND

Being in touch with your intuition is the key to psychometry because the intuition enables you to tune into the energy field in the object and make the close connection with the object's owner or user. There is nothing particularly mystical or supernatural about this process—you are just opening your intuition and becoming very perceptive.

However, once you start paying too much attention to the process itself through criticizing your impressions or wondering why you are picking them up, your logical mind starts interfering, which will turn off your intuition. The problem is, you cannot pick up information and question its validity or explain its source at the same time. After getting your impressions, you can analyze and interpret the images, thoughts, and feelings. But analyzing the images and impressions while you are having them will stop the whole process.

This is so with any experience. You can either observe it from the outside or you can experience it, but you can not do both simultaneously, unless you have a split consciousness, which is hard to develop. Some people have learned how to experience and observe at the same time, but most people find that observation distracts them from the experience or getting involved in the experience keeps them from observing.

Thus initially simply experience the impressions and shut off your logical mind. Stop any questions and criticisms and just focus on having the experience. Later, when the impressions stop, you can turn off your intuition and turn on your logical mind again, to examine your perceptions.

CHECKING YOUR ACCURACY

To improve your accuracy in both getting impressions and interpreting them, check to see if the information you received was correct and usable.

One method, if you are picking up information on someone you know, is to get feedback on the accuracy of the information you received, just as you might do after using conscious projection (i.e., projecting your consciousness into another place to pick up information; see Chapter 1). If you are getting information about an object or its owner, to verify it later, ask the owner how well the information fits. Likewise, if you tune in on someone doing something at a certain time, afterward ask if he or she was in fact doing it. For example, one man perceived newspapers lying around someone's house, and that person later confirmed his impression.

You can use this checking process even if the object or person you are trying to pick up information on is not present, since you can always put up an image of the person or object and get a sense of where that object or person is and what is happening to that object or person now. Similarly, you can work with objects or persons at a distance, and check the accuracy of your intuition when the object or person comes closer. Say you are on a freeway. You might project your energy into a car to sense what the driver and passengers are like. Then, when the car approaches, you can check on the driver's appearance or the number of passengers and their ages and sexes. Or perhaps you might tune in to an object held by someone at a distance, like a briefcase. When the person comes closer, you can see how accurately your impressions fit that person.

These techniques work because you are contacting and interacting with the energy of others or objects. And you can do this at any distance, although you may experience a stronger signal from this energy when you are closer.

You can play these accuracy-checking games at any time. Just project your energy into something or someone to make that energy connection and pick up information. Afterward, see if you were correct. For example, before entering a store or a house, try to sense how many people are inside. Then quickly check your accuracy.

KEEPING TRACK OF YOUR
EXPERIENCES AND IMPRESSIONS

Keeping track of your psychometric experiences and impressions can help you check your accuracy and gain insights from the information you have received. A good way to track is to record images and impressions in a notebook. Then you can review what you have learned and perhaps decide how to apply this information.

If your impressions are in the form of words or phrases, just write them down. For visual images, you can always draw pictures. Or if you get feelings, describe them in any way you can. Afterward you can look at what you have written to seek to understand these impressions further and attach meanings. Also, by keeping a record, you may notice patterns or themes. And you may notice the conditions under which you are accurate and inaccurate, which will help you improve your perceptiveness.

Exercise 12: **DOING A PSYCHOMETRY READING**
Although you can get information from objects and individuals whether or not they are present, in a typical psychometry reading, you will hold the other person's object, to get the strongest impression. You should also relax so you get into an intuitive, receptive frame of mind. In this state, try to perceive and experience whatever energy is in the object from its owner or other sources. The following visualization is designed to help you do this.

To begin, find a partner. If possible, work with someone you do not know very well, so you will not be influenced by what you already know about that person. You can read each other's object simultaneously, or you can take turns. The other person whose object is being read should try not to think about the object or send thoughts to the receiver so the receiver will pick up as much information as possible from the object itself.

As you each experience images or impressions, you can report them to the other person, or do so when you have finished. After this initial report, you can ask if the images mean anything to the other person. Or if you associate certain meanings and interpretations with the images, describe your own meanings before you listen to the other person's reactions. In doing so, you can better check your accuracy as well as improve your ability to pick up information.

The fit between your perceptions and the other person's associations can be amazing. In one case, a man who was reading someone's cane picked up images of a street, the color red, and a hand. After he reported his perceptions, the other man stated that he recently had to use his cane to defend himself against three rough panhandlers. When he refused them, one of the men struck him, and then all three fled, leaving him a little bloodied and bruised. So he felt that the receiver's images related specifically to this recent traumatic experience involving his cane.

During the reading, ask yourself questions to get more specific information. For example, as you hold the object, ask yourself, Who had the object? Where was the object? What was the object used for? Then just pay attention to whatever comes as your answer, whether in words, images or feelings. It is important to trust your ability to pick up the energy in the object and simply open yourself to the experience. As you practice, you will become more receptive and trust yourself more. In turn, as you trust yourself more, you will get more accurate images and thus develop more confidence.

If this is your first attempt at psychometry, you may find your images and impressions unclear, and you may not be sure whether these impressions are coming from you or from the object. But do not worry about this now. Just focus on being open and receptive, because as you practice and get more feedback, you will become more discerning, just as you will come in closer touch with your inner knowing and intuitions about everyday life as you tune in to them. The two abilities are very similar: in psychometry you use your inner knowing to tune in to a particular object; in daily life you use this knowing more generally.

Now, choose an object for this exercise. Ideally, the object should have a history known by the owner and not by the receiver. When you exchange objects, try not to project thoughts about the history of the object, so the receiver is not influenced by your thoughts (and ask the other person to do the same when you seek to receive).

Now get ready to begin. When you are receiving, focus on the object, touch it, hold it in your hand, and experience the images or impressions that come up. Let your mind relax into an unfocused, altered state. As the images and impressions come, try to get more specific details and comment on any special associations. Finally, ask the other to share what your images and impressions mean to him or her, and use this both to gain insight into the other person and test your accuracy. You can feel free to do this in sequence— one receiving at a time—or you can receive simultaneously and take turns sharing your experiences and associations. Do whatever works best for you. The following visualization is designed to guide

you into the process and direct you as you receive and share information.

Start off by holding the other person's object, and try to clear your mind of anything else. Now you'll get very relaxed, so start concentrating on your breathing. Focus on it going in and out. In and out. You're going to feel very relaxed, very comfortable, and you'll be very receptive to whatever you are experiencing. At the same time, you're going to stay alert and awake.

Once you feel very comfortable and relaxed, take the object you are holding and move it around in your hands. Notice what images come to you. Do you notice any words or phrases? If so, note those. You might also have certain feelings about the object. You might see some visual images too. Just begin by being receptive to whatever comes, without asking any questions at first.

Then ask yourself a few questions about the object. What is it? What was it used for? Who owns it? What is the owner like? And as you think of the present owner, maybe think back to the previous owners of this object and ask what they might have been like too.

Also be aware of any events affecting this object. Maybe it was used during a major event, or perhaps it was in the area where a major event occurred. You can ask yourself about this event and perhaps think about the person who had or owned the object when this event or activity occurred.

Now if you want to start sharing any of the images you are picking up with your partner, do so. As you share, you might have certain interpretations or meanings associated with your images or impressions, and if so, share those interpretations or meanings too. You can take turns doing this. Then, after each shares, the other can give feedback, if he or she wants.

Now wrap up your discussion with the other person and then you can go a bit deeper into picking up information.

Now that your discussion is complete, enter this relaxed state again. Just take a moment to refocus on your breathing going in and out and relax.

Now, as you feel very relaxed and comfortable again, feel this object you are holding again and form a picture or get a sense of the person you are working with. Then imagine what might be happening to this object or to the person who owns this object and notice what will be happening to this object in the future. Imagine that you are projecting your consciousness like a beam of light into the future, and this object is traveling along this beam of consciousness into the future too.

As you do, get a sense of where the object might be going next or where the person who owns this object might be going. You can obtain this knowledge of the future from this object, because the object can not only tell you about the past and present, but it can give you certain insights into the future too.

Again, as you get these images, briefly share them with the other person. As you do, you may find that you have been thinking about doing or planning to do something. You may also be aware of things that the other person hasn't thought about before, but with which he or she feels a certain rapport or connection. Or he or she may feel this insight will have a meaning for him or her in the future.

So, when you are ready, share what you have seen, thought, or felt about the future and perhaps get a little feedback from the other person about what you have seen. Find out how he or she relates to the information you have picked up.

Take another minute or so to wind up. And now it's time to come back so you can share the experiences you had. Count backward from five to one, and as you do, gradually come back into present time. Five, becoming more and more awake. Four, three, more and more alert. Two, just about ready to come back into the room. One. Completely back. And if you are ready, you can open your eyes.

COMMON EXPERIENCES AND EXPECTATIONS

When you do this visualization your images and impressions may seem very fragmentary and diffuse. Yet you should still report them, and you may find that the other person feels a connection to some of these impressions. If so, you can follow up by seeking to pick up additional related information from the object.

For example, in one workshop demonstration the receiver sensed that the piece of jewelry he was reading belonged to a woman's grandmother, and he began describing the grandmother. The woman confirmed his description.

Well, it is old like he said, and it did belong to my grandmother. And he did mention images of royalty, and I think of it as something that belongs to a royal family.

Also, he mentioned mountains and a feeling of power and strength in this person. Well, that could suggest my grandmother, because she wasn't a frail person. She was a very forceful woman, and she did live on a farm and she had broad shoulders.

In another case, a man picked up images of light, energy, and a higher spiritual focus from a cassette a woman had given him, and she felt he was picking up the high spiritual energy she had felt in recording it. As he stated:

What came through is something to do with relationships, and there was a picture of a strong light overcoming the darkness and a feeling of very high energy. . . . I felt a focus on this light and this energy, more than on any individuals. It was like this contained area was full of energy, and it seemed to be a somewhat spiritual area.

And she responded:

I just made that tape last night. And I feel one of the things that you were picking up is what was going on with me while I was making the tape, or the feeling I have that this spiritual power enters anyone when they listen to music. . . . I'm very, very much into that—the spirituality of music. And making that tape was a very strong spiritual experience for me, so I related . . . when you said you were picking up this higher guide and this spiritual energy. . . . For I see music as a way of having a relationship with your higher self or your higher energy. . . .

Thus this feedback and sharing can confirm your impressions of the other person. However, in some cases your perceptions may seem so vague and general that they could apply to anyone, so it is not surprising that the other person should feel a connection. Yet even if this is the case, reading someone's object can provide the basis for a deeper level of communication with the person, because you can follow up on what you have learned about the person through psychometry. Then too, the sharing may give you both a sense of closeness and connection which can help you get to know each other better.

For example, when one man read a woman's crystal, the information he received was quite general and unclear. But he reported:

> I feel I know Jenny a lot better than I did before, as a result of doing the reading. We did it as a light little social thing. But now I feel a strong feeling of connection because I have discovered some things about Jenny, and I feel very comfortable. . . . For example, I sensed some area that might have been Peru, because I picked up mountains, and I found out that she had a family in Peru when we talked about this later. . . . Also, I felt it was a very positive, pleasant object which she gave me, and it felt really good to be able to share that . . . and I feel closer to Jenny as a result.

Feedback can also help convince skeptics that psychometry produces real insights into and strong connections with others. One man with a scientific background reported that he had been very skeptical, but after the sharing experience, he felt he had observed something real:

> I got a good feeling about the object . . . and it made me feel good. Also, I sensed something about traveling, moving, and flying, and when we shared, the woman said she got the object when she went . . . she had been in Las Vegas. . . .
>
> Also, the experiment helped me to think about the whole miracle thing I have wondered about in this field. I tried to reject it for so long and I have thought that this . . . total bullshit.
>
> But at the same time, I've had enough experience with people in my life to think something is happening. So I've suspended my skepticism, or have tried to. And that's what I feel happened tonight. When it started, I felt like I was perceiving something real. But then, as soon as I started to think about what I was experiencing, that turned it off. Yet while I experienced it, I do think I was experiencing something real.

Finally, be aware that although you may be reporting your perceptions of the other person, your own point of view may also be shaping your reports. Accordingly, you may be using your own symbols and images, which have a certain meaning to you, to characterize another person's feelings or thoughts, which have parallel meanings but are expressed differently. One man at a workshop reported doing this:

I personally feel that most of what I was picking up was coming from me. . . . For example, the object I was using was her pen, and I picked up the image of concrete and the feeling of the air outside. Then I related this to my own image of what a city is like, and I thought of the civic center and its structure. There was an emphasis on structure for me.

Then, when she shared about the pen, she felt she was using it for a structure herself, for balancing her checkbook, and she felt there was a parallel between the way in which she tried to structure her life, such as with her checkbook, and the images of structure I reported with the images of the civic center.

Yet while you may be filtering your perceptions through your own point of view, to some extent you are also picking up the common associations you share with others. In turn, these shared associations can help you feel a connection with others, because you are able to apply your insights to others, even if these ideas have been influenced to some extent by your own point of view.

14

•

Psychometry
in Everyday Life

Once you have developed the
ability to tune in to objects and gain information from them, you
can use this ability in a number of ways every day. This chapter
suggests some of these uses, and you may think of others.

GETTING MORE INFORMATION
ABOUT THE PEOPLE YOU MEET

Psychometry can help you get more information about people
when you first meet or communicate with them. It helps if you
have a physical object associated with this person, but you can
also use the same receptive approach to pick up information from
the person's energy field.

For example, when you shake someone's hand, focus on the
hand or a watch. Or if you get a letter, focus on the energy the
person has put into writing it. In such cases, you might be getting
information from other cues, like the person's clothing or hand-
writing. Also, you might be influenced by information you already

have about the person, perhaps from someone who referred you to him or her. But the information you pick up through psychometry can serve as one more clue to better know the person.

SENSING SOMEONE'S FEELINGS

You can also use the psychometry process to pick up feelings and then help the person, if necessary. To do so, you might send out your energy and use it to feel around the person's body for signs of some problem in their energy field, as well as to pick up thoughts or feelings. If you sense that his or her energy seems abnormal, say you notice a hot or cool spot, feel some negative energy, or feel the energy unusually scattered, you might send back some of your own healing energy. On the other hand, if you get a very strong sense of illness or negativity and feel unable to deal with this yourself, you can move away to protect yourself.

In picking up this feeling energy, you are essentially reading the whole person as you would an object. To do this, you extend your own aura until you feel the other person's aura. Then you mingle your own aura with that person's aura, and you notice any images, impressions or thoughts. While it easier to read a person who is nearby, you can also do this with someone who is far away or inside a car, house, or other enclosed place while you are outside. You just use this technique of putting up a picture of this person, much like you would use the technique of picturing an object previously discussed. Then, you can use the information, send healing energy to the visualized image of this person, or step out of the way of any negativity you feel as you would if the person were present.

FEELING A CLOSER CONNECTION WITH SOMEONE

Another use of psychometry is to feel a closer tie with someone, which can help you get a better sense of that person and his or her motivations. For example, after reading a person's object, you may feel you better understand him or her and therefore feel more connected.

In turn, this feeling of connection can help you relate to that person, for you will have a better sense of his or her preferences. Suppose you are choosing a gift. By tuning in to the recipient and the object you are considering, you can intuit whether he or she will like it. You are picking up the personalities both of the person and the object, and sensing whether they mesh. If they do, this object would probably make a good gift for him or her.

GETTING AN OVERALL SENSE OF A GROUP OR ORGANIZATION

Not only can you pick up mental images or symbols from individuals, but also from groups and organizations. As with people, you can get this information by tuning in to an object associated with that group or organization (like a banner or brochure), or by examining an image of this group as a whole.

Particularly if you are thinking of joining a group, you might hang up a picture of the group or try to read one of its objects. Doing so will give you a sense of the group's character and help you decide whether you want to become a member.

READING A MAP OR PHOTOGRAPH

Psychometry can also tell you about a location on a map or about what is happening in a photograph. Put your hand over a particular spot on the map and move it over the photograph and then be receptive and open, as usual.

This technique can work well because the picture or map contains an impression of energy, and in some cases, this energy accumulates and becomes particularly intense over the years, as with a scrapbook photograph that brings back many important memories. Thus, if you put your hand over such a photograph, you might pick up a great deal of information about the people who are pictured.

PICKING UP NEGATIVE FEELINGS FROM AN OBJECT

Psychometry can help you sense when an object has been associated with negative people or events, and if it has, you may either want to cleanse the object or dispose of it; otherwise, you may pick up this negativity. At a workshop one woman described how such objects put her into bad moods:

I have found that objects can transfer their mood to someone else. For example, if I want to project joy to other people, and then I find that someone's in a stressed-out mood, I'm afraid to be around someone like that or have them touch me, because I can pick that up. And I find it's much the same thing when people have objects which have been stolen. They're like bad money because they have been earned in a bad way, or otherwise have a bad history. Those objects carry with them that desperation, and when I've met people who have those objects around them, I won't touch those objects. I won't use them, because I'm real sensitive, and I don't want any part of me to pick up those feelings from those objects.

There have been similar stories of people finding stolen objects and experiencing so much stress or guilt from these objects that they have had to relinquish them. For example, recently, a van dropped money in the street and a number of people took some home. But some of them felt so guilty, because it was stolen money that they had no right to, that they returned it. And there have been many other cases—people who have even sent back money they obtained wrongly many years ago, because they continued to feel bad while it was around.

Some of the bad feelings in cases like these may result from committing the wrong act itself. However, the object taken wrongly serves as a reminder of the wrong, so it acquires a power in and of itself to trigger the bad feelings and guilty reaction associated with the original act.

MAKING CHOICES

Still another use of psychometry is making choices about actions or directions. For example, if you are deciding which country, region, or neighborhood to live in, just put your hand over the appropriate map and move it around until you feel a special pull or tingling. Then look more closely at that area below your hand, because your response may be a clue that you want to live there. Or if you tend to respond visually, gaze around the map. You may suddenly feel an attraction to a certain area, suggesting this is the place for you.

You can also use this approach with a floor plan for an event. For example, before I attended a company-licensing show, I received a floor plan. I had a choice of three booths, and I tried to decide logically, based on neighboring booths, traffic-flow patterns, the location of the cafe, and other information provided by the sales representative. I felt confused by all the details and felt pressured to decide immediately. But after I did, my decision did not feel right.

So instead of using logic, I focused on the floor plan as a purely visual experience, without trying to make sense of it. I just tried to feel where the right place would be. And what felt right was a center booth. The sales representative's logic had not worked for me, but this holistic approach did. I felt drawn to this particular spot. So I called back to make the change, and subsequently I found this an ideal spot to be at the show—right in the middle of things, and near a few strong draws, which contributed to this being a successful show for me.

DECIDING ON PURCHASES

Psychometry also can help you decide about something you want to buy. You can make your choices more quickly, decide whether or not you really want something, and choose the item that feels right for you.

Some cases may seem too trivial for psychometry, but using it can speed up your purchasing decisions. For example, I have met people who waste time shopping because they rely too much on logic. An example is the woman who carefully examines the fruits and vegetables before choosing. By contrast, if she intuitively picked them without thinking, she might make just as good a purchase, in far less time.

The process can help you also make major, long-term purchases. Since you will be living with the item for some time, use psychometry to help you make a good choice. I do this when I select art for my home. I want to have a connection with the object. And sometimes that feeling can be extremely powerful—it draws me to the object. At a gift show, I once saw a red African mask which was quite expensive, so I moved on. But I kept thinking about this mask, and I felt I had to have it, so I was relieved to discover it was still there when I returned to buy it. Once I got home, I put it in the entryway to my house, and at once felt this mask was just the perfect object to go there. It was like a "watcher" or guardian object, with a powerful spirit of protection.

When you feel that kind of connection with an object, you may find that object is a real source of inspiration or power for you, and if so, you should probably obtain that object, if you can.

FORESEEING THE FUTURE

Furthermore, you may find an object can give your information about future possibilities. As you hold an object, you may pick up images, thoughts, or feelings which may not have much meaning for you now, but predict something that could happen if events continue on their present course. Then you can decide if you want to act to make this future possibility even more likely. Or you can reduce its likelihood if you want another outcome instead.

Exercise 13: **GAINING INSIGHTS INTO OTHERS**

You can also use a projection technique in combination with picking up information from an object, to gain insights into another person. Ideally, this person should be present when you do this, but that is not strictly necessary. Basically, you imagine an object in front of each of the energy centers in the person's body, noticing the qualities of that object and any transformations and then interpreting these images. The following exercise is designed to help you do this.

You're going to choose someone to get insights about. If you want to work with someone present whom you don't know very well, you can do this. Or put up in your mind the image of somebody you don't know very well or somebody you have seen only recently and would like to know a little more about. Then get very relaxed and again just concentrate on breathing.

Now display an image of somebody you know or have recently met whom you would like to know better and keep this image or the face of this person in front of you. Or if you prefer, you can just feel the presence of the person there. However, in whatever form you perceive this person, he or she is seated or standing in front of you. And you feel very comfortable, very relaxed, as you look at this person.

And now visualize, think about, or feel yourself sending out your own energy to this person. If you tend to get visual images, imagine this energy you are sending projecting out through your forehead, your visual center. Or if you are more likely to get your insights and information by hearing words, sounds, or phrases, or by thinking, experience this projection of energy coming from your throat, your center of communication. Or if you are more likely to have feelings about people, to get a total sense of them, feel this energy projecting out from your heart, the center of your feelings.

Just notice your energy going out, projecting into the image of this person in front of you, and as it does, it forms an aura of white light or radiant energy around the person. The person is being bathed in this energy you are putting out, and at the same time, the person is projecting his or her own aura or energy, which is merging into this pool or bath of energy you have put around him or her.

Now you can pick up information from this energy which he or she is putting out, which is blending with your energy. You may experience this information coming to you in the form of colors in his or her aura. You may see images appear there. Or you may experience feelings. Or you may experience words or thoughts coming to you. Just notice that as you perceive this information, it is as if your own energy is drawing information from this person to you. So you are able to really get to know this person from this information you draw to you.

To get even more information, you can do a scan of him or her by moving your eyes from neck to feet and notice the objects which appear as you do. These objects will give you even more and deeper information. They will help you know the inner person.

Start this scan at the top of the head. Just focus your gaze or attention there for a moment and notice any image, impression, or feeling that comes to you. As you look, you'll see an object emerge, or you'll feel its presence. Or the word for this object will come to you. It could be any object, perhaps a flower, such as a rose.

Notice what this object looks like, how it feels, or what you think about it. Then notice what happens to the object. For your experience might tell you a bit about this person and what he or she is like. For example, did the object seem full of energy? Did it light up? Did it change shape? Change color? These appearances and changes all can tell you a bit about the person, and since the object is at the top of the person's head, you are learning about his or her thoughts, ideas and beliefs because the energy center at the top of the person's head is the center of the person's mental and spiritual nature.

Now, dropping down a bit to the center of the forehead, again send out your energy beam and notice any objects or images that appear in the middle of the forehead. And if you feel the presence of these objects or have thoughts about them rather than seeing them, that is fine too.

Once again, notice what happens to these objects. Do they change shape or colors? Do they get larger, smaller, or transform into another object? And this time, as you notice these changes, think of what they might tell you about the person's outlook on the world, his or her attitude and perception about things, because this energy center in the middle of the forehead is the center of the person's vision.

Next drop down to the throat level, again send out your energy beam, and notice any objects or images that appear at the person's throat. As before, notice what happens to these objects. Do they change shape or color? Do they get larger or smaller? Do they transform into something else? And this time, notice what the images or impressions might tell you about how this person communicates, because the throat center is the center of communication.

Now go down a bit more and focus on beaming your energy at the level of the heart. And again, be aware of any objects that form in front of this energy center. Notice what happens. Do they get larger? Smaller? Change color? Shift shape? Just pay attention to whatever happens. And be aware that these changes might tell you a little about the person's feelings, for the heart is the center of emotion. So what happens to the object here might tell you about how the person relates to others.

Now drop down to the abdomen, send out another energy beam, and again notice any object that forms in front of the person, and notice what happens to it. Notice its shape, its color, and any changes. And be aware that this experience of the object might tell you something about the person's will, motivation, and level of energy. For the center of energy located in the abdomen is the center of will and power.

And now move down to the area between the pelvis and again send out an energy beam. Again put up an object and notice what happens to that object. Notice the size and shape and color of the object and any changes which occur. And be aware that this part of the body is the person's sexual center, so the object may tell you about the person's sexuality and sexual identity.

Finally, drop down to the base of the spine and put up one more object. Notice what happens to it. Notice its size and shape and notice if it changes in any way. This object may tell you how the person survives and manages in the world, since the base of the spine is the survival center. You might get some information about his or her financial situation, or about his work abilities and interests, for these are all aspects of the person's survival.

Now, after you have finished getting information from this last object, let go of that image, thought, or feeling and pull back. Then just observe, feel, or think about the person standing or sitting in front of you and notice that this whole range of objects you have seen before are all in front of the person now.

So observe these objects as a group and get a sense or picture of the whole person. For all of these objects you have observed are aspects of that person, and now they have come together to give you a total, holistic picture of the person. So just see this total picture, or have this total feeling or thought of the person as a whole. And perhaps you might even notice another type of object there before the person, representing that person as a whole.

When you feel complete with this experience, just let go of the objects and images you have seen. Also begin to pull back on the energy beam you have sent out. As you do, you can see or feel the aura around the person starting to disappear and dissipate.

Now, just continue to pull back this energy beam you sent out, and as it comes back in, you are feeling whole and complete and separate from this other person.

Now imagine that the image of the other person is also disappearing, and soon you are standing or sitting there alone, all by yourself, feeling very comfortable, very whole, and very complete.

And as you feel this completeness, start counting backward from five to one. As you do, become more and more awake, and start to come back into the room. Five, four, feeling more and more awake. Three, two, almost completely awake. One. Come back into the room. And when you're ready, you can open your eyes.

INTERPRETING YOUR PERCEPTIONS ABOUT OTHERS

During exercise 13, you may come to understandings about the person you are reading. Or you might take some time afterward to interpret your images and impressions.

Suppose you see an image of a rose in front of the person's heart, and the rose suddenly becomes more vibrant. That might suggest this is a very warm, loving person. Or if you notice a withered rose at the base of the spine, the person's survival center, he or she may be having financial trouble.

Do not be concerned if you do not see specific objects during this exercise. Some people may just see different colors of varying intensity. In this case, just interpret the meanings of those colors at each center. For instance, lots of grays or dark colors often suggest that the person is very solid and not very spontaneous. On the other hand, if you see lots of reds, the person may be very warm and vibrant. In turn, your own associations with these colors determine their meanings in any particular case.

When you do see particular objects, notice the details because these will reveal someone's personality too. If you see a hat on his or her head, ask yourself, What does the hat look like? Is it a witch's hat? A bowler hat? A cowboy hat? The appearance of the hat will tell you something about the person. Likewise, if you see a piece of clothing, concentrate on its appearance; notice if it is colorful, and so on.

When you first do this object projection, the images and impressions may seem fairly sketchy. But as you practice and gain more control, you can ask yourself questions and look at the images more closely. Also, if you are not sufficiently in control to examine images while you are experiencing them, afterward you can analyze your experiences logically. When you do this, review the images you have seen and ask yourself what they mean to you. What does a particular shade or intensity of color, or a certain kind of flower, for example, mean to you? Thus, in this follow-up, you essentially elaborate on your impressions, to draw even more meanings and connections from what you saw, felt, or thought.

CHECKING YOUR PERCEPTIONS ABOUT OTHERS

After you do an object reading of a person, it is helpful to get feedback on your accuracy, particularly when you are first starting, to help you hone your perceptual ability and give you confidence in the process. You may find you are quite accurate, which will help you feel more confident next time.

When I first learned this technique, I found its accuracy uncanny. We trained by putting a rose in front of people and observing its transformation, and we prepared for this by looking at the image of a rose in a vase for about a week to help us better visualize the image. (However, since you can do this process with any object that has meaning for you, or which you already have a clear picture of in your mind, you do not need this preparation time.)

In any case, after each object reading, the person whose image I had read confirmed my impressions. Once I worked on a woman I had just met in a class on body-mind relationships. I picked up many images of sadness, depression, struggle, and severed relationships, and she later told me that she had just gone through a serious illness and broken up a long-term marriage. Now she was trying to find a job, with little success.

APPLYING OBJECT PROJECTION IN EVERYDAY LIFE

Since this object projection technique takes some time, it is probably best for seeking in-depth information. For instance, it can be very useful if you are trying to decide whether to go into business with or work for somebody. Or it can help you decide if you want to begin a relationship or get more deeply involved with somebody.

Object projection is simply a more intense use of psychometry (getting information from objects). In turn, these objects provide just one more way of learning about somebody, and these intuitive insights can supplement your other sources of information about the person.

PROTECTING YOURSELF
FROM NEGATIVITY IN OBJECTS

As you become more sensitive to information from objects, you may also pick up negativity from these objects, just as you might from other people or your general environment. If you are sensitive to this negativity, you can do visualizations or energy projections to protect yourself. For instance, visualize a white shield of energy around yourself, or visualize yourself directing the negative energy to return to its source (i.e., the object or person sending it to you). You are creating a reverse shield, so if you do not want the energy you are picking up, you can send it back.

It is important to shut out such negativity, because in psychometry, you are opening yourself up and being receptive. But you can shut down your receptivity too, because an important part of receptivity is being able to turn off that receptivity when you wish. Also, if you do take in any negativity, you need to be able to eject it.

This process of protection is also done by healers. They need to cleanse themselves of the negative energy from the diseases they are treating; otherwise, they can pick up illnesses. Similarly, you need to cleanse away the negative energy after you get negative information from objects. Such information can be useful; for instance, you may sense that someone is unethical, and so you decide not to deal with him or her. But after you get this information, you do not want to make the negative energy a part of yourself. So imagine that energy cut down in size, or send the energy back.

There may also be times when you simply want to turn off your ability to pick up information, because otherwise you can experience psychic overload, just as anyone can feel overloaded by doing too much of one thing. A comedian or speaker does not always want to be onstage and may turn off that part of him or herself while offstage.

By contrast, people who can not turn themselves off at will can run into problems. For example, some psychiatrists and psychotherapists may be especially susceptible to psychological illnesses because they encounter so many psychological complaints, while doctors and other medical practitioners can be particularly sensitive to physical illness because contact with disease is a regular part of their lives. Likewise, people can make their work attitudes part of their everyday consciousness, although this may lead people to adopt undesirable traits. On the job, the trait may be essential, but it can create problems in everyday relationships. For example, lawyers can become overly aggressive, while police officers can become suspicious.

Similarly, when you work to become more intuitive and perceptive, you also have to balance this with your other activities. At times you do want to be very open and receptive. But at times you may feel you are receiving too much information, and so you have to be able to cut it off.

Accordingly, if you do start to feel overloaded, or you want to shut out or send back negativity, just turn off your inner receptivity or put up a shield or protection. When you feel ready, you can always take down that shield or turn on your receptivity again.

PART THREE

•

RITUALS

15

•

Using Rituals to Achieve Your Goals

The main purpose of any ritual is to raise power and focus your energy and intention on achieving a goal. You can similarly think about or do meditations on the goal to try to realize it. But a ritual makes this focus even more intense because you are using objects, magical words, symbols, and even creating a whole environment in which you can focus your energy on making that particular goal a reality. So the ritual in effect beams out your intent like a laser at your desired goal.

The goal you choose can be something you want in everyday life, or effect you would like to have on natural phenomena. Working with natural phenomena can instill confidence—that you do have these powers, so just as you can have an impact on the elements of nature, you can have an impact on what happens in everyday life. You can also take the experience of working with the natural elements and use your associations with these elements to give more power to the rituals you use to achieve personal objectives.

CHOOSING OR CREATING RITUALS

You can use a ritual that has already been developed by someone else or that is used by an established group. Or you can create your own ritual, based on your own personal style.

One advantage of an established ritual is you are using something with a proven record. It has already been found to work by those using it. In addition, if the ritual has been used repeatedly, like one that comes out of a long magical tradition, it has been infused with the energy, thoughts, and symbols of a large group of people over time, which can give the ritual even more power for you.

On the other hand, we all have our own approach, and in modern society, people have diverse religious and spiritual traditions and may feel more comfortable with different symbols. Thus, your personal rituals may have more power and meaning for you than a ritual that is ready-made.

Thus, as I describe different ritual techniques in this chapter, use them if they work for you. But if you prefer, I encourage you to develop your own ritual approaches. Or use a combination of established ritual methods and your own. The idea is to choose what you feel most comfortable with, for there may be certain symbols, techniques, or methods of ritual that have a special meaning or power for you.

Also consider whether you prefer a more complex or a simple ritual, since rituals can range from ones with a minimal number of words or gestures to very elaborate ones, like those practiced in ceremonial magic. Some of these practitioners incorporate symbolic associations with the phases of the moon, planetary configurations, objects, plants, the words and chants they use, and so forth, because this layering of associations and meanings has a reinforcing power for the practitioners. But there are many other people who find such complicated rituals detract from their ability to project and focus energy and thus prefer to do a ritual much more spontaneously. So choose whatever works for you at the time.

USING AN INTUITIVE OR DIRECTIVE APPROACH

There are two basic approaches to ritual. One is the intuitive approach, in which you focus on being receptive and do not plan your ritual in advance. Rather, you let your receptivity inspire you on the spur of the moment as to either the goal of the ritual, the nature of the ritual performed, or both.

Conversely, in the directive approach, you use your will actively to direct the ritual. In this case, you decide in advance what you want to do and then use a pre-planned ritual to bring about this goal.

The Intuitive Approach In the intuitive approach, which corresponds to the second-degree ODF ritual I described in *Shaman Warrior,* you are essentially opening yourself up to the energies of the universe, as if to say Here I am. I'm receptive. Then just see what kind of inspiration comes and act as you are inspired to act.

Suppose you are doing a simple ritual—standing in a meadow trying to experience a direct connection with the forces of nature. You might stand there quietly for a few moments, not sure what to do. And then you might feel that you should raise your arm, which might lead you to make other gestures, and this might lead you to think, Now I want to project power out of my arm. Thus one act would lead to another and this spontaneous flow would lead you to do certain magical things.

The underlying premise is that if you just open yourself up and be receptive, you will at a certain point feel inspired to act and do what is appropriate and will have the knowledge you need when you act. This process is a bit like having a dance with nature, in which you feel the presence of the forces of nature and show you are a part of nature too by being receptive.

In fact, when you are truly receptive and feel in touch with nature while doing a ritual, other people may be able to see this. For example, members of the ODF watched to see what kind of natural phenomena were produced during rituals, on the grounds that, if someone was in tune with nature, there would be an observable effect. If someone was working with the energies of earth, people would look for clusters of energy formed near the ground or around the nearby trees and bushes. If someone was working with the wind, people would look for noticeable changes, like the wind suddenly rising up. Or if someone was working with water, they would look for a change in the tides, like a sudden greater than normal surge. In other words, during an intuitive ritual out in the field, people would look for changes in the environment that transcended normal expectations. Then if something unusual did happen, it was seen as a sign that the practitioner was really in touch with and impacting the forces of nature through the ritual.

The Directive Approach In the directive approach, which corresponds to the third-degree ODF ritual described in *Shaman Warrior,* you decide in advance what you want to do and direct your energies toward that goal. For example, if you are working with the forces of nature in the field, you might tell yourself I'm going to work with the energies of earth tonight, and I'm going to try to evoke an earth elemental (an earth spirit or personification of the forces of nature). And to do this, I'm going to focus on sending out a beam of my own energy to the trees to get the energies there to form into an energy cluster. And then I'm going to have the cluster move around. Or if you are working with the wind, you might tell yourself, I'm going to try to get the wind to move as I do. In turn, any observers would notice if your intention produced the desired results.

Or if you are using the directive approach on a more practical everyday level, you might decide in advance that you want to achieve a certain goal, like getting a job or a promotion, and then you do the ritual to attain that particular end. If you achieve the goal, that is a sign that the ritual may have helped you do so, though other steps you took may have helped too.

TRUSTING YOUR OWN ABILITIES

Whether you use an intuitive or directive approach or a combination, it is important to trust in your own ability to attain your objective. You need that belief in yourself and in the power of the ritual in order to fully direct your energy and intention toward your ritual goal.

Part of this trust means believing that when you open yourself up to the forces of nature, the forces will be there to help you achieve your goal. Also, this trust means believing that if you need certain information to attain your objective, that information will be there when you need it. In short, you need to trust that the things you want will happen, and then you can let yourself go, feeling secure that this trust you have is valid—that you can indeed trust and let go.

In turn, you need this trust to help you put aside your logical mind, so you can move into an intuitive state of consciousness.

And you need to be able to move into this altered state because the essence of an effective ritual is to open yourself up to respond intuitively. If you stay in a logical frame of mind, nothing is going to happen because you will not be able to raise your energy in that state. You need an intuitive state to generate the energy necessary to direct your intent powerfully into achieving your goal.

MAKING A RITUAL LIKE THEATER

Whatever type of ritual you use, consider it a little like theater—a dramatic, intensifying device to help move you into an altered consciousness and heighten whatever energy you direct outward or whatever perceptions you receive. Or in much the same vein, compare the preparations of a ritual to a costume party. The costumes help create a different mood, as if they give everybody permission to step into another place where they relate to each other differently than they do in everyday life.

Similarly, in a ritual, you have a special setting, wear special clothing, use special objects, put on power jewelry, or otherwise mark the ritual as separate from your everyday activities. The ritual becomes like a stage or costume party where you step into another world for a brief period of time to focus your energy. Visualize your goal, and perhaps even imagine yourself as someone else with special powers, all to attain your objective.

BUILDING THE RITUAL

To create an intense ritual, set the stage with special actions, objects, associations, and symbols. This way you are layering the activity with many simultaneous levels of meaning, which contribute to the intensity and power of the ritual. Here follow a variety of suggestions.

A Special Place A special place can contribute very powerfully to this sense of specialness which surrounds the ritual and can help to transport it out of everyday time and space. You can choose a special room, or if you work outdoors, find a place that feels good for you, like a meadow, grove, or under a tree. Then, to feel in tune with the environment, take some time to get in touch with that space.

You may also have different places for different rituals (for example, a ritual on a beach for one purpose, a ritual in a meadow for another, and a ritual in a certain room for a third). The particular purpose for each setting depends on your associations and meanings. You might associate a beach with the qualities of water, like movement and spontaneity, so in a beach ritual, you might seek more change or freedom in your life. On the other hand, a certain location in your house might feel very warm, protective, and nurturing, and thus appropriate for a ritual to attain a more loving relationship.

Color Associations Another technique is to use color to create or intensify a desired mood. If you have certain associations with particular colors, use appropriate colors for your ritual's purpose. You can have objects, clothing, or candles in those colors—all to intensify the mood you associate with those colors.

Suppose you are doing a ritual to prepare for an exam. For many people, yellow is associated with intellectual achievement. If yellow has this meaning for you, you might use a yellow candle, dress in yellow, and surround yourself with yellow objects. Using the color with the appropriate meaning further intensifies the focus of the ritual.

Similarly, for other types of rituals, use other colors. For instance, you may associate green with healing. If so, in a healing ritual, use green candles, green clothing, green leaves, or other images of green to reinforce that association.

The point is to choose colors based on their meanings to you. While there are traditional color associations which you can readily use if you feel comfortable with them, you may have your own associations from past experiences. If so, recognize that any traditional associations are just guides, based on the common cultural experiences of the past. Use them if they fit your own outlook, but feel free to choose those that feel right for you, for we all have our own meanings, though we share a common culture.

A Magical Circle A magical circle can help you enter an altered consciousness and feel more focused and protected. You can create this circle in a number of ways. First, you can use certain materials to create a physical circle. Some people pour salt, which is associated with purification, around themselves to create the circle.

Second, you can use a physical object, like a staff or knife, to direct your energy to draw a circle. When I worked with the ODF, we would typically draw a circle by holding a staff outward and projecting energy through it, as we turned in a clockwise direction.

And third, just visualize a protective circle around you. Some people do this by imagining a bubble of light surrounding them.

However you create it, the circle becomes the space where you are going to do the ritual and so, the place where you are going to be separated from the ordinary world. And it is your choice whether to create this circle physically or just with your own energy and imagination.

However, you should be consistent when it comes time to break the circle, by simply reversing what you have created. If you have made a circle with salt, retrace your steps around the circle and sweep it away. If you have drawn a circle of energy with your staff, draw that energy back into your staff as you walk in the opposite direction. Or if you have created a bubble of energy, release that bubble. Then, with that circle released, you are back in the ordinary world; you have symbolically restored the natural order.

Objects You can also intensify a ritual by using objects—especially power objects which you have already worked with and charged.

As discussed earlier, there are two types of power objects—active objects and receptive objects. An active object, like a staff, knife, or sword, is especially appropriate when you want to do a purposeful ritual, because it focuses and directs energy. So you can visualize your energy projecting through the object and focus on directing that energy outward to attain your goal. You can always do this energy projection visually, without the object, but the object is one more way of intensifying and reinforcing your ritual.

You can use other objects for more receptive purposes, or to contribute to the layers of symbols, associations, and meanings you are using to reinforce the message of your ritual. For example, you might use a chalice of water for purification and a crystal as a receiver of energy. This way, in the course of the ritual, you use these objects in a way that reflects the powers normally associated with them. For instance, you might look into the crystal to make yourself more receptive and see what you experience. Or before you use the crystal, put it in the water to purify the message you receive from it. Or after you take the crystal out of the water, perhaps drink the water to symbolically transmit the receptivity of the crystal and the purifying powers of the water to yourself.

Creating and Choosing Objects for a Ritual Often, having special objects you use in a ritual can help you focus on the ritual purpose. You feel these are not just everyday objects—they have extra power because they are used only or primarily in rituals.

You can further add to this sense of specialness by doing a ritual to charge these objects with your energy and dedicate them to their ritual purpose. Also, you can make objects even more special or powerful by actually creating them in the course of a ritual and charging them with your power, as many people do in making drums or rattles, such as many American Indian craftsmen and women do. As they work, they may light a ritual candle, chant, or think about charging the object with certain energies, like the spirit of a particular power animal. You can do the same. Create a ritual setting, and as you fashion your object, charge it with power. Later, when you use that object in a ritual, it will feel even more effective in helping achieve your goal because you have created and charged it to serve this goal.

Likewise, you can create or charge everyday objects to help you achieve a purpose or create a mood. One woman in a workshop described how she charged kitchen knives while cooking: "I charge them in advance to create a certain mood. For instance, if I want to feel rested and calm, I'll charge them with that energy, so I'll feel that way as I make dinner."

Power Animals In some ritual traditions, people also work with power animals, based on the associations they have with those animals. They may draw on the power of an animal on a visual or intuitive level, or they may actually use objects in the form of that animal.

There are various ways of using these animals. You can call on the spirit or energy of these animals to help you, or you might even identify with that animal, take on its spirit or energy yourself.

As with power objects and colors, there are many traditional associations with these power animals, particularly among North American, South American, and Central American Indians. For instance, among many Plains Indians, the buffalo is associated with strength and endurance, the bear with contemplation, the eagle with clear vision, and the mouse with attention to detail. But again, if you have your own associations with certain animals, feel free to use these.

Incense Incense can be another means of creating a magical state. The scent that engulfs you during the ritual can both set the mood and alter your state of consciousness.

You can also choose among scents for different ritual purposes. For instance, if you are doing a light, uplifting ritual, use a light scent, such as a rose petal or other sweet flowery scent. Or if you want to emphasize power and strength, choose an earthier musky smell.

Sounds Sound can be another important factor in ritual. Music, chanting, or words of different types can all add intensity. In fact, as previously noted, some people use magical languages which contribute to the altered state and which are designed to communicate with other levels of reality (for instance, the Fermese language of the ODF, which Michael said was given to him by revelation). And many other magical and spiritual groups report revelations in which certain words or sounds are given to group members for use by the group.

Music can also set the mood. Members of another group I worked with would turn on music before a ritual, to help them attain an altered state, and their choice of music would depend on their goals. For a very powerful ritual, they would put on very powerful music. Or for a gentle ritual, they would use gentle music.

Symbols Images and symbols can also help to create the ritual state. And as you prefer, you can wear them (say as a necklace or embroidery on a robe), put them on an altar, place them around the area, or even draw them with your energy or visualize them around you.

For instance, some of the groups I worked with used a pentagram as a symbol of protection. One group focused on physical image during the ritual. But in the ODF, members simply created it with their energy. They would first draw a magical circle with their staffs and then draw a pentagram within the circle in each direction.

As with other ritual elements, use any symbols you feel comfortable with and which have suitable associations for you, such as for protection. This use of symbols is similar to some groups' use of the sign of the cross. And other people like using their own personal symbols. Different symbols vary in meanings and associations, depending on one's past experience and studies.

If you draw or visualize symbols, rather than using physical objects, charge these mental symbols with your energy and intent as you create them. Once created with energy, these symbols or images will remain there during the ritual, and if they are symbols of protection, they will help to keep out other energies that are not connected with the ritual. Afterwards, because this is real energy, you should release any images or symbols you have created by visualizing them dissipating or by making banishing motions at the end of the ritual. Otherwise, as practitioners report, this energy may linger on for some time after the ritual. You might somehow feel incomplete after the ritual, since some of your own energy is still left in the ritual space. Also, others who come by may perhaps feel this lingering energy, perhaps as a feeling of strangeness or heaviness in the area, which is why Michael always encouraged his students to be sure to banish any energy after a ritual, as a way of showing "common courtesy to others."

Calling on Spiritual Beings Finally, you may find it helpful to call on spiritual beings, spirits, angels, guides, guardians, or whatever you choose to call them. Different groups have different terms for these different energies, but they call on them primarily to seek their protection or assistance in performing their rituals and attaining their goals.

There are two ways to look at these beings or energies. Some people feel they are asking real beings and spirits for their help. Others feel that in calling on these energies, they are creating projections of energy from themselves, or discovering these representations within their higher selves. But once created, these beings are there to help, as manifestations of one's inner wisdom. Some people believe that either situation may occur at different times.

There is no way to prove either viewpoint. Decide what you believe and feel comfortable with it. However, in either case, when you call on these beings in a ritual, they can provide a great deal of help and support.

Clearing or Cleansing the Area for the Ritual It is often helpful to clear out or cleanse the ritual area, particularly if the area has been actively used for rituals or otherwise seems to have a lot of natural energy. A general cleansing or clearing of the space can also help you calm down and get centered. If you are overexcited after a very busy day, or if a negative experience has upset you, you may need to do this clearing.

Start by centering down, much as you would to prepare for a meditation. As you focus on finding your center, separate yourself from whatever has gone before. Then, for the clearing, do it both mentally and physically. As you clear your mind, clear our your surroundings so you have a purified, comfortable area to work in. This clearing is particularly important if you feel negative energy around you; even if you do not, clearing helps you get centered.

When you cleanse, this is also done both mentally and physically, and on yourself as well as on the area. Using certain symbols of cleansing may reinforce your efforts. For example, if you are cleansing yourself, you might run your hands down your head and shoulders and imagine drawing down any energy that is swirling around you. Then, as you shake your hands, imagine that you are shaking off that energy and scattering it around, much as a healer might shake away someone's negative energy.

You can also use specific gestures which traditionally symbolize cleansing. For example, make a clockwise cross, pentagram, or other symbol of purification with your hand or a power object, if you feel something negative around you. Or if you come from a tradition that calls on spiritual guides or helpers, ask these beings or spirits to help you cleanse the area. For example, I was once in a meadow with the ODF group where one of the members did a ritual using methods he had learned in a ceremonial magic group. He had been taught to command the spirits of nature, and as he arrogantly did so, he stirred up a lot of negative energy. Consequently, Michael did a purifying ritual to cleanse the area so that others could work there without being affected by this lingering energy.

Also, if you plan to work in an area where there have been problems, try reassuring the energies around you that the problems are over to create a smoother working environment.

However you want to do it, once you feel comfortable and calm yourself and also feel the energy in the area is cleansed and calm, you can proceed to the ritual you planned.

ACHIEVING DESIRED RESULTS

Once you have all the elements for your ritual—whether a very simple one or one with many ritual objects and symbolic associations—you can focus on the objective of the ritual: projecting your energy to achieve a goal, using any of these materials to intensify the energy.

One result of the ritual can, of course, be that the goal you seek happens during or soon after the ritual. Achieving your goal is not only satisfying in itself, but also confirms your own power or the power of your ritual. If you had a particular everyday goal, its achievement serves as direct confirmation. Or if your goal was to influence the elements of nature (for instance, to attract an earth elemental or affect the movements of the wind, fire, or water), getting the desired responses and having observed it, confirms your power too and suggests you can apply this power to influence everyday life. So this is an indirect confirmation of power.

In either case, you might question the real effectiveness of the ritual because you think you might have achieved that goal even without the ritual. And perhaps you might have. However, whether or not the ritual is an immediate or major factor, it can still help you feel more confident that the desired goal will happen and thereby increase your chances of acting to achieve it. Also, the ritual can suggest necessary preparations for achieving your goal. For instance, doing a ritual before a job interview might give you the confidence you need to get the job. Also, it might suggest ways to make a favorable impression. Or the ritual might simply be one more helpful factor—like having one more powerful card in your bag of tricks.

Also realize that if you seek a very powerful effect, you may need to do a ritual several times. Many people do a certain ritual every few nights for a few weeks, and each time they feel they are projecting more energy.

Thus, consider doing a series of rituals directed to one end, for by repeating the ritual you build the energy. Also, in a series of rituals, you may get other ideas to help you direct your intention or find new and more challenging goals.

ADAPTING A RITUAL TO THE SITUATION

The use of a formal or planned ritual, like those just described, can be especially helpful in focusing your attention on your goal. Yet you can also ease into doing rituals in the course of everyday activities. As one woman commented in a workshop, "It's not always that important for me to start the ritual by saying, 'Okay, this is a ritual. I am beginning a ritual and now I am ending the ritual.' Rather, in my day-to-day life, when I'm doing something, such as cooking, I may just think there's something I want to have, and I focus on getting that. So everything seems to overlap. I'm doing a ritual. But I'm doing something else too."

And that is fine. You can readily work a ritual into the course of everyday activities. However, there are advantages to setting certain times and places for special rituals. Likewise, in a stage play there is generally a fixed beginning, middle, and end. And similarly most people start a book at the beginning and read through until they finish it.

The advantage of clear beginnings and endings is that they help to demarcate the ritual space from the everyday world, just as seeing a whole play or reading an entire book in sequence can give you more of a sense of stepping into another world. By creating a formal circle or having a special ritual place, you enclose yourself in this special setting. Even stepping up to an altar can be a way of announcing that the ritual is about to begin.

But just as some people may prefer dipping into a book for a short time or just getting a taste of a play, so some people may at times prefer just doing a brief ritual on the spur of the moment or they have a more spontaneous style where they don't want to make clear separations of ritual places and activities from everyday life. Thus, if you suddenly feel inspired to ease into a ritual, go right ahead. Or if you would rather just be able to step in and out of ritual reality on the spur of the moment that's okay too. For you can use anything that feels comfortable as a demarcation to step into the alternate ritual world—it does not have to be a formal circle, altar, or special ritual place. Even just a word or thought that triggers the ritual will do. The formal ritual may be more intense and dramatic for most people, but these informal rituals are fine and they can be particularly useful for more limited, everyday purposes, like completing a schedule of activities on time or staying on a diet.

However you use a ritual, keep a balance in your ritual work. For example, after focusing and directing your energy in a ritual, release that energy. Rituals are good for creating more intense, dramatic focus and raising your energy and power for a particular purpose. But afterward, shift back into regular life and normal consciousness. After all, you do not want to spend too much time in an altered state.

16

•

Using the
Elements of Nature
in Your Rituals

Working with the natural elements or elementals—earth, air, fire, and water—can be another powerful tool in ritual, because getting in tune with them or demonstrating your power in influencing them can help you feel that sense of connection and power in everyday life. You can also use your associations with each of the elements in your visualizations and rituals to reinforce your intention.

MAKING ASSOCIATIONS WITH THE ELEMENTS

Use your own associations with the elements to make the ritual your own, although in coming up with your own categories, you can freely draw on traditional associations that have meaning for you. A good way to discover your associations is simply to think of each element in turn and notice the images, thoughts, and symbols that come to you.

For example, when they hear the word *earth,* many people think of solidity and groundedness. The earth is often associated with stability, persistence, continuity, and strength. Now think about any other associations you have. Later, when you work with these elements in a ritual, other associations may come to you.

How about air? Common associations are freedom or independence. People may think of birds flying, the spirit of imagination, creativity, inspiration. Then too, the movement and fluidity of the wind may suggest other associations.

As for fire, that is frequently associated with a very strong, assertive energy, activity, and power. There is a quality of unpredictability and spontaneity about fire. And you may have other associations with fire too.

Finally, you may find water often associated with cleansing and purification. Also, because of its free-form, flowing nature, water, like air, is often associated with spontaneity, flexibility, and creativity.

In short, look within yourself to see what associations come up for you. It is important to experience these associations from within, not just take traditional associations from outside, because these elements of nature are not only outside us, but also within us. In turn, as you get more in touch with these energies in nature, you can experience those energies within yourself too and draw on these elements to achieve your goals.

For example, before an important meeting, like a job interview, you might think of the strength of the earth so you will feel that stability and will not be flustered if asked a tough question. Or if you have to make a sales presentation, the image of fire might stimulate you and make you feel more powerful, which can make you very convincing and persuasive. Thus, there are many practical applications to working with these energies, which will be discussed in more detail in Chapter 17.

WORKING WITH THE DIFFERENT ELEMENTS

One of the keys to working with the different elements successfully, whether you see them as outside or within yourself, is to feel a sense of connection with them and to show that you are able to flow with them or influence them. You are demonstrating both your own sensitivity and your personal power. You can do this with the physical elements in an outdoor ritual, or on a more symbolic level, by controlling the elements, or feelings and responses associated with each of these elements, within yourself.

Generally, you will find earth the easiest element to work with and think about, because it is all around us. Thus, if you just look about, you can imagine energy forms which you can use. For example, out in the country, you might see a vortex or concentration of energy which you view as a center of power and strength. Then you can project yourself into that energy field or draw from it to add to your feeling of personal power.

By contrast, you may find the element of fire the hardest to control, because the flames seem to have a will of their own. For example, you might work with fire by trying to get the flames to move with you as you "conduct" them with your arm or as you shift your body from one direction to another. But flames may seem to go wherever they want as if they are playing with you.

Working with the air, you might imagine creating energy forms that fly like a bird or flow with the wind. Or perhaps see yourself moving in tune with the wind and imagine that you are directing it to rise or fall or change directions in response to your own movements or commands.

Finally, with water, you might visualize forms emerging out of the water on the horizon or focus on changes occurring in the waves or tide.

Starting Small When you first work with these elements, work with a small amount of that element or just seek a small effect. You will be more likely to succeed and can then go on more confidently to larger goals.

For example, instead of trying to influence the fire in a burning house, start with the flame on a little candle. Then you can experiment with this candle to get a sense of the flame's movement. Try directing your energy at the flame through your staff or with your hand and see if you can get the flame to move up or down, to the left or right, forward or back, based on your projection of intention. Or focus on bringing a simmering fire suddenly back to life.

Does It Really Work? When working with these natural elements, people frequently ask whether they are really affecting the elements or just imagining the results.

In some cases, your own energy appears to have some direct influence. When I first experimented with fire, I was standing in front of a small barbecue grill on a picnic ground. The fire had gone out five or ten minutes before, and the coals lay cold in the barbecue pit. I focused my eyes on the coals and imagined my energy going out in a beam to the fire in the pit. After two or three minutes, I saw a flame suddenly flare up and die again. I tried it again, and after a few minutes, there was another brief flash of light. It was as if the energy I directed into the coals triggered the fire, so it briefly started up again. Might the fire have spurted up again without my efforts? It's hard to say—but when this happened, I felt there was some connection, as if my energy were recharging that small fire.

You can also view your interaction with the elements as having a connection with nature, so that you feel what is going to happen next and flow with it. Thus, if you appear to influence a flame's movement, perhaps rather than actually directing the flames yourself, you are getting a keen sense of their direction because you are so attuned to the fire. So you can in effect flow with the flames, and by anticipating their movement, you seem to guide or lead them.

Likewise, you may appear to be directing the wind when you say "The wind is going to rise up now," but maybe you actually have a sense of its shifts. So before it rises up, you move up yourself, just following the natural movement of the wind.

You are not rationally planning your actions. Rather, you are so attuned to the elements of nature that you simply flow with them naturally. So you may feel you are really influencing or directing these elements, whether you actually are or are just flowing with them. Or possibly, by creating this connection with the elements in this altered state, you may get them to cooperate with you. In turn, they are responding because you are requesting, not demanding.

Whatever the reason for the elements' response, much the same process occurs with people, so your approach to directing the natural world can be applied to influencing others. Just seeking the elements' cooperation is more effective than trying to enforce your will on nature, so is it with people. If you demand compliance from others, they may submit out of fear, if they feel you are more powerful. But if they see your vulnerable spot, they may turn on you, and you can easily lose the power struggle. By contrast, if you cooperate with people, they will be likely to respond in kind. They will typically want to help you and will perhaps volunteer new ideas and suggestions. So you are flowing with people in the same way that you are flowing with nature, and thus you will be more effective.

Building a Ritual around Selected Elements To work successfully with these natural elements in ritual, select those elements you feel can help you in achieving a particular goal. Then use objects or symbols associated with those elements to reinforce your purpose.

Suppose you want to become a more flexible person, and like many people, you associate water with flexibility, fluidity, and receptivity. To achieve your goal, you might do a ritual with water and perhaps use plants you associate with water, like watercress. Or find a ritual setting near water, or display lots of bowls or glasses of water if working indoors. Then, in the course of the ritual, for further reinforcements, you can use words associated with water, have images of water, use the color blue, incorporate poems about water, and so forth. In short, choose ritual elements that intensify this association with water, because you associate water with the qualities you want to acquire.

THE POWER OF RITUAL TO DIRECT ENERGY

These rituals to raise and direct energy can be extremely powerful, and you can even see indications of the energy raised when you observe a ritual. For example, during outdoor rituals at night, members of the ODF would report seeing all sorts of energy forms, sparkles of light, aura images, and other signs that the ritual might be affecting the surrounding energy. Likewise, if you observe a ritual, you might see the following signs of energy:

The aura of the practitioner may expand or change. If the person is raising energy, the energy field around him or her may get larger. If so, it will look like a whitish afterimage or capsule of faint white light around him or her, and you will see it spread and grow. Then too, you might see his or her energy project out like a beam of soft white light, if he or she is projecting his or her energy out of a power object like a staff. Also, you might see flashes of light around the person. All these are signs that the person is actually raising energy, and observing the signs in a group will help confirm that you are seeing something real not just imagining it.

There may be energy movements around the area or in the air. If a person is focusing on sending out his or her energy, you might feel the air moving more strongly. You might notice clusters of energy forming; generally, these will look like dark or fuzzy, grayish areas against the blackness of night. For example, in the ODF, people sometimes reported sparks shooting out of the rocks, or concentrations of energy. Sometimes they noticed an energy form move, stop, and then move again. You might also see sparkles of light, or even animal or humanoid shapes.

The practitioner may vanish. This might happen if the person is so involved in the ritual that he has literally become a part of the environment. Members of the ODF reported this, and often the practitioner would report that he had been doing something especially intense at that time, like projecting a strong beam of energy outward or creating a gateway into an altered reality and stepping into it.

There may be a totally black area or a void where the practitioner should be. This is unusual, but it may happen if the practitioner does not really believe in his ritual or is doing something negative. Then you may see this blackness or void, as if the person has created a reverse energy field because he or she is not really projecting any energy and is not attuned to nature.

For example, as mentioned earlier, a member of the ODF tried to use ceremonial magic to command the elements and instead, only managed to project a stream of negative energy around him. Meanwhile, six observers reported seeing a black field around him, which looked like a black hole in the natural environment.

PERCEIVING ENERGY FORMS IN A RITUAL

When you start observing these energy projections and effects of rituals, you may experience them in a variety of ways, because in part you are influenced by your own system of perceptions and symbols. Yet at the same time, an underlying energy form may seem to be influencing you, because when groups observe a ritual often there is a consistency in observations. For example, when we observed rituals in the ODF, people might have somewhat different perceptions. Someone might report a clump of concentrated energy; someone else might report a dovelike form; someone else might claim he or she saw a cat. But consistently, people would see the energy, in whatever form it took, in about the same place.

Similarly, when someone was projecting his energy in the form of an aura around himself, observers would report a combination of different images linked by an underlying pattern. Some people might see this aura simply expand in size; others might see sparks suddenly start shooting; still others might see strong colors emerge. But these were all different ways of suggesting that the aura was becoming stronger and more powerful. By contrast, when the person was contracting his aura, the observers might report different images associated with that, like the aura getting smaller or quieter, or its colors becoming softer.

This combination of different observations linked by a common pattern may occur because when you observe energy in a ritual, your own perceptual system interacts with the energy field that the person is working with. This may occur because everyone perceives differently and draws on different systems of symbols, due to different past experiences. Thus, when you observe someone projecting energy, you may experience this energy form differently from someone else. For example, some people may feel things, but not see a lot, so they may simply feel the presence of the energy created in the ritual. Other people may have a strong sense of knowing and sense intuitively that the energy is out there in this way. And others may be very visual, seeing many things, although people may see in different ways because of their different associations and symbols. Thus, while one person may see a cluster of energy as just that, another person may experience that energy cluster as a dog, and another may see it as a small cat.

Likewise, different people may see different colors in the aura or energy field that emerges around the person doing a ritual. And again, these differences may result because people have different associations with different colors, although the underlying meanings of these perceptions may be the same. For example, one person may associate green with health and healing; another, with money and financial success. Or perhaps that color might have both meanings to someone, depending on the context in which it appears.

Thus, to be sensitive to the energy being raised, recognize that you will be perceiving this energy through your own perceptual and symbolic filters. So you will perceive whatever is there in your own unique way. You will stamp your own perceptual system on whatever energy forms you perceive out there.

CONFIRMING THE POWER OF THE RITUAL

If you have any doubts about the power of the ritual you are doing, your own ability to raise or perceive energy, or the reality of the energy you are raising, you can check to confirm actions or observations.

One approach is to compare your actions and perceptions with those of others. Have someone watch while you do a ritual and then project your energy in a certain way. Afterward, ask the person to describe his or her observations. Generally, you will find some parallels between your actions and the person's description, which will help to confirm the reality of the ritual's effects.

We did this frequently in the ODF. While one person did a ritual with the air, we would notice what happened to the wind. If the person moved his arms to the right as the wind shifted in that direction, that would confirm that the person was either influencing or attuned to the wind. Or if the person moved his arms up and the wind rose up, that would be another confirmation. In addition, we would also ask the person after the ritual if he or she had consciously intended a particular effect, to check if the person was aware of and in control of his or her actions, to try to rule out the actions of the person and of nature just happening to match by chance. So this was one more way to try to confirm what he or she was trying to do.

You can likewise experiment with these kinds of effects. If you work with fire, you might concentrate on having the flames rise up, lift your arms accordingly, and project this intent as you raise your arms. Then notice if the fire responds as you wish.

If you decide to work with the energies of earth and want to make some visual forms emerge, you may not be able to check this on your own, because when you concentrate on sending your energy to create or evoke an earth energy form, you are also suggesting to yourself that this is what you will see. However, to get more objective feedback, have someone else observe. Then proceed without telling him or her your plans. If his or her observations essentially match your actions, this serves as a confirmation.

It helps to do this checking in a group, as we did in the ODF, so you can compare observations. But you can do this with one other person, or on your own, if you are working with the wind or fire, because in these cases, you can readily check if your action is followed by the desired response.

This checking helps you to become more aware of the effects of your own ritual. Thus, you can get a firsthand demonstration of how you are having an impact on the energy around you.

SOME APPROACHES TO AVOID IN RITUAL

There are two major approaches to avoid when you do a ritual. First, do not try to order or command the elements or forces of nature. Rather, be receptive and try to cooperate with the natural forces and energies. Treat them with respect, just as you treat other people with respect and want them to treat you in that way. Perhaps another way to think of this is to imagine that you are honoring the energies that are all around you in the natural world, in others, and in yourself. Otherwise, if you are overly forceful or arrogant, you may find you have generated resistance or resentment. However, if that happens, you can always apologize and assume a humbler posture again, and then you will generally find the forces of nature more responsive, as if they have accepted your apology, just as most people will forgive you when you sincerely apologize. So if you ever feel that you have erred in working with nature or with other people, you can resolve the situation by being humble, opening yourself up, and acknowledging the error. Then you can proceed in the proper spirit.

For example, this process of disturbance followed by healing occurred when, as mentioned earlier, one member of the ODF tried to command the elements with techniques from ceremonial, or Western ritual magic. His actions left what to some ODF observers looked like a black hole of negative energy around the man, and swirls of smoky black energy forms filled with anger and confusion. When Michael saw the negative energy that had been generated, he told the man to stop the ritual and then proceeded to apologize to the natural elements in an effort to heal the area. After that, as everyone observed, the energies seemed calmer and people felt a sense of peace in the area. So, avoid that forceful commanding approach.

Second, avoid calling in strong negative entities or energies. Sometimes people try to call on demonic or other negative spirits in the belief that they have more power and therefore more ability to get something done, or simply because they wish to hurt someone. But generally, this negative energy comes back at you, so that any harm you create will only cause you harm, maybe not right away, but eventually.

From time to time, I have met people who have tried to deny this. For instance, while doing research for my book *The Magicians,* I spent a few months studying a group working with black magic. The group members seemed to believe they were so powerful that they could do anything with their magic and that no one could get in their way. However, again and again, they seemed to have disastrous experiences—planes nearly crashing, a close escape from a car that rolled down a hill, a roommate's suicide, major quarrels. Perhaps these events may have been pure coincidences. But as such negative experiences piled up in the members' lives, it was hard not to speculate that their efforts to work with negative energy in ritual and wreak destruction on others through magic were having some effect in creating these negative events.

Thus, since the people who do work with negative energy appear to get tripped up by their own efforts, it is a good idea to avoid working with negative energy in ritual. The risks of a potential negative return are just too great.

Exercise 14: **EXPERIENCING THE NATURAL ELEMENTS IN A RITUAL**
The following exercise is designed to help you experience what it might be like to work with the different elements of nature in a ritual.

Start off by getting relaxed. Begin by focusing on your breathing. Let it go in and out. In and out. And as it does, you're feeling more and more relaxed, more and more centered. At the same time, you're going to be able to stay awake and alert.

Now see yourself on a meadow. It's a nice sunny day, and the meadow feels warm and very comfortable. You feel very safe and very protected there.

Now, notice a path leading off from the meadow. Walk down this path and down to a beach.

Down there you'll be experiencing the different elements, and you'll be seeing how you might use those elements when you do a ritual, to work on achieving a goal or objective.

Now come out and stand on this beach, near the water. Really feel that beach under your feet. If you want, take off your shoes and just feel the strength of the earth or sand under your feet. The sand is very firm because it's near the water.

Now, just think of your associations with this earth under your feet. You may think of its strength or its solidity. And maybe you have other associations with this earth too.

Walk around the beach a little now, and as you do, you may notice different qualities of earth. You may notice that the earth near the water is a little bit smooth, a little bit more fluid and flexible. But as you move away from the water, off the sand, you feel the earth is even stronger and harder. You may also notice that there are rocks on the earth near you, and if you stand on these, you will feel they are even stronger and firmer under your feet.

Be aware that these qualities of the rocks and the earth you have just experienced are all part of you. They are outside you in the rocks and earth, but also within you, for you can draw on those qualities of the rocks and the earth. And you can feel yourself being part of the rocks and earth as well.

For a few moments, just experience yourself being like the earth or merging with it and having that strength and that stability and that solidity. And think of any other associations you might have with the earth or the rocks. And know that these qualities are not only in the earth and in the rocks, but they are within you too.

Start moving away from the rocks and move back across the beach toward the water. And now you are standing there looking at the water.

And as you look at the water, notice how it's moving and feeling very fluid. Just get a sense of that water and, if you want to, step into it and become a part of it. And you feel very safe and secure as you do.

Then, if you wish, imagine that you are a fish and just like a fish, you can move and swim with the water. As you do, think of the associations you have with water. It's fluid. It has a purifying quality. It flows.

Experience these qualities for yourself. And notice any other associations with water that come to mind as you move through it and feel the water a part of yourself. For all those qualities of water are within you too. And you can call on those qualities when you need them.

Now swim back to where you started and get back on the beach again. Then notice the air above you.

And as you look up into the air, notice the qualities that you associate with the air. You might feel the coolness of the wind as it goes by. Also, you might get a sense of movement, of speed, or perhaps of the gentleness of the soft wind. Or if the wind is strong, you might feel its rising power.

Then too, as you look up in the air, you might notice a bird and think of the independence and freedom which the bird feels as it flies through the air. Then, if you want, experience yourself rising up into the air, becoming very light as you go up. And if you wish, imagine yourself flying like a bird or being that bird and feel this quality of being in the air.

Now, as you move about through the air, notice any other associations you have with air and be aware that the qualities you see in air are also qualities within yourself. You may feel a light, enlightened feeling in the air, or maybe you associate it with spontaneity, with creativity, with ideas, with free thought. Just notice whatever qualities you associate with air; just feel like air and experience those qualities being a part of you. And know that you can always call on those qualities too, when you want them in a ritual.

Now come back down from the air and land once again on the beach. And now notice off to the side that there is a barbecue or camp fire.

Go over to it now and you'll see a fire there. As you stand before it, notice the associations you have with fire. Maybe you experience the fire as pure energy. Other associations might be the power, the aggressiveness, the assertiveness of fire. You may notice it darting around. You may observe its activity and energy. Or maybe you experience its playfulness.

So think of any other associations you have with fire. And again you might imagine yourself blending with the fire, becoming part of it and feeling very comfortable as you do. Then feel yourself moving with the fire, darting around quickly like the fire. For you truly feel the fire; you are fire.

And know that the fire is also a part of you. And all the associations you have with fire are a part of you too. And you can draw on those powers and qualities of fire whenever you want.

Now move away from the fire and come back to the part of the beach where you first started working with these elements.

Now, on the beach, imagine some situation that's affecting you. Maybe it's a conflict. Maybe it's a problem. Maybe it's a challenge in your life. And just think of how these different elements might be able to help you with that particular problem or issue. Think of the qualities of those particular elements and think how you can apply them to your particular problem or challenge.

You might use just one of these elements. You might use the associations you have with earth, like its strength or solidity. . . . Or perhaps you might call on the powers of water, like its fluidity, movement, or its cleansing, purifying quality, whatever you associate with water. Or perhaps you might find the associations you have with fire helpful, like its energy, its strength, its power, its activity, its excitement, and its enthusiasm. Or you might find help in the associations you have with air, like freedom, independence, spontaneity, or creativity.

You can use whatever qualities you associate with those elements to help you and you can draw on as many elements as you need. So just imagine yourself drawing on those different associations and elements and applying them to your particular problems or goals. In fact, imagine yourself using these elements in a ritual and see yourself directing your energy with the help of these elements, to achieve your particular goal.

If you are finished with that particular problem or issue, put up another one to look at. See it come onto a screen in front of you in the air, or perhaps it is occurring on the water in front of you, or on the earth.

And again see those qualities that you need and know that you are able to apply them as you want.

In the same way, know that if you have any other problems or challenges, you can also draw on these qualities. You can do a visualization like this, or you can draw on them in a formal ritual.

It may also help to have the objects around you which you associate with the qualities you want to draw on or acquire. Or perhaps you may be able just to visualize these objects around you.

For you can draw on these qualities to help you focus your energy to do whatever you want to do, and then you can draw on the particular powers and qualities you need to achieve your goal.

Now, just see your objective. See that goal being accomplished by yourself. You have obtained your desire, and you are aware of these energies and elements that have helped you do it. So now you feel very complete. And you know you can always call on these elements and draw on these qualities again when you want, if you need more help in this area or in achieving another goal.

So now, feeling very satisfied about what you have done, just let go of that image, association, feeling, or thought, and come back into yourself as you are standing on the beach, feeling very comfortable and very protected. You feel a kind of closure, a sense of being done.

So now, as you feel ready, turn around and start out on the path again, going back toward the meadow. Now you are on the meadow again, where you started. Count backward from five to one, and as you do, become more and more awake and come back into the room. Five, four, becoming more and more awake. Three, more and more alert. Two, almost back. One. You're back in the room. You can open your eyes, feeling very good.

WORKING WITH A COMBINATION OF THE ELEMENTS

While thinking of the elements separately helps to develop your associations with them, you can draw on some or all of them simultaneously for assistance. For instance, if you are starting a new job, drawing on qualities associated with both earth and air might be very helpful. You might use your associations with earth, like stability and solidity, to give you a feeling of security and strength in your new position. And then you might draw on your associations with water, like flexibility, movement, and change, so you can adapt to a new environment. During a visualization, you would imagine yourself imbued with these qualities as you go to work. And later, when you actually go to work, you would continue to draw on the feelings and images provided by this earlier visualization.

DEALING WITH THE LACK OF A GOAL

Sometimes when you do exercise 14, an image of a goal may not come to you. If so, perhaps you are not quite ready to see a goal. You may be in a period of transition, or may be uncertain about what you want, or you may not want to think about future goals right now. Then too, sometimes you may not experience a goal if you feel satisfied and there is nothing in particular you want.

In either case, if you do not see a goal, don't worry about it.

Just let go of any concerns and do not try to come up with a goal now. Later you can try the exercise again when you feel more ready and you really do have an objective. After all, a ritual is done primarily to attain some particular goal, so if you do not have one for some reason, postpone the ritual, unless you enjoy doing it for its own sake.

Also, your goal does not have to be a major one. It can be anything from simply evoking a being or natural response to achieving a life goal. And the life goals you consider can range in importance and scope, from the purpose of your life to day-to-day issues like controlling your weight.

So feel free to use these techniques of drawing on the natural energies for any level of goal—from the spiritual and serious to the everyday and relatively trivial. And if you have trouble thinking of a goal, just let it go, for you may not be quite ready for one.

DEALING WITH FEARS OR NEGATIVES THAT ARISE

During visualizations or rituals working with the forces of nature, you may be concerned about possibly drawing on any negative forces. Generally, you do not have to worry about this, as long as you approach the visualization or ritual with a good intention, because your positive thoughts will normally draw only positive images and associations.

However, if you want additional assurance, do some positive preparation before the visualization or ritual, to keep out any negative forces your activity might attract. For instance, do an advance meditation in which you imagine putting up a protective bubble around yourself. Or if you worry that something negative will come around you during the visualization or ritual, alert yourself to this possibility in advance, so you can imagine yourself pushing out the undesired intruder.

However, generally, when you do these light visualizations and rituals, negative intrusions do not happen. So this should not be a major concern.

17

•

Ritual in
Everyday Life

There are numerous reasons to use a ritual to intensify your efforts to achieve a goal. This chapter will suggest some specific applications.

PROJECTING ENERGY AT PEOPLE
TO INFLUENCE THEM

You can project your energy to influence people positively because when you send out energy, people respond in kind (which is one reason not to pass on negative energy).

If you want a warm relationship with somebody, send out warm energy to this person. For instance, send out positive energy to the driver as you get on the bus and he may smile at you, which he would not normally do. Or if you have had difficulty with somebody at your office, send him or her friendly energy, although you naturally tend to regard that person negatively, and he or she may suddenly be friendly and the difficulty may be quickly resolved.

PROJECTING ENERGY FOR PLANNING

A ritual can also be effective to plan an undertaking and help you focus on what you expect or want to happen. Doing so helps to prepare you to act to achieve your goal.

For example, before going to meet the manufacturer who published my game *Glasnost, The Game of Soviet-American Diplomacy,* I did a miniritual in my mind, to visualize the outcome I wanted. Also, I mentally prepared my approach. I imagined him accepting my proposal to share the start-up expense and to make this a joint venture, and that is exactly what happened.

Then, before a second meeting a few weeks later to work out the final arrangements, I again did a visualization ritual. We had left the arrangements very open, since I had convinced him to accept the start-up agreement by proposing a joint venture, showing my faith in the project, offering to put up as much as five thousand dollars myself. But in fact, I wanted to work on a royalty basis. I imagined the approach I really wanted: he would handle the artwork, cover my costs, and pay me a royalty. And at the meeting, that is exactly what he suggested, since his accounting system had no way to figure the profits on a joint venture.

I got exactly what I wanted by setting my goal, planning the best approach and directing my energy to make it happen. So the actual meetings were like playing out scripts I had already prepared in my mind. And I think if I had not done this foreseeing none of this might have happened.

So you can apply planning rituals, in which you map out your strategy, to many situations.

EVERYDAY RITUALS TO SET THE RIGHT MOOD FOR AN ACTIVITY

You can also do small rituals to get yourself in the mood for an activity. The rituals are almost like daily habits that prepare you for an activity, because they have become associated with that activity. Doing these rituals is like telling yourself, After this ritual I'll be ready to do that act. For example, making coffee helps to prepare me for writing. The coffee itself is a stimulant, but I think the process of making it and bringing it into the room where I write has become a signal that tells me, Now you're going to write.

Similarly, many people have little rituals they use as preparations and stage setters. For a smoker, lighting up can serve as a ritual to facilitate social interaction.

USING AN ENERGY-RAISING RITUAL
TO UNBLOCK YOURSELF

Rituals can also break through energy blocks that keep you from doing something. Since you are focusing and directing your energy in the ritual you can literally cut right through the energy block and begin your work.

For example, when I first started writing, I used a little energy ritual to break through the blocks that writers sometimes get, often because they are afraid their writing will not be perfect. I would visualize energy rising from the earth into my feet and then spiraling around in my body. And next I would imagine energy from the air coming in and spiraling around. The two energies would come together in my center to form a big white ball of energy inside me and I would then visualize that energy pouring out of me. I would go to the typewriter with that image, and the energy seemed to pour out of my hands, helping me write. After a while, I became so conditioned to writing when I sat down at the typewriter that I no longer needed that energy visualization ritual. I was automatically ready to write.

Likewise, if you feel yourself blocked from a task, use that kind of energy visualization or create another little ritual to get yourself moving. It could be almost any visualization, action, or gesture, like chanting, ringing a bell, or any signal you feel comfortable with. After you complete the ritual, simply position yourself to do your task. For instance, if the task is writing, sit down to write, knowing that you have just done a preparatory ritual so you are ready. The first time, nothing may come. You may just stare at the typewriter blankly.

But even if you feel this block at first, just say to yourself, I'm going to do whatever it is I want to do. Thus, if your intention is to write, tell yourself, I'm just going to sit here and I'm not going to worry about it. I'm just going to let it happen. After you have expressed your determination to sit it out, just wait.

Even if nothing comes because the block is still there, spend some time meditating on the activity you want to do, to remind yourself that you have set aside this time for this activity and you have the intention to do it. Then, on the next occasion you want to do this activity, say the next day, do the ritual again. Go and again position yourself for the activity. After a few times, this barrier will suddenly open up and you will be able to start the desired activity. For in effect, you are creating a link between the ritual, your intention, and the desired activity, so the repetition of the ritual linked to the activity helps to raise the energy needed to break through the barrier blocking your action. Once this break-through occurs, you can readily act, for you can draw on the intense force of the energy you have raised in the ritual.

Or perhaps another way to think of the process is that your active will has set your energy in motion, once you have decided to do your task. So you are using that energy raised in the ritual to help you direct your will.

However, even after the ritual, you may still have to exercise your will to carry out the activity. For instance, say you are trying to write; distractions may arise, like a sudden desire to check the mail. When such distractions happen, just acknowledge them and let them go (i.e., you tell yourself, Yes, I would like to check the mail). But then don't do it. Just stay there, committed to your intention.

Thus, besides doing ritual to encourage your commitment, you may also need to discipline yourself so you keep at the desired task. However, after you continue to hold yourself there by will for a while, the resistance will start to subside because you are not letting anything distract you. So after a while, perhaps out of bore-dom, or because you recognize that this task is the only thing you are allowing yourself to do, you will do it. For you have broken all energy barriers and distractions standing in your way.

PRACTICING TO MAKE YOUR RITUALS MORE EFFECTIVE

As you work with rituals more, you may find your rituals becoming more effective. As with any first effort, your first rituals to achieve a goal may not seem to have much impact. For instance, you may have trouble making associations or connections when you visualize. But as with anything, like trying to have more dreams or pick up more information intuitively, the more you practice a ritual, the more it will become second nature and the more effective it will seem.

You can practice on two levels. First, you can work with the more intuitive rituals, in which you focus on receiving information. Here you can try to develop your receptivity. Second, you can work with the more directed ritual, in which you project your energy to achieve a specific intention. In this case, focus on developing your ability to project your energy and your will. In either case, this practice will help fine-tune your abilities, so you can be more receptive or directive, as you wish.

Yet even if you want to develop this ability to project energy, remain receptive so you can be ready to respond or change as needed. For even as you exercise your will and intention, you should think of yourself as doing a dance with nature or trying to flow with the energies and people around you. In other words, ask for something to happen, yet be ready to flow with the experiences you have and accept what comes. This is part of seeking a balance between your directive and receptive moods and staying in tune with the overall flow of events in the universe.

RECOGNIZING AND RESPONDING TO RESISTANCES

When you do a ritual, at times you may experience resistance. This is a sign that maybe you should not be doing it; maybe the time is not right.

Suppose you decide to do a ritual to further a particular love relationship. But you find all sorts of resistances as you do it, like feeling tense. Or maybe you feel the ritual is not working, or you find it difficult to focus and direct your energy.

When you get such resistance, look at the reasons for it. Perhaps there is something wrong with your goal. Or your approach. In the case of the relationship, maybe you are being too manipulative, or maybe this person is not ready to have a relationship and you are trying to force it with the ritual. While a ritual can prod events if the time is ripe, you can also encounter strong blocks if the timing or purpose is wrong.

Thus look at such sources of resistance, because they may indicate that you should not be doing this ritual with this purpose at this time. Or you may simply need to work on being more receptive or directive, or letting yourself go deeper into an altered state.

ATTAINING DEEPER ALTERED STATES IN RITUALS

The rituals discussed here involve primarily everyday, light re-laxation states, which are generally easy to slide in and out of and which generally do not require special protections. The suggestion that you will feel comfortable and safe and have a pos-itive experience is usually all you need in working with these states.

However, there are much deeper states you can enter, and at times, you may find you are going too deep instead of staying in a light altered state, or you may feel a need to protect yourself from thoughts, images, or perhaps spiritual beings you believe are both-ering you.

If you want to enter the deeper state, that is fine. But if you want, you can use a trigger to pull yourself back or disrupt any negative thoughts or experiences.

Entering Deeper States Since this book is not designed to deal with the deeper states, I will just suggest the possibilities here. You can use various techniques, like repetitive sounds or dance, to enter a deep, trancelike state, and sometimes in this state, you may even lose a conscious awareness of your actions. You become so recep-tive that the conscious or controlling part of yourself slips away. You are much more aware and can see more directly into other realities; without your normal awareness or control mechanisms in place, you are much more vulnerable to negativity. So you need to be especially careful to do this in a safe environment, to be with people you trust, or to enter the state in a positive frame of mind or with protective images or feelings (like surrounding yourself with a bubble of white protective light).

Generally, to get into this deeper state, you have to chant man-tras, or dance, or use rattles or drums for a half hour to an hour, or even longer, until the constant repetition brings you into this state. Yet there are some people who can simply slip into this state with very little suggestion, moving quickly from an intended light relaxation state into a deeper trance.

In any event, you may find yourself so deep in this state that you remember nothing. A classic film, *Dance and Trance in Bali,* shows people dancing until they enter a trance. They poke them-selves with swords and roll on the ground without getting hurt, and afterward, they have no recollection of this. Yet they experience a catharsis that makes them feel good, as if through their trance they eliminated their evil or unhappy, negative feelings.

So if you undergo a period of change or have negative experiences, an intense ritual can help you release these experiences and put the past behind you. It can be a way to achieve a break through catharsis. When you wake from this altered state, you may feel like the past is completely over.

Also, in the intense ritual you can identify with and express deeper parts of yourself, so you feel more complete and connected to your identity. Some people do this by taking on another form, like that of an animal or object.

I saw one woman do this quite dramatically, when I was working with the ODF. The woman was doing a ritual in which she responded to the inspirations of the moment, and she began by wanting to feel very close to the earth. She lay down and meditated to feel this closeness, and then, after standing up briefly, she began rolling on the ground and then started dancing. Next she curled up like a rock and experienced its deadness. And then, when she emerged from being the rock, she let her hair loose and started running like a cat. And next she lurked in the grass like a panther.

As she explained later, she really felt she was the animal or object whose form she assumed. She was not just going through the motions. And although she had not told the observers about her actions, because she did not know in advance each time, we could tell what she had become, because her identification with the object or animal was so strong.

By the end of the ritual, she had raised so much energy that she felt an explosion or catharsis within, and afterward, she returned to her normal state. As she felt this catharsis, the moon suddenly appeared from behind the clouds, the meadow became illuminated with a brilliant white glow, and she suddenly gave a loud, piercing yell, which was followed by a sudden gust of wind. So the experience was not only a dramatic catharsis for her, but it seemed to be paralleled by natural events. Then, as she calmed down, the wind subsided and the clouds covered the moon again.

Maybe it was a coincidence that all the changes in nature happened while she was in this intense trance state. Or perhaps her energy state influenced or responded to the environment around her, to create this perfect synchronicity. In any case, the ritual had a powerful intensity, and afterward, both the woman who experienced it and those of us who watched, felt a sense of awe by what had happened.

Avoiding a Deeper State Generally, you will not enter a deeper state or be bothered by negative forces while in a light relaxation state. However, if you tend to go too deep or find yourself bothered by negative energies, there are several ways to avoid this.

One way to avoid this is by having a trigger for yourself to pull yourself out of this state. For instance, you might have a hand signal—you snap your fingers and pull yourself back. Or perhaps wear a chain that you can pull on if you feel you are going too deep. In turn, by triggering yourself to pull back, you may not need to worry about protecting yourself against negative feelings or spirits, because you have pulled yourself back up to a more ordinary level.

You do not usually have to worry about these negative forces in the visualizations and rituals discussed in this book, because in that light relaxation state, a part of you is still very much in control. The altered state enhances your receptivity and your ability to project your will. But at the same time, a conscious part of you is still alert. So you are watching yourself do the ritual, and if you feel uncomfortable, your consciousness can always intervene to pull you back or push away anything negative.

Second, you might also protect yourself from going too deep or encountering any negative energies or spirits by giving yourself advanced suggestions (i.e., surround yourself in a bubble of light or tell yourself that you can push away any negative forces).

A third approach might be to look more closely at whatever you are afraid of encountering in a deep trance, if you feel comfortable doing so. But if you do not feel comfortable doing this, perhaps it is better simply to use a trigger or a bubble of protection.

If you do explore, ask these negative energies or spirits questions like, Why are you coming here? Why do you bother me? What do you want of me? Who are you? Often this process can be very illuminating, because in a sense, these energies or spirits are aspects of yourself that you maybe do not want to face, or symbols of unresolved issues. When you ask these entities why they are here, they may tell you, so you will better understand yourself and know how to resolve a troublesome issue. In fact, you might even plan such an encounter by meditating on it before you enter a deeper state. In this meditation, give yourself the suggestion that these energies will show up and that you are going to confront them with these questions.

Think of the whole process as talking to a deeper part of yourself. It is as if you are splitting yourself into two parts, so that one is talking and the other listening and answering with some deep inner information about you.

Finally, if you are concerned that you may go so deep that you will not remember what happened, tape the ritual. Then, as you pose your questions and hear the energies or entities respond, you can record what they say.

CREATING YOUR OWN RITUALS

You can use a traditional ritual structure from a group you are working with, like the ritual forms I have described, or you can create your own structure, using whatever objects and symbols you want. Set up a ritual circle if you want one, or don't, if you prefer. Use an altar if you feel comfortable with it, or keep your ritual setting very simple. Likewise, you can use a staff or other power objects if they help you, or create your ritual with just a visualization or projection of your feelings or thoughts.

The key is to decide on your purpose and then choose the elements of ritual to achieve that purpose. To this end, you can draw on suitable elements of nature individually or in combination. You can choose appropriate words and symbols and use the materials or objects that feel right for you. Together, all of these parts of the ritual should combine to create a feeling of unity so they merge together to reinforce your purpose and focus your energy and intent on achieving that goal.

In some cases, as in Western magic, people use a very structured ritual form, because those classical symbols with their layers of meaning create a total ritual context, where all elements are carefully chosen to focus on a particular goal. However, others find a structured ritual deadening, because there are so many things to remember that it is hard to get into the flow. They prefer a more spontaneous ritual so they can freely improvise on the inspiration of the moment, which is what I prefer. But either approach is fine. If you can learn traditional symbols and methods without feeling inhibited, this traditional approach might work well for you. But if you find learning all of these meanings and procedures a real struggle, a more spontaneous, free-form approach might be better for you. Or perhaps start with a more traditional ritual form for inspiration; then develop your own ritual forms.

In short, whether you use traditional forms or are more spontaneous, the key to an effective ritual is using whatever elements you choose to direct your energy to your goal and developing your own personal style so the ritual becomes a part of you. It is not just an outer form you are using; in essence, the ritual is you. It has truly become your vehicle, infused with your energy and your purpose, and so you can ride it, as if on a freeway, on a clear and direct route to your goal.

SHARING RITUALS

Creating rituals with others can work well, if everyone has a similar purpose and similar associations with the objects and symbols you use. There are, of course, numerous groups in which members learn to do rituals and come to share certain symbols and meanings.

However, beyond these more formal group rituals, you may find it especially powerful to share a ritual with a person you are close to, as a way of bonding more closely, or you might even use a ritual to express your sense of commitment to each other.

Group rituals can have a great deal of energy because everyone in the group focuses on the same thing and raises energy for that purpose. Group rituals also create a sense of communion. This intensification of energy is much like going to a movie theater. The effect is more powerful than watching television, not just because you are watching a big screen, but also because you are watching with so many others and picking up their energy. Thus, other people's laughter intensifies your own, and as you have other feelings, they are intensified too. You can become aware of this if you watch a movie in a deserted theater. The experience may feel less intense than it would if the theater were filled with people. And so it is with ritual—the shared power of the group makes the energy of the ritual that much stronger.

The group ritual also gains even more power because each member gets a sense of permission that helps him or her let go and step into a high-energy, altered state. This occurs because everyone is doing the same thing at the same time. Also everyone appears to share the same belief system, and so people can more strongly believe in the power of the ritual to make things happen. Thus, for all of these reasons, the group setting generally intensifies the energy of the ritual. In turn, this heightened power of the group, with everybody doing the ritual at the same time, helps lead each member into this altered state.

Finally, in a group ritual, it is important to have a leader to unify the group, so it directs and focuses its combined energy toward a desired goal. However, with only two or three people, a leader is less important because in a small, intimate group, members jointly plan the ritual and readily share or take turns in the role of leadership. Or in some cases, the members of a small group may be so in tune with each other that they literally act as one, which is a tremendous source of power.

Exercise 15:

PERFORMING A RITUAL TO GET INTO AN ALTERED STATE

Purely mental rituals can also have great power to lead you into an altered consciousness state, where you can focus your energy and intention on your goal. One way to get into an altered state is by focusing on an object. The following exercise is designed to help you do this.

In the following ritual, you will be looking at an object and imagining yourself going into another reality on the other side of the object. As you do, you will be able to acquire certain qualities you want for yourself.

Start by getting relaxed again and just concentrate on your breathing going in and out. In and out. But at the same time, you're going to stay very alert.

Now, with your eyes open, pick a spot in the room to look at. It could be an object or something on the walls that has a center point, where you can visualize yourself going through the center.

Just start looking at this, and as you gaze at it, let your eyes go out of focus. You may notice that the object vibrates, and you might imagine that this means it is opening up into another world for you and you can project yourself through that opening into that other world.

Now, with that thought, association, or image, continue to look at this spot. And as you do, imagine that the center is opening up, letting you through. You may notice that your consciousness is like a beam of light projecting through this opening, and on the other side of this opening you might find a source of information. Or you may see some spiritual guides or beings you might talk to. And they may have some information to give you, or they may have certain qualities which you would like to develop, and they can give you those qualities.

So just imagine yourself going through the opening to the other side, and as you go through, you acquire these traits you are seeking, and you experience a great sense of power.

You might also think about the different qualities you want to acquire. If you want more confidence, more knowledge, more willpower, more skill in something, more creativity, whatever you want, you can focus on continuing to move ahead in this other world, and you know you will be able to acquire these qualities and find the assistance you need.

In fact, maybe you now feel those qualities surrounding you, as if you are putting on a suit of armor or a cloak of several colors. But instead you are putting on a cloak made up of qualities, of traits, that you want to acquire.

So feel those qualities becoming part of you as you beam yourself through that opening and explore this other world which you find. Just keep concentrating, in turn, on each of the qualities you want to acquire, and experience yourself being that quality. You feel that quality. You are that quality.

Experience that, and know that you can always come back here and do this again. So you can experience this quality once more, or you can experience another quality, and you can get the information or advice that you need, and when you return, the person or guide you have spoken to will be there again to help.

Also know that you can look at any kind of object and project yourself through it. Or even if you don't have an object, you might create a screen in your mind and imagine yourself going through it.

Or if you want to, set up an altar with an object in front of you and then look through that. Also, you might set up candles and incense to help you project yourself, and you might use objects or symbols that you associate with these particular qualities that you want to acquire. You might also put on music which you associate with these qualities. You might use words or chanting to help you intensify your experience too. For all of these symbols and associations will help you to reinforce this image or feeling of the quality that you want.

Now, as you keep looking at this object or spot, start letting go of the people or beings you talked to in this other reality. Start pulling back your consciousness. As you do, you see the hole into the other reality closing. And you see this object or spot becoming just an ordinary object or spot once again, as your consciousness returns to normal.

Now count backward from five to one, and come back into the room and you'll be totally alert and awake. Five, four, letting go of the other world. Three, two, letting go of the object you have used. One, you are back to normal consciousness, fully awake and alert in the room.

In exercise 15, it may be especially helpful to choose an object which does have a clear center, like a mandala. Then it will be easier to see yourself being pulled or moving into this center opening, for all of the lines or images are directed toward this center.

If you feel any resistance to going through, do not worry. That generally just means you are not quite ready to go through or do not feel comfortable doing it right now. But maybe next time you'll feel more comfortable. Also, with practice, your ability to visualize and focus your energy will improve.

USING RITUAL ETHICALLY

Done appropriately, ritual can be an extremely powerful tool for directing your energy to get what you want. But at the same time, because ritual is so powerful, it is important to use it ethically. That means you have to respect the space of other people whom you might be affecting in your ritual. Thus, while you may want to do a ritual for your own gain, be sure that this gain will not directly hurt anyone else. If it does, that harm will eventually come back to you, because of the basic principle of cause and effect, karma, or justice in the universe.

As a result, you must approach rituals in a spirit of goodwill and good faith. Ritual is much like entering a contract. It is assumed that this contract is governed by an understanding of good faith and fair dealing and you should bring the same spirit to a ritual.

Perhaps think of doing a ritual as making yourself more powerful or taking on a position of power. A sense of responsibility comes with that power. For instance, we have higher standards and expectations of people, like public officials, who have more power than others. We think they are supposed to set an example.

Similarly, if you are working with magical power in a ritual, you should take responsibility for what you do. Consequently, as you become more powerful, you should be even more responsible and more ethical, and if you are not, many negative things can happen, because as you work with more power and energy, much more power and energy can come back at you, if your intentions are negative.

Thus, for both practical and moral considerations, you should use ritual ethically, in a spirit of good faith and goodwill for positive goals, and make sure you do nothing to hurt anyone else in the process. In turn, you will find working with this positive higher energy more powerful, because this higher energy is much stronger than any negative lower energy. So this higher energy will eventually push aside the lower energy, just as the more powerful energies of fire and light operate in nature, banishing cold and darkness. Likewise, you should use your rituals for a higher, positive purpose, and doing so will help to sweep away the lower, negative energy barriers to attaining your goal.

In short, using ritual effectively can bring you great personal power. But in turn, you need to use this power wisely and well, in keeping with the laws of the universe, for then the laws of the universe will reinforce your own positive energy and intuition.

A FINAL NOTE

In this book, I have described a variety of mental imagery and visualization techniques for rituals. I have also incorporated certain images and symbols into these exercises. These are particular images and symbols which have worked for me and which I have used in a series of workshops based on shamanic teachings. However, I have tried to emphasize that there are many different approaches to shamanism based on both ancient and newer traditions. Any of these approaches can be effective, whichever feel comfortable for you, and you can develop your own techniques, using the images and symbols that have special meaning for you.

Most important is to understand the underlying principles, whatever you call your system—shamanism, magic, spiritual science, and so forth. Essentially, the major principles are based on working with energy and visualizations and focusing your intention on your goals.

If you work with a shamanic tradition, you will use symbols like earth, air, fire, and water, and you may do rituals outdoors, or perhaps work with rattles or drums. But if you work with another tradition, you may have other symbols and associations. However, the underlying process is the same.

The key, whatever system you work with, is to use the symbols and associations you choose to help you better raise and focus your energy and direct your intention into your goal.